Marion Harland

The Royal Road

Marion Harland

The Royal Road

ISBN/EAN: 9783743397460

Manufactured in Europe, USA, Canada, Australia, Japa

Cover: Foto ©Lupo / pixelio.de

Manufactured and distributed by brebook publishing software (www.brebook.com)

Marion Harland

The Royal Road

THE ROYAL ROAD

OR

TAKING HIM AT HIS WORD

THE ROYAL ROAD

OR

TAKING HIM AT HIS WORD

BY

MARION HARLAND

AUTHOR OF "ALONE," "EVE'S DAUGHTERS," "HIS GREAT SELF,"
"A GALLANT FIGHT," ETC.

NEW YORK
ANSON D. F. RANDOLPH AND COMPANY
(INCORPORATED)
182 FIFTH AVENUE

Copyright, 1894,
BY ANSON D. F. RANDOLPH AND COMPANY
(INCORPORATED)

University Press:
JOHN WILSON AND SON, CAMBRIDGE, U.S.A.

TO MY BROTHER,

S. H. H.

IN RECOGNITION OF THE STEADFAST AFFECTION THAT,
IN FIFTY YEARS OF SUNSHINE AND OF SHADOW,
HAS NEVER FAILED ME,

This Book is Lovingly Dedicated.

MARION HARLAND.

One evening, when Luther saw a little bird perched on a tree to roost there for the night, he said:

"*This little bird has had its supper and now it is getting ready to go to sleep here, quite secure and content, never troubling itself what its food will be, or where its lodging for the morrow. Like David, it abides under the shadow of the Almighty. It sits on its little twig content, and lets God take care.*" — FROM THE GERMAN.

CHAPTER I.

Hast thou, my Master, aught for me to do
    To honor thee to-day?
Hast thou a word of love to some poor soul
    That I may say?
For see! this world that thou hast made so fair
    Within its heart is sad,
Thousands are lonely, thousands sigh and weep;
    But few are glad.

ELIZABETH PRENTISS.

THE ROYAL ROAD.

CHAPTER I.

MENDEBRAS AVENUE is not in a fashionable quarter of Brooklyn. It is, however, unquestionably respectable. Many of the houses are of wood, — evidences of a time, not many years back, when the district was one of numerous villages which have been overtaken and run down by the hurrying city. Such neighborhoods have a bewildered look and a general air of being ill at ease. So might stand and gape a group of country children surprised by a bevy of city cousins, and invited to take part in their games.

The region about Mendebras Avenue was especially confounded when the municipality raced up to it and swallowed it. Against its will, it was sliced into six blocks one way, and ten the other. There were once gardens there, and orchards, and commons, where carpets were beaten spring and fall, and the boys played ball on Saturdays. Before the march of improvement, brick houses in twos and threes and fours were wedged into the gardens; streets and avenues (Brooklyn is affluent in avenues) trampled the orchards out of sight and memory; each vacant lot was filled with tall rows of houses, — some thinly faced with brown-stone, others of pressed brick in front, cheap brick in the rear. In certain streets, most of these houses had several door-bells apiece. There were Nottingham lace curtains at the front windows; and the various tints of the Holland shades testified to the diverse tastes of the families occupying the several floors. The trees lining the sidewalks were generally poplars, a good deal the worse for years and wear, and supercilious young maples.

Trees were leafless, and the vines clinging to the porches of the "old residents" leafless sticks, one November night when the street-lamps struggled conscientiously with a tawny fog that would bleach into rain as soon as it grew a little heavier. Right in the middle of a block, with a pair of new brown-stone fronts crowding it on one side, and a time-blackened cottage giving it elbow-room on the other, was the Jeremy Taylor Memorial Church. It belonged to the days when the district was a township, and had once stood in the centre of its own court. Middle-aged people could recollect the fine elms that shaded the western windows, now darkened by the cataract of the dead wall of the brown-stone front. There were then tomb-stones in the quadrangle behind it, and the bell in the square tower rang out resonantly across green and garden.

It had rung twice on this evening, at seven and again at eight o'clock, it being prayer-meeting night.

The Jeremy Taylor people, as they called themselves, — life being too brief in a fast-growing city for saying three words when two would do, — were regular in attendance upon church ordinances. They said complacently that there were fewer "itching cars" among them than in the majority of Brooklyn congregations. A goodly number of them were from New England, and "calculated" upon going to church as regularly as upon crossing the Ferry in the morning and coming home to supper at night. One pastor had folded and fed them for twenty-five years. He was "getting along" now, — rising fifty years of age, — but they craved nothing younger and livelier. They knew his ways, and he knew theirs. Blessed is the people who is in such a case, and thrice-blessed the pastor.

The chapel was behind the church, an oblong room, plainly furnished with cushionless settees, a platform and desk, one armchair and a melodeon. The minister was of medium height, spare in build, and wore eye-glasses. His coat was buttoned across a narrow chest; and, as many New York and Brooklyn preachers have a habit of doing, he cleared his throat of the catarrh-breeding fog frequently while speaking. Seventy-three people were present, — a gratifying attendance for a wet night.

The pastor's wife was at the melodeon; in the intervals of prayer and addresses, a gas-burner back of the pulpit hissed and blew alternately; the subsiding hum of the city was like the far-off roll of sullen surf. The air of the chapel, hot with furnace-breath, was yet humid, oppressing lungs and spirits. In a distant corner, a brother had succumbed to it, and snored intermittently, but under his breath, as befitted place and occasion.

The text of the lecture following the preliminary exercises was: —

"Before faith came, we were kept under the law, shut up into the faith which should afterwards be revealed."

The Rev. William C. Barnes constructed his discourses, major and minor, upon models received into a good and honest mind more than thirty years ago in Princeton Seminary, making liberal use of the stock ecclesiastical phrases which orthodox Bible students are supposed to comprehend. The men before him to-night belonged, one and all, to the mighty middle-class of the community. Every man of them worked for a living, and, without exception, worked hard. Back of each sedate visage were experiences in the battle of every-day life that would have astonished the owner's right and left hand neighbor, had he revealed them. Their faces were criss-crossed by lines which were as truly scars as if made by a branding-iron. The women's faces were tired and discontented, or tired and resigned. Under one or the other of these types may be classed most of the countenances of native-born United States women. Of the fifty in the chapel that raw November night, perhaps forty "did their own work," and probably thirty-nine did it well. These are the true yoke-fellows who fill the settees at prayer-meetings, and seldom get leisure for other evening engagements. These are likewise they who do not drowse during the services, even when the lecture is upon Justification by Faith, The Perseverance of the Saints, or Reprobation. They are, as a body, too weary to do much thinking, and familiar platitudes glide, like bland warm oil, over rasped nerves. It does them good always to go to church, they will tell you with significance imperfectly comprehended by themselves. The House of God is to their soul the gate of heaven, be the ministrations of His earthly servants what they may. Gleams of light, sweet airs, and snatches of celestial melody escape to them through gracious crevices in the blessed portals. There are calming influences in the voice of prayer, and refreshment in the dear old hymns.

Dr. Barnes was also tired to-night. He had made six pastoral calls in the afternoon, and in the morning gone to Cypress Hills Cemetery behind the hearse of an utter stranger whose first cousin had, ten years ago, attended "the Jeremy Taylor" when she went anywhere. He had, according to his custom when he had an evening service, eaten no supper, spending the hour given by his family to that meal in his study, "thinking up" his lecture. When tired, he was didactic. Jaded memory did not go afield now for apt illustrations, and imagination dozed as stupidly as the brother in the distant corner. There was not the rise of an inch to the mile in the commonplaces of his comparison of the "Old, called the Mosaic Dispensation" with the "New, otherwise the Christian." He cited passages relative to the Law from the New Testament, until a hearer unversed in such matters might have inferred that every apostle was a member of the legal profession; he dwelt upon the impracticability of living up to the strict letter of the Law, "rubbing it in," to steal a slang phrase, as if every tried and tempted parishioner had not had the terrible truth burned into his soul by a thousand failures; he described Faith in neat formulas learned from professors and notebooks, and exhorted the impenitent — all within the sound of his voice being church-members in good and regular standing — to choose the better part, and begin the study and practice of saving Faith before the judgment of the Law overtook them.

The Rev. William C. Barnes was a good man, sincere in belief and faithful in teaching, to the best of his ability. But he had conducted a prayer-meeting once a week for over a quarter of a century; and human nature is very human, mortal flesh very weak when weary.

The prayers, of which there were four beside the pastor's, were in the same key. To those who "offered" them, these services were likewise an oft-told tale. Had they ever heard the anecdote, each, had he dared and had he been blest with a sense of humor, would have plagiarized the man who was so eloquent in public prayer that an admirer listened at his chamber-door one night in the hope of being edified by his secret devotions: —

"Dear Lord," sighed the disciple, as his head sank into his pillow, "Thou knowest how weary I am! Thou knowest, also, that *we are on the same old terms!*"

"There still remain three minutes before we close these exercises," said the leader's patient tones. "I hope the brethren will occupy the time."

It was obviously an economic, and not a devotional, instinct that drew the fourth brother to his feet to enunciate a prim ascription of praise, a confession of sins many and heinous, a thanksgiving for mercies received, and a supplication for a continuance of divine favor. Men of his age and religious training, consciously or unconsciously, adopt the formula of devotion prescribed by an eminent teacher of "pastoral theology," wherein the monosyllable ACTS is indicated as a sacred combination for the lock of the divine treasure-chamber.

With an involuntary sigh, the patient pastor arose to announce the closing hymn. The time had been honestly occupied; but in nothing that had been uttered in prayer or exhortation had anybody followed his lead. They had danced dutifully, but not to the tune he had piped. For any reference that had been made to the "line of his remarks," he might as well have preached, like the old English clergyman of *The Spectator*, from "Adam, Seth, Enoch."

A sense of incongruity between the words, "We will conclude our services," and the perfunctory character of the exercises from beginning to end, had something to do with the sigh, and the undertone of pathos in which he read one stanza of the hymn he had selected: —

> "I need Thee every hour,
> Most gracious Lord!
> No other voice like Thine
> Can peace afford."

The melodeon stirred and spoke feelingly under the skilful touch of the minister's wife. She was the daughter of a wealthy man, had cultivated her musical talent in former days, and never allowed the accomplishment to lapse into desuetude. The somnolent brother in the dim corner also stirred, and, mightily refreshed by his sojourn upon the Mount of Privilege, stood with the rest, with the over-acted aspect of wide-awakeativeness, which imposes upon no one the belief that Eutychus has found edification behind the drawn curtains of his eyes. Mrs. Barnes raised the tune with voice as with hand, nearly all of the little congregation singing with spirit, if not with understanding.

At the second verse a new voice arose, with startling effect, from a seat near the door. Dr. Barnes, supplying a light and original tenor to his wife's fine, true soprano, faltered on a high note in momentary surprise, and glanced over his glasses towards the quarter whence the sound proceeded. Several other heads were turned in the same direction.

A woman of thirty-five or thereabouts, dressed in mourning that, without being new or fashionable, did not detract from the impression of refinement conveyed by her face and carriage, stood there, removed from the rest of the audience by the width of two empty settees. Her hands, clasped loosely upon one another, lay upon the back of the seat before her; her face was upraised slightly; her eyes were wide, and fixed upon a point above the pastor's head. It was plain that she was removed in thought, no less than in body, from human companionship. Her voice was full and rich, with that indescribable vibrant quality we call "carrying well;" but it was the passionate fervor of appeal, the cry of the soul in every note, that went to the listener's ear and heart: —

> "I need Thee every hour!
> Stay Thou near by;
> Temptations lose their power
> When Thou art nigh."

It rose and swelled in the chorus like the call of grieving earth to a pitying heaven: —

> "I need Thee, oh, I *need* Thee!
> Every hour I need Thee!
> Oh, bless me now, my Saviour!
> I come to Thee."

With the thrilling echo still calling to the depths of his soul, the pastor bowed his head to pronounce the benediction. When he raised it, the back seat was empty.

Two of the deacons were waiting for him in the vestibule when he came out. After a word of greeting he inquired, with a professional interest, if either of them had noticed a lady dressed in black, who sat in the last seat of the chapel, quite close to the door.

"She has a remarkably fine voice, as I observed in the singing of the last hymn. But my attention was first drawn to her by her manner of listening to the lecture. I do not think she lost one word of it," he subjoined, with the frank vanity which, although not confined to men of his calling, is seldom so outspoken in other professions. "She has an intelligent face, and one that seemed strangely familiar to me. I have probably seen her in some other church when I have exchanged pulpits with some of my New York or Brooklyn brethren. Should she come to us again, we must look her up. We cannot be too attentive to the stranger within our gates."

Neither of the deacons had noticed the stranger until they were singing the last hymn, and neither had any idea who she was. Both agreed with Dr. Barnes that she had a wonderful voice, and one thought she "sang like a professional."

When they turned up the street, and Dr. and Mrs. Barnes down, the latter had something to say.

"I saw that woman when she came into the chapel." Belonging to a more modern and less formal school than her husband, she said " woman " instead of " lady." Being one of the laity, she had no flattering delusions upon another point. " But I don't agree with you in thinking that she listened attentively to the lecture. She kept her eyes on you, yet it looked to me more like the polite trick of a well-bred person, accustomed to appear interested in a speaker, than real hearing and thinking of what one hears. She has an eager, intense face, and, unless I am greatly mistaken in her physiognomy, she is intensely miserable. I never saw a sadder gaze. Her mourning is not new, so her trouble must be of some other kind. I don't believe, moreover, that she is in the habit of attending prayer-meetings regularly. She just happened into ours, in passing. She did not come in until after the second hymn, and dropped into the first seat she came to. There was a *hunted* look about her that struck me at once, and, combined with the impression that I had seen her before, made me uneasy. It set me to thinking of stories I have read of women meditating suicide who stole into churches on the way to the river. I was glad that you gave out that last hymn; and her way of singing it confirmed me in the idea that it was just the word in season for her."

"Upon my word, Annie, you seem to have made more use of your eyes than of your ears during service." Dr. Barnes had an excellent disposition, and was loyally fond of his bright helpmeet; but one or two things in this speech grated upon his ear. "While I make no pretensions to being an entertaining preacher, it is within the range of possibility that this stranger, who, I am convinced, has heard me somewhere before, may have followed my humble remarks with more attention than you imagine probable."

"My dear William! I assure you —"

"I have the floor, I believe, my love!" with a vexed little laugh and a show of extreme politeness. "I was about to question if it is consistent with Christian charity of thought — as practised by *men* at least — to jump to the conclusion that every woman who comes late to prayer-meeting, and has the bad taste to listen intently to what is said, and to look solemn after a searching, practical discourse, must, of necessity, be an abandoned creature bent upon self-murder."

Sensible Mrs. Barnes, a clergyman's wife of over a score of years' standing, recalling to mind that her spouse had had a trying day and was still fasting, quickened her pace a little, and glanced up solicitously.

"Is that a drop of rain upon my nose?" she cried blithely. "You were sensible in not wearing your new hat to-night, and I foolish in venturing out in one which I cannot afford to have spoiled; but I do not care to pay too dearly for the lesson."

A favorite supper dish, kept warm over hot water until he had finished the day's labors, and a cup of fresh black coffee made by his wife's deft hands after they got home, did their part toward restoring the good man to his wonted serenity, and banishing the now unwelcome image of the intelligent stranger, who, after all, might have simulated rapt attention to a plain talk prepared for the more spiritually-minded of his own flock, who would compose his audience on a wet night.

The more imaginative wife did not dismiss the subject so easily from her silent thoughts.

"That woman's face haunts me," she soliloquized over her mending-basket, when her husband had withdrawn to his study, renewed in body and spirit. "I could not keep my eyes from wandering to her while William was speaking. And the voice too, I could be sure went with it in my mind. Poor, dear William!" here she smiled in affectionate amusement, " it was thoughtless in me to rub his fur the wrong way by my inconsiderate talk. I never dreamed of intimating that she was a bad woman. There was not a sign of that sort of thing about her except the misery in a face I seem to recollect as happy and smiling."

Half an hour afterward she tapped at her husband's study door. Gentle birth and breeding had made her punctilious in the practice of the smallest courtesies of life.

She said, "I beg your pardon," when she failed to catch the hurried or mumbled speech of a servant, and never entered the door of a member of her family without knocking. She was a comely body, with perfect teeth, expressive brown eyes, and the clear brunette complexion was, like Olivia's, "ingrain." Just now her face was youthful under the flush and flash of excitement.

"William, dear! I am positive that I know that woman!" was her introductory outburst, as the opening door revealed the reverend student bending over his desk.

He looked up with labored mildness.

"What woman, my love?"

"Excuse me! What a blunderer I am! The stranger at the chapel this evening. And so will you when I remind you that you were at her wedding eighteen — almost nineteen years ago. Don't you recollect Alice Lanier, who married that handsome, fascinating, shiftless Ernest Paull? She and I were dear friends at school, and until we were both of us married. I declare I have no patience with myself for not recognizing her at once to-night. Yet she is so sadly changed that I never thought of my old friend. I saw the notice of her father's death two or three years ago, and ought to have written to her. There is no doubt of that. But you know how selfishly we let such opportunities slip by; and I had lost her address, and other matters crowded upon me, — and so I did n't do the decent and kind thing. The last I heard of her, she was living away up town, near the High Bridge somewhere, — and New York is such a howling wilderness. There must be something akin to sin in a life so busy, such absorption in one's selfish interests, as to leave no time and thought for others, no matter how dearly we loved them once. I was very fond of Alice. She was one of the cleverest, most affectionate, and altogether charming women I ever knew. It hurts me to the quick of my heart to compare her face as I saw it an hour ago with what it was on her wedding-night."

She had run herself down at last, and sat down to pant silently, while her husband availed himself of the gap to insert some judicial questions.

"'Shiftless' and 'fascinating,' did you call her husband? What else do you know of him? Were you acquainted with him before their marriage?"

"Very slightly. I never saw him after the wedding. You may recollect — and you probably don't — that we could not attend the reception given to them at her brother's, Mr. Roger Lanier's, on their return from a year abroad, — their bridal tour. Elizabeth was just six weeks old, and I could not leave her."

"Woman's chronology!" interpolated Dr. Barnes, indulgent of the weakness. "That fixed the date of the marriage in your mind."

She nodded decidedly, coloring as she laughed.

"Of course it did! Some poet has made a calendar of the flowers. The mother's way of reckoning time is prettier and more poetical too, to my mind, to say nothing of its infallibility. Never dispute a date determined by a baby's age. I wonder if poor Alice has living children. I cannot describe to you with what a shock I identified as my gay-spirited, prosperous school-fellow the stranger in mourning that was almost shabby, and with such a woe-worn face. I felt as if I had seen a ghost. What could have brought her to our chapel, or to Brooklyn at all? and out alone on such a disagreeable night, — and in Mendebras Avenue, of all places in Brooklyn? There is a mystery about the whole affair. Then the way in which she broke out in that last hymn! Her voice sings in my ears yet. William, I cannot forgive myself for not recognizing her then and there. The conviction is so strong upon me that she is in some trouble."

"My blessed child, how you run on! Even if the to-you-mysterious stranger be your old acquaintance, — which, mark you, I do not admit as a certainty, — the incident is simple and unremarkable. For aught you know, she may be living in Brooklyn, and have felt some curiosity to hear the husband of her former friend preach, granting that nothing else led her to attend divine service. It is clear that she did not recognize you, or she would have waited to speak to you. Eighteen years have changed you as well as herself. For the better, allow me to say," the genuine affection that underlay the thin crust of conceit fostered by parish adulation, breaking through in an appreciative gleam as he surveyed the matron who was ten years his junior, and looked fully fifteen years younger; "but time exacts tribute of us all.

The comeliness of forty-five is not the bloom of twenty."

For once the wife was unmindful of the conjugal compliment. Her elbow on the arm of her chair, her cheek on her hand, she was gazing into the past.

"Maybe she shrank from meeting me," she said thoughtfully. "Times have evidently altered for the worse with her. She was always proud. She came of old Huguenot stock, and they thought a great deal of family honor. There were three sisters. One lives in San Francisco, another in England; both are older than Alice. The only living brother, Roger Lanier, was especially fond of her. He was one of the best, yet proudest, men I ever saw, — a model of business integrity. I see his name in the papers now and then in connection with benevolent and religious enterprises. He is very rich, I imagine. I shouldn't think he would let Alice suffer for want of money."

"It is highly improbable!" said Dr. Barnes, dryly, glancing at his manuscript. It was Friday night, and his first sermon for Sunday was unfinished. "Perhaps she is a widow."

"Oh, I think not! It is more likely that he has been unsuccessful in business. She was not in widow's weeds. You asked what I know about Ernest Paull. He was a banker, or a broker, or something that sounded rich, and promised to make him richer. Papa thought him visionary and unstable, I recollect, and only 'hoped my friend had chosen wisely.' You know what that means when a man like papa says it. But" — starting briskly up and apologetically — "I won't detain you any longer. I could not help rushing in like a whirlwind the instant the truth broke in upon me. You won't sit up late, will you, darling?"

As she passed into the hall, the monotonous drip of rain upon the skylight overhead caught her ear, and she drew herself together with a shrug of conscious comfort, as a bird tucks his head under his wing when "the north winds do blow." Home and family warmth were blessings worth being thankful for on a stormy night. She went downstairs to lock up the house for the night. William would not think of it for hours to come. Instead of closing the front parlor shutters, she lowered the gas, raised the window, and looked out into the street, moved by an impulse she could not define. It was, in English phrase, "a nasty night," — the sidewalks and round paving-stones shining greasily under the street-gas, the rain falling in hair-like streams, close and steady. Without being bitterly cold, the air made her flesh crawl. The pastor's wife was not, it is superfluous to remark, a rich woman; but her nest was cosey; her life, albeit not exempt from the trials incident to the changes and chances of clerical existence, was sheltered and honorable. Her William had his ways like other men; but love had piloted her among the reefs, whirlpools, and shallows of these for twenty-two years, and she no longer feared or was annoyed by them. She had perfect trust in his sterling virtues, in the sincerity of his piety, and in his love for herself. Experience had taught her the marvellous art of supplementing her partner's deficiencies without letting him suspect that she did him this good turn, and, a more marvellous thing still, without lowering her own respect for him.

All this passed so rapidly through her brain that she could hardly have traced the links of the chain of revery. Thoughts of the three children given into arms that opened in rapturous gratitude to receive them as God's choicest earthly gifts; of troops of friends, tried and true; of opportunities for serving the Master, and her kind, — overflowed her heart with a sudden glow and rush.

"Dear life! sweet life! *full* life!" she breathed inarticulately, tears warming eyelids already chilled by the misting rain.

A woman's figure passed between her and the street-lamp nearest the minister's house. It was wrapped in a long black cloak, glistening with rime. The eyes looked straight forward; the yellow light struck across a face that was haggard and rigid.

"Alice!" called Mrs. Barnes, tentatively.

The apparition was so unexpected that she could scarcely credit the fidelity of her own eyes. She might also, she reasoned swiftly, be mistaken in fancying that the woman was the same she had seen in the chapel. Much thinking upon the incident might have heated her imagination. She could have believed that the figure, already quite beyond her window, faltered, and glanced from right to left. Mrs. Barnes leaned over the sill, and repeated the cautious call in wooing intonations: —

"Alice! Alice!"

Then she ran to the front door, and opened it. The street, as far as she could see up and down, was empty of any living presence. The dimmed lamps and the close web of rain had the night all to themselves.

CHAPTER II.

The hardness of our task lies here: that we have to strive against the grievous things of life while hope remains, as if they were evil, and then, when the stroke has fallen, to accept them from the hand of God, and doubt not they were good. — J. MARTINEAU.

CHAPTER II.

ALICE PAULL had gone out that evening because she could not stay in the house. She had never tried to delude herself by giving the title of "home" to the two-and-a-half-story frame house with a high "stoop," on the humble avenue with the high-sounding name, into which she had removed with her family last April, yet it was all the home they had. Neighbors and neighborhood they had none. One can, if so disposed, as easily live in Brooklyn six months, or six years, without knowing so much as the names of the people next door to her, as in the bigger city across the river. It is a common error to suppose that this sort of indifferentism is confined to the rich and worldly.

Without guessing at the truth, the Paulls were the more effectually isolated by the impression created by the household stuff transported from the vans to the two-and-a-half-story house. Every article of furniture, however ingeniously muffled up, was detected and criticised by the denizens over the way, and on either side of what figured in the real estate agent's advertisement as "that desirable cottage residence, at 363 Mendebras Avenue, between Post and Pillar streets, and combining all the advantages of town and country." There was not too much furniture for a small house, but the pieces were too large for the rooms and altogether too handsome for the vicinity — decided the spectators, standing well back in their upper chambers, not to be seen through the windows. Mrs. Gaze, at 364, settled in her mind at a glance that the big carved buffet must be set in the back parlor. "It couldn't never no way at all be shoved into the basement dining-room, without they tore the front of the house out." Mrs. Pryor, at 365, "wondered the new folks next door had n't traded off that big grand piano for a small upright." She "admired to see things suitable, and that lumbering elephant of a thing would take up the front parlor."

The crowning offence was a billiard-table, to admit which a basement window had to be taken bodily from the casings. It set the stamp of disreputableness upon the whole establishment in the estimation of the steady-goers thereabouts. Such appurtenances might do for the private residences of rich New Yorkers who tampered with all sorts of soul-destructive playthings, but it was not what Mendebras Avenue, where so many people owned their houses, was used to.

The Paulls kept but one "girl," Scotch by birth, fifty years old, and an inveterate stay-in-doors, except on Sunday, when she went a mile and a half, clear to Williamsburgh, to attend a Scotch Presbyterian Church. Thus much was gleaned by a boy who went down on a street-car with her one Sunday morning, and saw where she got off. She did all the marketing, bringing her purchases home in a covered basket, and taking in the ice at the basement door with her own hands, never allowing a strange foot to cross the threshold, and resisting all neighborly blandishments looking toward chats over the back fence, and while sweeping the sidewalk. Yet the tale somehow got about that the new folks ate in the back parlor, the billiard-table being devoted to the purpose for which it was made. Mrs. Keeneyse, at 366, had "hoped that it was a second-hand affair bought cheap and meant to be used for a dining-table. As it was, she had n't a word more to say, except that times had changed, and Mendebras Avenue was no exception to the rule."

When the weather grew warmer, the secret of the novel scandal was soon out at the open windows. More than one passer-by on summer nights was reported to have been misled as to the respectability of the neighborhood by hearing the click of the ivory balls, and men's voices in merry conversation in the front basement.

The family proper consisted, as was soon ascertained, of father and mother, a lad of seventeen or thereabouts, a girl somewhat younger, two boys of ten and eight, and a little girl of six. Eight souls, all told, counting in the immortal part of the Scotch "girl," — and a close fit for No. 363. True, the father, who must have been a splendid figure of a man when young, was away from home for weeks at a time. They did say that he travelled for a New York concern — silk, some thought, and others, straw goods. All the family except Mrs. Paull and the Scotch girl were away in July and August. Somebody — nobody could specify whom — had said that they had swell relations who owned " places " at Newport or somewhere else, and took a sight of notice of the children. The oldest boy was off at boarding-school, or maybe college; and the biggest girl, she went away early Monday morning and came home on Friday night, so she was most likely in a school in New York. Twice, on very stormy Fridays, she had been brought home in a bang-up private carriage.

Taking all these drawbacks into consideration, the Paulls went ill with the setting in which some reverse of fortune had placed them. The sturdy, honest pride of their neighbors did not revolt at the almost certainty that the new people had once been wealthy, and in circles of which they — the Mendebras Avenueites — knew nothing except by hearsay. Nor would the "bang-up" brougham have held them back from "neighboring" with the pale woman in black who was rarely seen beyond her doors by daylight, but who had been met a mile away after dark, more than once, walking fast and noticing nobody.

Brooklyn is the safest place on the globe for unescorted women by day or by night; and this Mrs. Paull carried herself so like a lady born who minded her own business and let other people's business alone, that she would not be insulted even in New York. But — and the "but" was deep and broad and long and high — there was the billiard-table in the front basement, and a something everybody felt and nobody succeeded in defining, in the general air and tone of the household, that deterred sober housekeepers and householders from making advances to the strangers in their midst. And, finally, the new folks did not appear to have any regular church connection. When the father spent Sunday at home, he sat near the front windows, looking like a picture, or a nobleman on the stage, in a black velvet smoking-jacket, and read the thirty-two pages of the paper while church-goers trooped by, to and from their various places of worship. In the summer months, when Mrs. Paull and Elspeth held the fort, they went to church somewhere every Sunday, without fail. Since the children got back, the mother usually accompanied them, presumably to some place of worship, on Sunday forenoon, but they went sometimes up-street, sometimes down, — a circumstance that pointed to spiritual tramphood.

In Brooklyn, a church home — to wit, a pew, the rent of which is paid promptly, and participation in Sunday-school or parish work, together with a kindly desire to do good and to communicate to one's fellow-Christians — constitutes a passport to the hearts and homes of "regular residents." It may be a primitive state of society in cosmopolitan eyes, but it is apostolic — and Christ-like. The household of faith is not an empty phrase; the band holding together the communion of saints is strong and of pure gold.

Thus stood affairs with the Paulls in their immediate neighborhood on the evening of the twenty-second of November, the Friday preceding Thanksgiving week.

Within doors, Scotch Elspeth, sitting over her tea in the kitchen, heard her mistress's step in the lower hall, and arose mechanically as Mrs. Paull entered. The fifty-year-old girl had "gentle-folk ways" in such matters. Unless deprived of the use of her lower limbs, she would as soon have thought of standing on her head as of remaining seated when receiving orders from an employer. The entrance of the latter was to her like the drill sergeant's "Attention!" to rank and file.

Mrs. Paull was dressed for walking. She was never florid; to-night her very lips were colorless. There were livid semi-circles under her eyes which were dull and deep; but her voice was even, and she spoke, as always, pleasantly to the elderly servant.

"Elspeth, I have put the children to bed, and am going out for a long walk. My head aches badly, and the walk may do me good."

"It's very damp, ma'am."

Elspeth had been an American for forty years without ridding her tongue of the North Country "burr." She was secretly vain of her excellent English, firmly persuaded in her own mind that nobody would ever guess her nationality from her speech, whereas she betrayed it in feature, voice, and accent to the least observant. When excited, she lapsed into the vernacular. On this occasion, she did not quite say "verra," but the *y* suggested the broader vowel, and she rolled a pair of *r's*.

"I never take cold, you know, and I have my waterproof. Please leave the kitchen door open that you may hear the children should they awake."

"I will, ma'am. Do not give yesel' ony uneasiness aboot them. They'll likely not stir till ye get back."

"Thank you. I hope they will not be troublesome."

The domestic never betrayed inquisitiveness, however eccentric might seem the behavior of any member of the household. Her scorn of gossip extended to her self-communings, yet she shook her iron-gray head at the clang of the closing front door, and poured out a third cup of tea with an audible sigh.

Mr. Lanier, Mrs. Paull's brother, and a trustee under their father's will of her portion of the patrimonial estate, had spent a long time with his sister that afternoon. He looked grave and preoccupied when Elspeth admitted him, and to her eyes Mrs. Paull had worn an unnatural aspect ever since. True, she made talk with the three children over their evening meal, only cautioning Tom not to laugh too loudly, for "mamma had a headache." She chatted cheerfully with them on the way up to bed, too, and would make Elspeth go down to supper while she undressed Gladys with her own hands.

"But she's aye one to keep hersel' to hersel'," reflected the discreet Scotch girl.

She had almost deserved the name when she took service with Mr. Lanier twenty-five years before. At "Miss Alice's" marriage she had asked to be allowed to go with her to her new home as chambermaid and seamstress, and had followed her young lady's fortunes faithfully ever since. Until after the birth of Tom, the third child, she had had assistants in the housework, sometimes three or four fellow-servants. Then began the gradual decline in the apparent prosperity of the wedded pair. There was a bad crash about the time Gladys was born, five years ago, — a crash so loud that the world heard it. Ernest Paull's business career for fifteen years had been a descending scale: one year a hitch, another a break; a third a drag, with wheels that creaked dryly. His father-in-law had set him up in divers businesses of various degrees of promise, once and again, and as everybody knew, although not from him or his son, had lost heavily from hitch and crash, having furnished the oil for the creaking wheels.

At his death, two years prior to the date of our first chapter, he had left his daughter Alice twenty-five thousand dollars in real estate and stocks, but so tied up by legal knots that she could not touch the interest without the consent of her trustees and her father's executors, while the principal was strictly entailed upon her children. The purport of the testament was unmistakable. Mr. Lanier, Sr., did not mean that his son-in-law should profit directly by any more of his money.

Elspeth had assuredly never been told what were the provisions of the will, or why they should be particularly obnoxious to "Miss Alice's" husband, but a pretty accurate knowledge of the state of family politics had filtered into her mind. Mr. Paull had broken out several times when she was within ear-shot into caustic gibes relative to his wife as a property-holder, and himself as her pensioner, and, whereas, up to the senior Lanier's decease, Ernest had been upon apparently friendly terms with his brother-in-law, it was yet more apparent now that the relations between the two men were strained to the point of parting.

Once, while removing the dishes from the table, the discreet hand-maiden had heard the master of the house say in reply to a question from Edwin, the youngest boy,—

"'Why don't I stay at home like other little children's fathers?' Because, my son, this is not my home any more. It is mamma's house, and everything in it belongs to her. She holds the purse-strings, and your Uncle Roger tells her just how much money she can have to support you and your brothers and sisters. If you were older, you would understand that the interest of twenty-five thousand dollars at four-and-a-half per cent (your uncle doesn't believe in a higher rate than that) won't lodge, feed, and clothe eight people. Especially, when one of the eight has been brought up as the daughter of one millionnaire and the sister of another. Poor papa, having spent all the money he has made in the last twenty years upon his wife and children, must scuffle for himself for the rest of his life."

His wife's eyes had blazed indignantly at him from a deathly white face, as he said it, but not a word escaped her.

The scene was one of many that made Elspeth return thanks morning and night that she "belonged to nae mon, gentle or simple, but could gang her ain gait wi' nane to say, 'Why do ye sae?'" Her mistress's economies would have enlightened her partially as to the financial stress that had overtaken the family, had none of these streamlets of information trickled into her ears. The faithful creature had to be taken into confidence so far as to be made to comprehend that Mr. Paull had had heavy losses, and that since the children must be educated, there was little to spare for luxurious comforts, nothing for superfluities. She knew what Marie, the elder daughter and her mother's intimate associate, did not seem to notice, — that Mrs. Paull had not bought one new article for herself since she put on black for her father, that napkins and table-cloths, sheets, and even towels, were darned as long as the old threads would bear the new, and that the children's underclothes, frocks, and jackets were mute miracles of the mother's skill in repairing and making over.

Mr. Paull's costume showed no sign of thoughtful thrift. To be well dressed was a part of the stock-in-trade of a "man on the road." He had travelled for several houses in the last five years, his handsome face and pleasing address going further in recommending him to employers and customers than anybody but himself suspected. If he ever reckoned up his assets, he put these down at double their real value. He had no trouble in getting a position. Keeping it was another thing. In the "dull season," he found recreation at the Rangeley Lakes, Les Chenaux, or the Adirondacks. As a crack shot and expert fly-fisherman, he had what he would have described as "a national reputation," and was welcome wherever sportsmen congregated. The air of these resorts and the society found there were absolutely necessary for building up his health and spirits to sustain the hardships of the next winter's campaign.

As he informed his wife, he made barely enough to meet his few personal expenses and to pay the rent of a house in which his family could live. He had no home, and never expected to have one until his wife should buy a six-feet-two lot for him in Greenwood. There was an insurance of ten thousand dollars upon his worthless life, he would add jocularly. Without alluding to the fact that Mrs. Paull paid the yearly premium upon it, he liked to jest upon the profit she would derive from his death. Perhaps she might prevail upon her trustee to spare her a few dollars for a slate headstone; or one of marbleized iron would make more show for less money. As to lettering, there would be no sense in wasting her wealth in epitaphical lies. "Here lies a failure!" would cover the whole ground, and unite truth and pathos.

He was sentimentally fond of his children, particularly of his pretty daughter, Marie, whose resemblance to himself was delicious flattery. Had he spent more time with them, he would have vitiated the mother's wholesome influence. As it was, with all the love and respect they bore her, they were inclined to pity him as the victim of circumstances, and Marie to wonder that mamma did not sell houses or stocks, or make some other effort to enable them all to live together the year round. When a hint of this veiled feeling transpired, Alice Paull held her peace. What was there that she could say?

She had never uncovered the grinning skeleton in the closet of her heart even to the brother who was her confidant in all else, or so much as confessed to him that her husband had a fault.

He had visited her on this afternoon upon a painful errand, and as a man of sense and feeling, had done it without cruel delays. So-called preparation for bad news is but so many additional turns of the rack-screw.

Ernest Paull had gone abroad that morning, leaving a letter to be delivered to Roger Lanier after he had sailed. It commissioned him to break the truth to his sister. Mr. Paull had speculated with money collected by him for his late employers, and lost it. Since he had no private resources on which to draw for reparation of the misfortune, he had but one resort, — flight.

Where he obtained funds for the voyage and the proposed sojourn in a foreign land, he did not see fit to specify. The date of his return was, in the circumstances, so remote and uncertain that his wife would act wisely in basing no calculations upon the event. She must shape her future course according to her own judgment and her brother's advice. This would be the easier, inasmuch as these had been the rule of her faith and practice for many months. Her husband, since his severe pecuniary losses set in, had been such an insignificant factor in her existence that his withdrawal from the scene of action would not affect her seriously, except so far as it wounded the Lanier pride. For himself, he had found this same pride an expensive — he might say a ruinous — luxury for a poor man.

Her marriage — before her judgment was matured by the influence of heredity and advice — to one whom she had chosen to treat as a cipher on the wrong side of the unit representing her potent personality, was the fatal blunder of her life.

"I forbear to add, of mine also, conscious as I am that that would count for little in her opinion and that of her counsellors. My heart is wrung to bleeding by the thought of leaving my children (God bless and keep them forever!). Had I been permitted to exercise the sacred privilege, I would have proved myself more to them than a father in name only. As man and husband, I will not interfere with their mother's management of them. Sometimes I dream that in the days to come, when she sees reflected in their innocent faces the lineaments of the unhappy being whom she once believed that she loved, whose misfortune, not whose fault, it has been to forfeit that affection, — she may so far compromise with her stern sense of rectitude as to let them speak of the exile now and then, and affectionately. I cannot bear to think that my darlings will forget me utterly. I know that she will refrain from poisoning their minds against me. In this I trust to her magnanimity.

"This is the sum of my requests to your sister, Mr. Lanier. Knowing, as I do, how severe are her ideas upon certain subjects, how relentless her prejudices against every form of speculation; that she esteems all games and operations in which chance has a part as inventions of the Enemy of souls, — I comprehend fully what degree of charity will be used in computing the iniquity of this, my latest and heaviest disaster."

Such was the letter placed in Alice Paull's hands by her brother with the simple preface, "My dear sister, I am the bearer of disagreeable news. It is all written here in your husband's hand. May our Heavenly Father grant you strength to bear it and to live for your children!"

She read the four closely written pages through, down to the signature, and turned back to the letter-head to see that it bore the date, — " Fifth Avenue Hotel, Thursday morning, November the twenty-first, 188–," and letting her hand with the letter fall in her lap, looked down at it as at a horror that had changed her to stone.

"He is a thorough villain, — a hypocritical villain!" said Roger Lanier, in wrath the deeper for his enforced self-control. "He knew every word he has written concerning you to be a lie, deliberately planned to wound in the tenderest sensibilities the best, most patient, most heroic wife that was ever bestowed upon one so utterly unworthy of her."

She turned the letter over in stunned bewilderment, seeming to study it for further light.

"I have not been patient, brother; I have tried to do right, but I am not naturally amiable, as you know. Perhaps I have never understood him; never made allowances for the temperament and education that were so unlike mine."

"You have ruined your life for his sake!"

"I gave it to him when I married him — that and everything else I had or hoped to have — 'for better, for worse, for richer, for poorer.'"

The low, hopeless tones, the dry eyes, worst of all, the wan, lightless smile that went with the words, cut the listener to the heart. He burst out with an impatient ejaculation.

"Alice! I cannot, I will not have you blame yourself. You shall not attempt to excuse him. Have I not seen the several steps of your disillusion, yet was obliged to hold my tongue? Ernest Paull has proved himself a specious, utterly selfish braggart, unstable in principle, in action — in everything but evil. You cannot conceal this from yourself. Why try to make me think that you do?"

She raised her eyes, blank and miserable, to his face.

"Must the children hear of this? He is their father, Roger. He loves them, and they love him. Or is it inevitable that the story should be made public?"

"We will do our best to hush it up. I have seen the men to whom he owes the money. There will be no prosecution."

She took him up on the instant.

"Because you have made good their loss!"

"Hush! That is neither here nor there. His name is the same as yours and your children's. My chief concern is your comfort and happiness. This man must be a stranger to you from this time forth."

"I am his wife, Roger!"

He started up, strode to the window, and remained there, his head bent, his fingers knotted behind his back, seeming to stare into the little yard where Elspeth was stretching dish-towels upon the line. Her stuff skirt was folded back above her knees, he observed, and pinned so tightly he wondered that she could walk. There were eight towels, and three were patched. Elspeth had a blue cotton handkerchief tied about her head like a turban.

His sister joined him, laying a timid hand upon his cheek, her voice breaking as he drew her head to his breast. He stroked back her hair as he would his own little daughter's were he compelled to deny her petition; his brow and lips were unbent.

"Roger, dear, don't be displeased with me! I think my heart is breaking with the sorrow and the shame of it all. And what he says is bitter! bitter! But he is my husband, and, as he reminds me, my children's father. I vowed to forsake all others and hold to him,— to love, honor, and obey. Nothing can release me from that obligation."

"Except — except — " the blood flooding his forehead darkly — "Alice! — sweet sister! believe me that I would not tell you if I could help it — I made it my business before coming here to see his employers and others who were yet better conversant with his life of late. I have long suspected that he had other claims upon his means than you know of. He has not gone abroad alone. I saw the entry in his own handwriting in the office where he bought his tickets. He registered 'Paul Morgan and wife, Cincinnati.'"

She dropped back as if struck by a bullet. Her brother caught her and carried her to a sofa. She had not swooned. Insensibility is a boon seldom granted to women of her mould. There was a minute of voiceless gasping ; her hands, groping convulsively as in the dark, found and fastened upon one of her brother's. She raised it to her lips and pressed it there before she said hollowly, —

"If you can come over to-morrow to see me — we will talk of what it will be best to do. Or — shall I go to you?"

This he would not allow. He would call soon after breakfast. His time — his means — all that he had or could do — were at her service.

Then he asked — for he knew her as few could know her, —

" You would like to be alone now ? "

" Don't think me ungrateful — but it would be better — perhaps. Thank you for understanding me."

She had spoken truly in telling Elspeth, three hours after this interview, that her " head ached."

CHAPTER III.

How long? How long, O Healer? Thou dost know
   It is not in me to hold still;
In meekness, like Thy saintly ones, to bow,
   A reed before Thy gracious will.
A Sunset Prophecy.

CHAPTER III.

THAT man does not live — he has never lived — who comprehends the iniquitous mystery of a woman's "constitutional headache," — the foe who never omits an opportunity to spring upon his prey, and has all seasons for his very own. Sometimes he is provoked to attack by a fast; sometimes by a feast; often by insomnia, and occasionally by too-sound slumber. Now he creeps by almost imperceptible inches to the acme of torture; again, leaps, fell and furious, from his lair as the sleeper awakes at morning to the horrors of demoniacal possession. With one victim the agonies of nausea augment the pains in the head; with another, one lobe of the brain throbs with mad anguish, and the other is dull and heavy as lead. A third cannot lift her head from the pillow without the agonized conviction that a ball of hot metal, pulsing as in a boiling kettle, rolls from one side of her cranium to the other.

There is the headache that assails the base of the brain and the adjacent cords of the neck, and still another form which lodges in the temples, and one variety, the seat of which is the frontal bone and the eyeballs, making light intolerable and sight a torment. No more excruciating form is or can be experienced than that induced by mental pain, — a sudden shock to nerve-centres and sensibilities. Then the frightened blood retreats to the citadel-brain, and will not be lured or compelled back to the clammy extremities; shivers run over the surface of the body, and the congesting pores alternately contract and gape, reducing the skin now to freezing coldness, anon to the dry heat of fever. Delirium is a not infrequent accompaniment of the last-named phase of this plague of feminine flesh; an insane disposition to talk! talk! talk! until exhaustion or stupor intervenes, or the wild longing to escape from the place of torture, to find surcease from suffering in the wilderness, in the woods, in the sea — anywhere, be it in the grave itself, so long as unconsciousness follows flight.

Once in a while, one reads in the daily prints of an unfortunate — sometimes the loving and beloved mother of a respectable family — who leaps from an upper window while suffering from nervous headache, or, wandering away from her bed in the dead of night, is found, after days of anxious search, in the river or at the bottom of the well. Or, a healthy, happy woman complains of intense pains in the head, and after some hours of agony, dies in convulsions.

Ah, dear friends! much of tragedy lurks in the jests passed upon the all-convenient headache of the novel heroine and the every day-woman of real life.

"Synonymous with heartache?" Ay! and oftentimes the synonym of the death-throe of heart and brain.

Elspeth was used to her mistress's headaches, and played the skilled nurse when the "constitutional" malady routed the gallant will and laid the wrecked woman low. She was used, too, to seeing her set off upon the long lonely tramps, as often as not in the evening, after the children were safely folded,— walks from which the sufferer would return languid and tremulous, but able at last to sleep off the duller ache that had superseded keener pangs. She surmised — this shrewd and reserved servitor — that a business talk had brought on the attack. Had she had an inkling of the real condition of the thoroughbred who quitted her kitchen with a level chin and firm tread, she would have barricaded the front door to keep her in — as a countrywoman of hers had hundreds of years before — with her living bone and flesh.

The humid chill of the outer air was grateful to the pedestrian's hot forehead. She halted at the foot of her porch-steps to draw in great breaths of it. The gloom of the ill-lighted streets, where gas fought feebly with the falling fog, was welcome to eyes strained with staring into a future peopled with dreads.

She had loved her husband through indifference and open neglect and active unkindness; had served him as a dog his master, after she knew there was nothing to be gained by fidelity of service. Years ago — after long striving, at first sanguine, finally desperate — she had resigned all hope of winning him to a higher manhood; had tried to accept him as he was and must ever remain, and to make the very best of the poor remnant of her happy dream of their united lives. Only He whom she besought without ceasing to give her grace, wisdom, and patience, knew with what ingenuity she had endeavored to cloak

Ernest's faults, and to make home attractive to the unsuccessful man sour with discontent, and at war with fortune.

The billiard-table was put into their New York house against her wishes. But when it was a fixture and her husband's solace in moodiness and petulance, she became his pupil, and learned to play a better game than most of the boon companions he liked — and she dreaded — to see about him. She made it convenient to be much in the room when billiards were played; and in her presence there was none of the betting she was confident ran high at other times. She detested all games of cards, as her father had before her, but Ernest encountered nowhere else so clever an opponent at backgammon and chess. Music was his most innocent recreation; and she devoted to her piano-practice whole hours of the day which she knew she must make up by toiling late into the night over her needle. His fastidious ear must not be offended by slovenly execution or false notes when he took it into his head to ask for a musical evening.

Love in such natures as this woman's is of a hardier growth than respect. Her stubborn fealty to her husband never allowed her to confess in her inmost thoughts that she despised him. She was too honest to pretend, in thought or in prayer, that she had honored him for the last ten years.

She could have told the day and hour when respect died an unnatural death. Ernest Paull was the treasurer of a charitable society connected with the church to which he and his wife belonged, and he had appropriated, to purposes of his own, funds held by him in trust for the organization. He had used the money for necessary expenses, he stated briefly to his wife. A woman of her breeding and tastes entailed upon her husband the obligation to live beyond his income. He dragged a lengthening chain of debt, and expected to do this while he lived; but this five or six hundred dollars — maybe it had mounted up to a thousand by this time — must be made up in some way, and speedily, or he was ruined. To be sure, there was the river, or a pistol-shot, or prussic acid, as an alternative, but there might be a disagreeable degree of publicity connected with that expedient. All this he uttered airily between the puffs of his cigar, eying her quizzically — as if curious as to the effect of the communication upon her mind.

With strange composure, that ought to have warned him of volcanic changes going on beneath the placid surface, she insisted upon knowing the exact amount of the defalcation.

"An ugly word to ears polite, my love!" interrupted her husband.

"The thing is uglier. Tell me the whole truth, Ernest. Of course, I must get the money if you cannot."

"From your father, I suppose?" looking up from the row of figures he was at work upon.

"To whom else can I apply? I shall not tell him why I want it."

"Naturally not!" with a faint sneer. "While you are tapping the parental pocket, you may as well ask for two thousand as one. There are other liabilities."

"Will three thousand cover everything?"

He assured her eagerly and seriously that it would — and more. In fact, it would set him straight with the world.

When she went to her father with her request, she stipulated that the money should be a loan to her personally, to be deducted from whatever portion he might have intended to leave her, should she survive him. In indorsing the check that put the whole amount into Ernest's hands, she frankly told him of the condition named by herself. A glare she had never seen there before flamed up in his handsome eyes.

"The woman who could do such a thing as that when her husband is the dupe of her sharp practice, is false to her marriage vows and capable of any depth of degradation," he said with incisive coolness. "After this, nothing you do can surprise me."

But he took the money.

The straight sheet of November fog was, to her heated fancy, the canvas upon which memory projected this and a succession of scenes, similar and yet more revolting. This man, calling himself a gentleman, and controlled in bodily exercise by the traditions of his class, had never lifted his hand against his wife, or failed in external demonstration of the deference due from his sex to hers. He would not, for example, have lowered himself in his own eyes by passing out of a door in advance of her, or by sitting while she stood; he would not have helped himself to an easy-chair when there was none for her, or kissed her with his hat on, or failed to raise it, if he met or parted with her on the street. His manner to his wife was cited as an example for other and less attentive husbands by their enviously admiring spouses. In society he was "simply and altogether charming." Society, reasoning after the superficial style peculiar to itself, inferred that he must be yet more charming in the bosom of his family.

An exclamation of intensest self-disgust passed her lips. A boy, loitering homeward with a parcel that looked like a loaf of bread under his arm, turned to look at her : —

" Eh ! what say ? "

Getting no reply, he stared hard at her and strolled on, rattling a stick against the palings and whistling a familiar hymn-tune. Brought back by the interruption to her actual environment, Alice Paull became aware that many voices near by were singing the same air, —

" Even me ! Even me !
Let some droppings fall on me ! "

She had never, to her present recollection, noticed until now the plain church wedged in between its neighbors on the right hand and on the left, and standing further back from the street than either of them, as if trying to make more room for itself. The singing was in a building at the rear. She turned in at the gate and walked down the narrow brick walk, — an insatiate soul-thirst gaining upon her.

The familiar melody was the murmur and cool-sounding ripple of a forest rill to the traveller upon the scorching highway. A wizened little sexton with thin white hair pushed open the inner door for her silently, and motioned her to an empty seat. The singing ceased as she sank wearily upon the settee — which was the last in the house — and leaned her head against the wall behind her. Every limb ached, and every nerve was a tense chord upon which pain smote fitfully — always with force.

This was the house of God, — the courts in which David, in his hour of fever and thirst, longed to be a doorkeeper.

"*The Lord bless thee and keep thee; send thee help out of Zion and strengthen thee out of the sanctuary!*"

The words must mean something, or they would not be in the Bible. If she were not in perishing need of help and strength, where in all the universe of the all-pitiful Father was there a wretch who was in extremity great enough to entitle her to claim the promised succor?

"Pass me not, O gracious Father!
Sinful though my heart may be."

Was that the way the hymn ran? Was there no balm for sorrow as for sin? These looked like good and sincere people, — above suspicion as to respectability. She was in the right place on that back seat.

"And thou begin with shame to take the lowest place."

"Grant one poor sinner more a place,
Among thy saints, O God of grace!"

Not even that belonged to her of right. She had never rented a pew in Brooklyn. Severe economies, bound upon her by circumstances unsuspected by the world outside of her home, had debarred her from that privilege. She had told Ernest one Sunday on her return from church, that she felt like a religious poacher. He was in a merry, kindly mood that day, or she would not have broached a subject fraught with humiliation of spirit to herself. She came of church-going people, who held as part of religion the obligation to support the public ordinances of the church. When she married Ernest Paull, he was superintendent of a Sunday-school and a deacon. He resigned both of these offices when he "went on the road." In four years he had not darkened the door of a church, and family worship was omitted when he was at home. In his absence, she gathered the little ones about her morning and night for Bible reading and prayers.

Had she failed in her duty to her husband in ceasing to remonstrate with him upon the duty he owed to God and the church He had ordained? Yet would it have made any difference in his behavior had she worried him with argument and entreaty?

She supposed nothing made any difference in anything now. She was a deserted wife. The name transmitted to her by a godly ancestry who had kept it clean was likely at any hour to be breathed upon by public scandal; would, perhaps, to-morrow be dragged through the filth of newspaper notoriety. Perhaps her picture and Ernest's would figure in black outlines all out of drawing, — just below the heading in fierce capitals, *Embezzlement and Elopement*.

Dear Father of pity! how wretched she was, torn and bleeding, and dying of thirst, soul and body!

"*Who, passing through the valley of Baca, make it a well; the rain also filleth the pools.*"

That tired-looking preacher must have quoted the text. It could not have come to her of itself. It had no relevancy to her case, except that parching thirst actually suggested water.

> "As pants the hart for cooling streams,
> When heated by the chase."

Ernest and she used to sing that together. He had a glorious voice. In the lower register the tones were like a bass drum; the higher were pure and mellow.

Why did she say "had" and "were," as if he were dead? He was never more alive than at this very moment. They would be well out to sea by now. She wondered, dully, between the spasms of pain, who "Mrs. Paul Morgan" was, and why she had never suspected her existence until Roger reluctantly told her that her husband had taken another wife with him. There had never been anything like this before in the Lanier family. They would take it hard, — her sisters and her sister-in-law. Maybe they would blame her. The wife is always blamed in such affairs.

Was she talking of herself? this woman sitting among respectable Christians, and thinking such things while they listened to the words of the man of God? She — she — Alice Paull — was a repudiated wife — disgraced forever! Between her and the sharpest blast of the world's scorn was not even the thin veil of a decent pretence of social caste. Her husband — the lover of her youth (and how she had loved and believed in him!), the father of her children — had turned loose all the furies of the bottomless pit upon her, and from afar, jeered at her misery.

"*All Thy waves and Thy billows have gone over me!*"

"All, Lord! not one is spared me. Out of the depths — ah! Thou, who rememberest our frame, knowest out of what depths — I cry unto Thee! Look upon my affliction and my pain! my affliction and my pain! my *pain!*"

She had not known where she was for a while, in the temporary stupor that yet did not release her from the sense of suffering. Her head lay against the hard wall; the heavy lids drooped until the eyes were almost hidden, while the neat little prayers, well put together and singularly correct in phraseology and grammatical construction for a plain, middle-class congregation, were addressed to the throne of grace. For aught they asserted or implied, every brother — and, judging by association, every sister — there had had precisely the same temptations and the same deliverances from temptations, the same sorrows, and joys as like to one another as impressions stamped by one and the same die.

As the rustle of consciousness that the duty of the evening was done, ran through the audience with the rising of the pastor to announce the last hymn, Alice Paull sat upright, a movement that concealed from her the face of the woman at the melodeon. A nameless quality in the touch upon the keys sent a faint thrill to the clammy hands and feet; as the flexible soprano, tenderly devout, took up the words of the sacred song, the heart of the stranger within the sacred gates was moved to longing that had in it some element of hope, — a wave of passionate desire, bursting bounds in the strain that electrified the hearers.

A wave, the undertow of which swept her out again into the outer night.

She was never able to recall, and Elspeth could only guess by her drenched clothing and hair, and the mire clogging her boots, how long or how far she walked after the service was over. She may have wandered around and around in a circle, a dim sense that she ought, by-and-by, to go home to her children keeping her in the neighborhood of Mendebras Avenue, if hers was the figure that passed her old school-fellow's window at ten o'clock. It was about eleven when the old servant, keeping watch at the darkened parlor-window, saw her mistress come laggingly up the steps, and hastened to open the door for her.

"Ah, Elspeth! You should not have sat up for me. Are the children all right?"

She brought out the words with an effort, taking short breaths between them. While speaking, she gained the stair-foot and began to go up, without waiting for an answer. As she climbed, she caught at the balustrade and lifted her feet with evident difficulty.

"It's yesel', ma'am, I should be speiring after, I'm thinking."

Elspeth said it behind her teeth, and followed her mistress to her room at a discreet distance. She brought forward an easy-chair, and as Mrs. Paull mechanically sank into it, began to undress her as she might Gladys, if the child had been caught in a shower, — swiftly and silently.

Mrs. Paull submitted without demur. When her bonnet was removed, she let her head drop against the cushioned back of the chair; her hands were limp, and cold as clay. Not a sound was heard in the room but the dull "frou-frou" of the soaked garments, as the servant drew them off and shook out the moisture, and her stepping to and fro. When a wadded wrapper was put on over the night-dress, Elspeth folded a thick shawl about the lady's knees, and, sitting down upon the floor, took the cold feet in her lap and chafed them fast and hard.

The languid lids were partially lifted, one lax hand moved toward the Scotchwoman's shoulder, but fell back without reaching it.

"Faithful among the faithless found!" said a hoarse whisper.

She dozed off again, not awaking while Elspeth wrapped her feet in warm flannel, laid them upon a cushion, and went to the bath-room for hot water with which to fill a rubber bag to put between the sheets. The sealed lids did not flicker even when she was lifted in a pair of strong arms and deposited in the bed.

"Miss Alice! my dear mistress! wull ye please tak' a sup o' this?"

It was more the unwonted sob in the voice that spoke than the call itself that reached the lethargic brain. Elspeth had slipped one arm under the heavy head, and held a steaming cup in the other hand. A strange smile drew the lips apart; the patient bent them to the draught, and swallowed it eagerly, as if consumed by inward fever. As the servant returned to the bed after setting away the empty cup, she met the full gaze of eyes that had in them mysterious meaning.

"Elspeth! I heard my mother call me three times to-night. I think — I hope that I am going to her!"

"It wad be nobbut yo' fancy, ma'am. Ye are oftentimes light o' head wi' th' headache."

"No! my head is a little confused now, but it was clear then, — quite clear. I was walking fast, and certainly not thinking of her. There was nobody in sight in the street, for it was raining. I heard her as distinctly as I hear my own voice at this instant. She called, 'Alice! Alice! Alice!' tenderly; oh, so sweetly and lovingly! I am glad that she wants me!"

CHAPTER IV.

There is a plan working in our lives; and if we keep our hearts quiet and our eyes open, it all works together; and if we don't, it all fights together, and goes on fighting till it comes right, somehow, somewhere. — ANNIE KEARY.

CHAPTER IV.

ON the southwest corner of Mendebras Avenue and Post Street stands a yellow frame house, two honest stories in height, and with a twenty-five feet front. The effect of comparative height and breadth is to make the old-fashioned dwelling appear " squat " among the tall lean apartment-flats near to it on the same side of the way, and upon the opposite corner. If you survey the premises from Post Street, you will see that the house is three rooms deep, and being on a corner, that all the rooms must be light.

There are two bells beside the front door, the Dutch stoop of which is raised but two steps from the street. Above the upper bell was once nailed an oblong strip of tin, painted white, lettered in blue: " MARY WILLIAMS, NURSE, &c."

The " &c." was her own unassisted device, and I believe the idea to be original. Those who had the best reasons in the world for knowing what they were talking of used to say that, admirable as she was as nurse, the " &c." was the best part of her. We will leave our story to define what entered into it and glorified the cabalistic characters.

" &c." may have something to do with some or all of the half-dozen invitations which " Nurse Williams," as people in whose houses she worked professionally preferred to call her, — using the title generally as a pet name, — had received to eat her Thanksgiving dinner at that number of tables. She had declined them all, gratefully, with the large, slow smile that belonged to the " &c." side of her, and in the round gentle voice that could not have gone with any other smile. It was not only that the voice was round, but it was cushiony as well, never chopping or harsh, and with never an edge to one of the agreeable inflections.

Nurse Williams had had a busy season thus far, what with whooping-cough, malaria-dregs left over from the summer, and what figured in her note-book as "pneumonia," in her every-day speech as "new money" (*o* long). Patients and their families said she had been wonderfully successful, even for her, with all her cases this fall, — "a sickly time," by the way. She had told her pastor, Rev. Dr. Barnes, of the "Jeremy Taylor," last Friday night, when he expressed his pleasure at seeing her again at prayer-meeting, that she "felt to praise the Lord for His goodness, and for His wonderful works to the children of men."

"By the time folks get to your age and mine, doctor," she had added, "that is an old story, but it is one we are never tired of telling."

In her secret thoughts she had meditated — "if the Lord did not object — to have a real rest-day treat" at home on that Thursday, and to spend it after her own fashion. Accordingly, she had betaken herself to the butcher's, the baker's, and the green-grocer's on Wednesday, and laid in sundry stores suitable to the occasion to be honored in the observance of sixty millions of happy people on the morrow.

Among her acquisitions were a fat turkey, — "a little dear!" she had pronounced it, to the smiling butcher's gratification, — only a six-pounder, but it would surfeit one lone woman for a week if she had not known where to send what would be left over by Friday morning; a pumpkin pie, with a rim of flakey crust like the setting of a big gold-stone brooch; cranberries to be made into jelly that night, and to be turned out, a tremulous scarlet, semi-transparent mound, next day; a can of French green peas; two oranges; two pippins; a bunch of black Hamburg grapes; a pound of fresh butter sent from a New Jersey creamery by a former patient; a loaf of cake from another; and from one of the "new money" convalescents, a box of superb chrysanthemums, — Japanese, with sweeping fringes of shaded yellow, cream-white, and royal purple. Generous moisture suffused the pleasant gray eyes as she made ready her banquet at one o'clock, and sat her down to the discussion of the same. There had been a praise service in the chapel of the Jeremy Taylor at half-past nine; and she attended it in preference to the union service in a grander and more fashionable church, where the music was sure to be magnificent, and municipal reform and political corruption would be the burden of the thank-offering to the Lord of the harvest and Author of peace and concord. She was at home and out of her Sunday clothes by eleven o'clock, and was glad and yet more glad of her own nest with quietness withal, as the snowfall that had lightly powdered her best bonnet on the way to church, and coated the sidewalks an inch thick when she came out of the chapel, increased in weight.

It was a damp snow, as most Brooklyn snows are, hence, a beautiful, trimming the boughs with ermine, and changing the tiniest twig into the semblance of white coral. It muffled footfalls upon the stones, the roll of carriages, and the tinkle of horse-car bells. Nurse Williams's one personal extravagance was an open grate fire in her sitting-room; and she added a generous lump of coal before drawing up her chair to the round table set in the middle of the room. It was one more visible manifestation of the gratitude bubbling over the brim of her heart.

She asked a blessing aloud (she had never learned to call it "a grace," being an humble soul), bowing a chastened countenance over the hands joined under the edge of the hot plate awaiting a help of the little brown turkey.

"Our Father who art in heaven! bless to our use the food Thou hast provided for our use upon this happy, happy Thanksgiving day, and may we draw from it strength to do and to bear Thy holy will! Have mercy upon the poor, and incline the hearts of the rich to be liberal unto them, as Thou, Lord, hast been to *them*. We ask all for our Saviour's sake. Amen!"

In secret prayer, she always said "we" and "our" and "us." In rising heavenward, her thoughts and sympathies broadened too much to be confined to the first person singular.

It was a bountiful first person, and pity it was, and

is, that the sample should be so singular in a world where man so needs bountifulness of mercy and largeness of Christian charity. She was five feet four-and-a-half inches in height, and weighed one hundred and sixty pounds. To look at her cheeks, where winter roses bloomed healthfully, the kindly mouth, the well-opened gray eyes that looked straight and never boldly into yours, at the plump capable hands, the backs of which, together with her wrists, were dimpled like a baby's, — you would have agreed with me that she could not, in the natural fitness of things, bear any name but that of "Mary," and that the honest every-dailiness of "Williams" finished it off as a twilled galloon binding a substantial jacket. She wore a small cap over the abundant gray hair, a cap with a fluted lace border, and a bow of inch-wide pink ribbon just above the somewhat wide tract between the eyebrows. Her gown was of a sensible shade of gray, darker than her hair. About her waist, compact, albeit not small, a full white apron was tied behind with broad starched strings. The apron had capacious pockets, and when she was on professional duty, the pockets had so much to do with the "&c." that I should never get to the middle of my narrative were I to begin to descant upon their properties and uses.

That turkey should have been photographed in two shades of brown, and done duty upon Thanksgiving bills-of-fare as the bird of gracious plenty. Nurse Williams was the very princess of caterers to people of slender appetites, and patients with no appetites at all; a firm believer in "kitchen physic," as many knew to their comfort and profit. Her jellies were always clear, and consistent without being tough; she made tea with boiling water, and did not let it stand in the pot until it drew all the bitterness out of the leaves; she understood to perfection the art of keeping the juice in chops and steaks; she knew as many ways of cooking eggs as she had varieties of broths; her dry toast was never scorched, and her cream-toast was a revelation of deliciousness. The tiny dish — a mere saucer — of so-called mashed potatoes, flanking the picturesque turkey upon one side, had not in truth been mashed at all, but whipped to a *soufflé* with a spoonful of hot cream in which a bit of butter was melted. A coffee-pot, that might, for size, have belonged to a toy tea-set, was upon the hob, the dry ground coffee within it warming into willingness to give up all its aroma by the time the boiling water should be poured in.

Nurse Williams had made but one cut into the turkey when a bell rang. The knife was arrested midway; the plump hands caught the expression of expectancy from lifted chin and fixed eyes.

"There now! I do hope no poor dear creature is taken bad on Thanksgiving Day!"

By special arrangement, the little daughter of the "folks downstairs" answered the nurse's bell, and took in messages and notes in her absence.

A hurried run up the stairs, a stride from the upper landing to the sitting-room door and a double rap were followed by a burly figure overtopped by a good-humored face.

"Good-day! good-day, Nurse Williams! Bless my

buttons, if I have n't surprised you in a regular carouse, and no mistake. Hi! hi! hi!" walking around the table to get a better view of what it contained. "This is what comes of being a fashionable nurse with no expenses to speak of, and the right to send in thumping bills nobody dares dispute. And I, a poor dog of a doctor, have n't had a mouthful since I was jerked violently from the breakfast-table, and shall think myself well off if I get time to steal so much as a drum-stick at seven o'clock to-night. Things are not evenly divided in this world, — no, not if it is Thanksgiving Day!"

"They 'll look evener to you when you 've sat down in this chair and helped me eat my dinner."

She bustled noiselessly about, setting down a second plate to warm on the fender, getting knife, fork, and tumbler, talking all the while in placid inattention to the stream of expostulations poured forth by the doctor.

"I understand now," — he heard her say when he desisted in comical despair, and let her push him with gentle urgency into the vacant seat, — "I understand perfectly now why I was let to put off my dinner until one o'clock when I had meant as much as anything to have it at half-past twelve. A bit of the stuffing, and a tiny slice of the breast?" heaping his plate. "Now, gravy! Oh, yes! I know that you high-flyers don't dine until other people's supper-time; but you 'd ought to have a hot luncheon to keep the snow-air out of your stomach and lungs, and you can talk better while you are eating than when you are empty, and be better able, when you start out again, to study what's the matter with your patients and what's good for their complaints, if you are full than if you are fasting. There, now!" resuming her seat with a long breath of benevolent content, "this is what I call a providence! I'm never, so to speak, lonesome; but it did seem a shame, if not a sin, for one lone woman to be sitting down to a genuine Thanksgiving dinner on a snowy day, with never a soul to speak to."

The doctor's hunger was as genuine as the excellence of the dinner. One whiff of the savory air of the room had assured him on this head; one mouthful told him that he had seldom tasted anything more toothsome in his own house. Moreover, he and Nurse Williams had worked together professionally for a dozen years; and he knew that the surest method of getting his way with her was to let her, in the first place, have hers. He could not help laughing out, in his jovial fashion, now and then, at the holiday adventure; but, being a gentleman at heart, he forbore to intimate how much of his amusement arose from the anticipation of describing to his wife over the seven o'clock family dinner, where there would be a dozen of his relatives and hers, where and how he had lunched.

He liked to shock the pretty woman who had married him after his success in his profession was a foregone conclusion, and he could picture her incredulity of dismay.

Out of kindness to his hostess, he refrained from "talking shop" until he was sipping the best cup of coffee he had tasted in twenty years.

"You have guessed, I suppose, that you are wanted," he said then, dropping his tone of good-humored banter. "It is a case of brain-fever, — a woman. An ugly case, too, I'm afraid. Some things point to possible pulmonary complications. It seems that she had a bad headache last Friday night, and tried to walk it off. You may recollect that it began to rain about nine o'clock? She came home wet to the skin, and slightly delirious. I was called in on Saturday by her brother — a Mr. Lanier, of New York, who had happened to come over to see her, and saw at once that she was in a bad way. Her daughter, an intelligent, handy girl of sixteen, or thereabouts, is at boarding-school in New York, but came home on Saturday to spend Sunday, and would not go back on Monday and leave her mother so ill. She does her best in the sick-room, and so does an elderly Scotch woman who is a sort of maid-of-all-work in the family, and a capital nurse at that. But there's a houseful of younger children, and all that, you know; and the time has come, as her brother and I concluded this morning, when other assistance is required. Can you go?"

"Right away?"

"I'm afraid I must say 'yes;' brain-fever is n't a thing to be trifled with."

She nodded gravely.

"You're right. Is she out of her head still?"

"Raving — when she is not in a stupor. Eyes glassy; disposed to roll her head and to pick at the bed-clothes. Temperature an average of one hundred and five. You know the signs. Knows nobody, and calls constantly, when awake, for her husband, who is abroad, and for her mother, who is dead. Came home Friday night with a story of having heard her mother call her by name three times on the street. Took it for a sign, and keeps referring to it."

"Such things have happened. It's a very thin curtain that hangs between us and them who have passed out of our sight, and we are leaning all our weight against it most of the time. 'T ain't surprising that it should give way in spots once in a while."

"Yes, yes! but, you see, my good sister, this woman is my patient, and I don't want that curtain to give way under her weight, for good and all. You must help me darn those thin places you talk about so coolly, — out of simple humanity, if professional pride don't move you. There are all those little children, you know, — not to mention the husband."

"It's as well not to mention some husbands sometimes," retorted the nurse, with grim pleasantry aimed evidently at him. "But children can have only one mother" — relapsing into seriousness. "I'll be off in an hour, if that will do. As you say, this sort of thing can't be fooled with, and it seems to have got pretty well under way already. Where is it?"

"Not far away. No. 363 Mendebras Avenue. The name is Paull."

"I had three cases of measles at 362 last year. They know that I am coming?"

"I promised to send a trained nurse before dark. I am uncommonly lucky in finding you at home, and disengaged."

"Speaking after the manner of men, — yes!"

Dr. Bacon's eyes twinkled as at a challenge. He stood up, brushed a few crumbs from his knee, and glanced at his hat and the overcoat he had tossed upon a chair.

"What ought I to say if I spoke after the manner of women?" he queried quizzically.

"Depends upon who the women are."

She was clearing away the remnants of the dinner, rapidly and with surprisingly little noise for a woman of her size. Plates did not clatter, glasses did not ring, or silver rattle.

"You'll excuse me going on with this work," she said, apologetically. "I haven't a minute to lose, if I'm to be on duty before dark."

"If you were the woman, for example," pursued the doctor, teasingly, "what should I say then of my luck?"

"I should say there is no such word in my dictionary; nor in God's Word; nor in His world either, for that matter. It is His will, His wise and merciful planning for our good — which we call providence — that brings all things to pass. Nothing happens by chance."

Dr. Bacon took up an argumentative position upon the hearth-rug. He knew that he was wasting time here, but he was loath to rush off immediately after swallowing a hearty dinner; the room was cosily warm; the out-door prospect more and more disagreeable by contrast. He would be amused, and "laze" for ten minutes more, before he took himself by the shoulder and turned out into the storm.

"I've heard you say so often enough for me to begin to believe it if I could elevate my opinion of myself, or of any other ordinary mortal, to the point of fancying that the Maker of the universe concerns Himself about my hourly goings and comings."

"If *you'd* taken the pains to make a valuable machine, I guess you'd concern yourself to look after it, and see if it was running regular and smooth," interposed the nurse, quietly.

"But I have n't learned the secret of perpetual motion, you see, and He has got it down fine. According to my way of thinking, He has established general laws for the government of whatever He has made; and these laws go on, acting and reacting, from year to year, and from century to century. Men are born, and live, and die; keep well and get ill; make money and lose it; are happy or miserable in obedience to these general laws, — just as trees put out leaves in the spring and shed their leaves in the autumn. Some fruit comes to perfection; and some drops to the ground and decays unripe. Some men live to a good old age; and as many, who are born into the world, die in infancy. We can account for the death of one as well or as poorly as for the other. The individual man is no more in the eyes of Deity than one of those snowflakes out there, that flutters from the clouds to the ground to be melted as soon as the sun comes out, and be soaked up by the earth."

"Yes?" in civil reserve of her opinion. "I beg your pardon, doctor, but there's a hair upon your sleeve!"

She plucked it off with a respectful thumb and finger, and regarded it attentively, holding it between her eyes and the window.

"It's a gray hair too!" meditatively.

"Probably. There are as many of that kind as there are brown upon my head and face. I look more and more to myself like a gray raccoon each morning when I stand before the mirror."

She was still gazing at the hair. One might have detected a shade of reverence in her manner of inspecting it.

"He says that He has counted them all," she began, musingly. "Every one in your head is a reminder of the close watch He keeps over you."

Still gently, she let the hair fall upon the hearth, and turned toward the window.

"I was a-pitying the sparrows just a while ago. A row of 'em sat on my window-sill. They know when I'm at home as well as if they'd rung the bell and had their answer at the downstairs door. I keep a pile of crumbs on the window-sill for them, but to-day the snow had covered them up. So I swept it off clean, and spread their table again for 'em. While they were a-eating, it come to me how many city-sparrows must starve if the snow lay long on the ground; and as quick as that thought popped into my faithless and foolish mind, I recollected that He who made 'em keeps account of their needs, and of every one that falls to the ground, and how He has said in so many words — not leaving us to work out the sum for ourselves — that we are of more value than many sparrows. It's the cheapest bird in the Holy Land, so I've heard tell; and pity knows, for all the good they seem to do, or the use they are as human creatures' food, they are dear in America at any price. I should calculate now" — her head on one side, her eyes measuring his goodly proportions, with never a glimmer of a smile — "that a man like you, in whose hands are the issues of life and death (under the Almighty) for hundreds of people every year, must be worth more than fifty millions of them noisy little birds."

Dr. Bacon's sides shook with his jovial laugh.

"The sparrows might think differently if you were to leave the decision to them. Thank you all the same, for your good opinion, and for the Thanksgiving sermon. I haven't been to church on Thanksgiving Day for thirty years, that I recollect. I should probably go to sleep if I did. Your lecture has kept me awake."

He moved toward the door, but stopped midway to look at something hanging on the wall.

"Halloo! You have been treating yourself to some new decorations since I was here last. What is it all about?"

CHAPTER V.

Our life is determined for us; and it makes the mind very free when we give up wishing, and only think of bearing what is laid upon us, and doing what is given us to do. — GEORGE ELIOT.

What is meant by our neighbor, we cannot doubt; it is every one with whom we are brought into contact. It is every one who is thrown across our path by the changes and chances of life, — he, or she, whosoever it may be, whom we have any means of helping.

DEAN STANLEY.

CHAPTER V.

THE doctor's overcoat lay over the back of a chair, where he had tossed it upon entering, and immediately above it was the new frame that had arrested his attention. It was a tasteful affair in white-and-gold, and within it was what looked, at the first glance, like a testimonial or certificate, engrossed upon white vellum, with an illuminated border.

Mrs. Williams smoothed her apron with both plump palms, and approached her visitor, gratification beaming from every line of her visage.

"Ah! you may well stop to look at it. Just read it aloud, won't you? And then I'll tell you how I came by anything so nice."

Dr. Bacon settled his gold-bowed eye-glasses upon his nose, and complied. He read with deliberation, pausing after each verse, as if to satisfy himself that he had rendered it with proper emphasis and discretion. The nurse hearkened with the eagerness of one who had never listened to it before, — her eyes serious, her mouth smiling tenderly; once in a while a gentle nod signified her appreciation of a favorite passage.

> As the shepherd lifts the hurdle
> Daily set about his sheep,
> Shifts afield the wattled girdle,
> Wills the flock to feed and sleep

THE ROYAL ROAD.

Within bounds his wisdom orders,
    Faring as his love assigns,
Pining not for richer borders,
    Chafing not at strait confines, —

So, O Father! when the morning
    Grayly steals into my room,
Be it promise and not warning,
    Earnest of perfected bloom;
Of wise willing and wise giving;
    To my restless spirit say,
" All thou hast to learn of living
    Is to do My will TO-DAY."

Yesterdays — their prayers, their sinning,
    Bootless cares and futile tears,
Thwarted end and rash beginning, —
    Are with Thine eternal years,
Tales all told, and sealed pages —
    Turn I steadfastly away,
And from out the coming ages
    Reverent take the virgin day.

Grace sublime of simple trusting
    Grant unto Thy servant, Lord!
Without friction, without rusting,
    I would take Thee at Thy word.
Nothing boding and naught asking
    Of the dim and outer land,
Glad to do the tender tasking
    Daily laid unto my hand.

It may be the safe surrounding
    Of Thine angels' banding wings
Shall appoint fair meads, abounding
    With the dews of Baca's springs.
If, instead of beauty, burning
    Be the measure of Thy will,
Let eyes made by faith discerning
    See the shining ones there still.

"I am not much of a judge of poetry," remarked the reader when he had finished. "But that sounds pretty and pleasant. It's awfully unpractical, of course, but poetry doesn't set up for that as a rule."

"There was one gentleman who wrote for the papers, whose wife I nursed, who found a scrap of paper with those verses on it, lying on my bureau, and he said it was 'good religion, but poor poetry.' I cut it out of *The Congregationalist* in the first place, and I'd read it over so many times it was quite threadbare when he got hold of it. I told him he'd maybe like it better if it had been in better shape. I took such a fancy to it, not being literary enough to know poetry from prose, that I got into a way of singing it when I was by myself. It goes well to Greenville, Nettleton, or Autumn, or any other eight-by-seven tune."

"It is handsomely copied and decorated," said the physician, kindly suppressing a smile.

"Isn't it?" said the nurse. "You see, when poor little Willy Barnes was so bad with the whooping-cough, and the other two down,—I never saw children have it harder,—and I was called in to help with them, Willy would go to sleep in my arms to that hymn sooner than to any other. And Mrs. Barnes, a-hearing me going over it again and again, and him a-begging for 'the sleep-song, nursie,' would know where I got it, and all about it. After the children got well,—and, as I needn't tell you, doctor, I just couldn't let my pastor's wife pay me a cent, for, as I told her, I came out of her house richer and fuller in spirit than if she'd given me double price for the little I'd done, — she sent me the two little boys' pictures and that poem, all elegantly framed, just as you see it, and the loveliest letter I ever read. I told her I'd ought to have a border painted around that, and frame it too.

"You see" — pointing — "in that corner is Willy, and me a-rocking him to sleep; you'd know my cap and apron in Madagascar, but the rest of it is altogether too good-looking for me, as I told her. And over there is the shepherd a-driving his flock before him, when the old grass inside the wall is all eaten bare; and the border at the bottom is the hurdle. She explained about it to me, and the meaning of 'wattled.'"

She stopped to laugh here.

"Would you believe it? I had some sort of a notion that it had something to do with a turkey-gobbler, and kind o' skipped over the word in my singing and my thoughts. Not being educated is a drawback sometimes. And at the top, — don't you see how the border is all angels' wings, a-touching and a-lapping one another and a-shining? They are the 'shining ones there still,' you know. I never mistrusted what Mrs. Barnes was up to when she asked me to let her copy the piece I'd worn into rags. I was 'most ashamed to have her see it, but newspaper won't stand much wear."

The doctor recovered himself with a start from a critical inspection of the really clever etching, brightened effectively by artistic gilding and coloring.

"By Jap!" People forgave the enigmatical adjuration because he was never heard to use any other under the strongest excitement. "You have made me waste a good half-hour here in feasting and folly when I ought to be at work. I'll see you again about six o'clock. I left orders with the Scotch woman that would hold until then. She is a faithful creature, and behaved better than could have been expected when we told her we must have in another nurse. She is very much attached to her mistress, and has worked like ten horses since she fell ill. Yet I shall feel easier when you are to the fore.

"Good-by, and thank you again for a first-rate luncheon and an A. 1 sermon. As a human sparrow, — unless you prefer to class me with the snowflakes, — I ought to be better for both."

The genial smile had not faded out when he signalled his carriage, which was toiling up and down the street, with clogged wheels and whitened horses.

"That woman is a character!" he soliloquized, after he shut himself in and was on the way to his next patient. "She may be a fanatic, but she is the happiest, jolliest, most useful soul I know."

Not a falling intonation or shade of expression had betrayed to him her disappointment at the failure of her plan for securing her "one real rest-day." The deep easy-chair that had descended to her with her name from her grandmother already stood midway between the grate and the front windows, where the light would fall over her left shoulder; and on a stand beside it that was as old as the chair, lay a well-thumbed copy of "Stepping Heavenward." Mrs. Barnes had introduced her husband's parishioner to the incomparable religious classic, which had straightway become a chief favorite with the woman who had little time for reading of any kind. She was wont to speak of it as "the only novel she had ever cared to read more than once." She was on the fifth perusal now, and had meant to devote all the daylight that remained after the dishes were washed, the white cloth superseded by a red, and the hearth swept, to enjoyment of pages which always helped and never tired her. She had hoped, when twilight should steal between her and "Stepping Heavenward," to treat herself to a refreshing nap, her feet upon a footstool, the fire making cheer on one side, the snow curtaining out the world on the other. She had promised to take tea with the friendly "folks downstairs," and at ten o'clock would be in bed "trying to get slept out," after vigils many and wearing.

As it was, she summoned the little girl from below, and sent to her mother everything left over from her Thanksgiving dinner. There was no telling when she would be able to sit down again at her own table. At four o'clock, the cozy comfortableness of the "living-room" had given place to the chill formality of preparation for being left "all right." The chairs had retreated to the walls; the table-cover was on wrongside out; the Holland shades were drawn down; the still warm grate was empty; and Nurse Williams, setting her capacious satchel, packed and locked, down upon the floor, knelt to commend herself and the task she was entering upon to Him who feeds the birds and clothes the grass of the field. As for herself, as she confessed to this ever-hearing Friend, the utmost skill she could command could not make one hair white or black, or keep in the passing breath for the thousandth part of a minute. She was, at her best, only a willing tool in the hands of the Master-Workman. All that she could do was to get it clean and to offer it, with the handle held toward Him, until He was ready to use it.

The snow had been shovelled from the sidewalk and the steps of 363. The inhabitants of other houses on the block were apparently content to await the slackening of the storm before attacking the drifts. It was little past four o'clock when Nurse Williams ploughed sturdily through these, yet it was quite dark. The street-lamps were lighted, and transmuted into a golden shower the falling flakes within a radius of a few feet of each. Above the doors, and through the windows of the dwellings on both sides of the way, yellow and ruddy lances of light stabbed the gray outer glooms. Here and there, a shade had been forgotten, or purposely left up by a charitable householder, willing to share his holiday cheer with the wayfarer, and the nurse had a picture of an interior that, in her unspoken thought, "kind o' chirked her up." She was thankful that other homes were bright, warm, and happy, although the fire upon her hearthstone had been extinguished.

Her subdued ring at the door of 363 was answered promptly by a raw-boned, high-cheeked Scotchwoman with gray hair and shrewd eyes.

"I am the nurse sent by Dr. Bacon. My name is Williams," was the visitor's self-introduction.

Quiet tone and straightforward address were an

instant recommendation. Elspeth was a true Gael in her readiness to form prejudices, and her reluctance to dismiss them.

"Ye are welcome, and ye can come right up, so soon as ye've had a word with Mr. Lanier, the mistress's brother."

There would be no words wasted in preliminaries between these two. A gentleman appeared in the doorway of the parlor while Elspeth was speaking.

"Good-evening, Mrs. Williams. You can take her valise upstairs, Elspeth. She will be up in a few moments. Wait for her in the upper hall."

He spoke courteously, but with authority; his refined face and bearing bespoke the gentleman; his expression was grave to sadness.

"Please step into this room," he continued, standing back to let her precede him. "I'm Mr. Lanier, of New York. Mrs. Paull is my sister. Mrs. Lanier — my wife — is confined to the house by a severe cold, or she would be here. In her absence, the responsibility of superintending the arrangements for Mrs. Paull's comfort devolves upon me." He bent a scrutinizing gaze upon the matronly face, respectful and interested. "I need not explain to you how useless a man is in a sick-room. My sister is very dear to me, — and to my wife, — and she is dangerously ill. I wish you to spare no trouble or expense in her behalf. Dr. Bacon's recommendation is security for your skill, and for your discretion. I wish you, furthermore, to be perfectly candid in your reports of her condition from day to day. I may say, also," — another and longer look, — " what it is well for you, as an intelligent nurse, to know before going to her, — that this illness has been aggravated, if it was not brought on, by mental anxiety. If possible, keep your patient from raving, or, should she have lucid intervals, from asking questions. If she will talk, promise anything in reason — or out of it — that will pacify her. Say to her, should she intimate a desire to discuss her anxieties with me, that I have promised to do all in my power to bring matters out right. Ask her to trust me until she is strong enough to think and talk.

"Perhaps" — seeming to gauge the moral force of the listener by a test of his own — "you have scruples against deceiving or even equivocating to a delirious patient? You would not be willing to do even so little an evil that a great good might be brought about?"

He looked so kind, with all his seriousness, that she answered frankly, —

"There is no lie — ever — in saying that everything will come out right, sir. I'll do my best for the poor lady, and may the dear Lord of us all help me!"

"Amen! and thank you!"

To her surprise, — for she had set him down at first sight as "a genuine high-stepper, and no mistake," — he shook hands with her and dismissed her, saying that he would remain in the house until after the doctor's next visit.

Elspeth was waiting, according to instructions, in the upper hall, and showed the nurse to a chamber where she might change her dress, designating the door of the sick-room as they passed it, and telling her to come in when she was ready.

"And the sooner the better!" she subjoined.

"Why do you say that?" demanded accents, the sharpness of which contrasted strangely with the youthful quality of the voice.

A pretty girl, with golden hair put back carelessly from her face, and blue eyes too weary and dry for her years, met them upon the threshold of the hall bedroom to which Mrs. Williams had been directed.

"I did not go upstairs to lie down as you told me to do," she went on to Elspeth, noticing the new arrival only by a slight and haughty inclination of the head. "I would not go out of hearing of my mother. I am able and anxious to watch with her to-night, and every night. I cannot see the necessity, as you and Uncle Roger do, of bringing in any one else to help us. I am accountable to my father for all that goes on here in his absence — remember! Whatever nurse you engage must not be left in ignorance as to who is the master of this house."

"There is no danger of that, Miss Marie," rejoined Elspeth, with no show of temper.

Mrs. Williams slipped into the door, and the serving-woman closed it upon her. Whatever colloquy followed the withdrawal of the third party to the little scene was unheard by her. There were, evidently, other complications to be dealt with than pulmonary in the new case.

Dr. Bacon found her in full charge of the chamber of illness at his evening visit.

"You have made your mark already," he told her when, after ten minutes spent at the bedside of the patient, the nurse obeyed his summons to follow him into the adjoining apartment.

He spoke in a professional undertone, nodding backward at the interior visible through the half-open door. "Got all ship-shape in there, I see. Close-reefed and ready for rough weather. There's nothing like the touch a professional nurse gives to the sick-room. Where's the daughter?"

"Elspeth coaxed her to go to bed, I believe. I only saw her for a minute when I first came."

"Good! I had my fears that she might make things a little more lively than agreeable, poor thing! She is awfully cut up by her mother's illness, and has an idea that everything depends upon her young shoulders while the father is away. Was very tart with her uncle when he told her in my hearing that we must have you in. She is wonderfully bright and capable, but, delirious as the mother is, the daughter's worry affected her unpleasantly. There are times, as you and I know, when relatives — especially affectionate and anxious relatives — are not the proper people to be about a sick person. There's something exciting in the very atmosphere under such circumstances. Well! what do you think of the outlook?"

"She's a very sick woman. And I mistrust that she's been ill longer than people know. She's likely kept up when she ought to have been in her bed. Like walking-typhoid, you know. I've seen her before. For a half-hour or so, I couldn't just think where. By-and-by she tried to sing, — a pretty poor try it was, with her hoarse voice and short breath, — and it flashed in upon me. 'T was last Friday night at a prayer-meeting in our lecture-room, — the Jeremy Taylor, you know. She got in late, and there was a sort of queer look about her. I was right across the aisle; and I saw presently that her color had all gone out, the same as the flame of a candle, and she turned so pale and her mouth was so drawn that, being as I am a nurse, I could n't but feel that 't was right to keep an eye on her from time to time. I was afraid she was going to drop in a faint."

"So you watched while the others prayed?" unable to deny himself the joke.

"I watched between the prayers, sir," answered the nurse, not without dignity. "I could have made sure she was asleep sometimes if her hands had n't squeezed one another hard, and her face twitched now and then. So I was fairly taken off my feet, as you may say, when the last hymn was sung, and she joined in all on a sudden with a voice like an angel's, — a strong angel, too. Mrs. Barnes, she sings most delightful, and she raised the tune, — there being no man there who could do it, — and was a-carrying of it well; but this strange lady just took it away from her, and led us all along with her, so pitiful and so earnest-like that I could n't think of anything but — ' I will not let thee go, until thou bless me!' The words were, ' I need thee every hour,' and, thinks I to myself, ' There 's one that means every single word she 's singing.' It gave me quite a turn when she started up the same tune awhile ago."

Dr. Bacon lent an attentive ear.

"The fever was upon her then; there is no question of that. It was lucky for her — I beg your pardon, it was providential — that she did not wander away and get lost.

"Well, nurse! we've got to roll up our sleeves and fall to in good earnest, if we are to pull our patient through. Mind and body are both against us, I suspect, not counting in the author and forwarder and general backer of all disease, — the evil principle you call the devil."

Thus began, over the prostrate body of Alice Paull, the hand-to-hand fight that lasted without respite for ten days longer. The doctor did his part gallantly; Mr. Lanier's purse and time were at his sister's service; at his suggestion, two New York medical magnates, whose very breath might be reckoned as currency, so costly was every word, visited the patient three times in consultation with the physician in charge.

Foremost and indefatigable, the nurse fought in the breach. She seemed to live without sleep, except for the two hours of the forenoon when the sick woman was most quiet, and Elspeth insisted on sitting with her. In all that week and a half, Mrs. Williams did not leave the house; never lost heart; never raised her voice above its accustomed pitch, or hurried her even speech by so much as a quarter-breath. That hushed upper chamber was her world; and within it, she effaced herself so far as consideration of her personal ease was concerned. The one created being in all the universe for her lay there, parched by fever, moaning in delirious agony, the demon in possession tugging at the tense, attenuated thread of her existence.

It was like the tossing of a frail boat in a storm, each pitch and wrench grinding the cable upon the toothed rocks of the beach.

CHAPTER VI.

Ask God to give thee skill
In comfort's art,
That thou mayst consecrated be
And set apart
Unto a life of sympathy;
For heavy is the weight of ill
In every heart,
And comforters are needed much,
Of Christ-like touch.

ANONYMOUS.

CHAPTER VI.

"WHAT has become of the picture that used to hang there?"

The query, faintly but coherently uttered, called the nurse to the bedside.

Mrs. Paull had slept without stirring for four hours. It was a season of suspense, during which nobody but Mrs. Williams was in the room. This was by the doctor's express orders, which none — assuredly not his leal coadjutor — thought of gainsaying.

The house was as silent as the grave, and, although it was not yet noon, shades and curtains tempered the light to the dimness of evening. The woman in the chair that commanded a view of the sleeper's face, was as motionless as she whom she watched. A score of times she hushed her own breath to listen for that which was the only token of life in her patient.

One of her sayings was, "It's a thousand times easier, no matter how lazy you may be, to be up and doing, than down and waiting."

Long practice had made waiting a part of her religion. She had learned, through much tribulation and many lessons, "having done all, to stand." When God said, "Be still!" she moved not. When action no longer availed, she gave herself unto prayer, every sense on the alert for the next word of command. Resting upon her arms did not mean sleeping upon them.

Her practised ear detected instantly the alteration in Mrs. Paull's voice and articulation. The languid legato movement of the words was that of feeble but intelligent speech. Her heart gave a great bound, the hurrying blood beat upon the drums of her ears, but, without rustle or flurry, she arose and moved slowly forward. Mrs. Paull was gazing at a vacant place upon the wall over against her bed.

"We took it away because you were ill, Mrs. Paull. The less furniture there is in a sick-room the better, or so the doctors say nowadays."

Too weak to be greatly moved by surprise or curiosity, the patient turned her eyes to the unfamiliar face.

"I must have had an unusually bad headache, have I not? It has taken all my strength, I think. Where is Elspeth? And why has she left you to take care of me?"

"Elspeth's busy, getting the children's dinner ready, I guess. Shall I call her?"

"Not if she is busy. She has too much to do when I am unable to help her. But I am afraid this is an imposition upon you — "

"Not a bit of it. I'm Mrs. Williams, one of your neighbors; and seeing that Elspeth did n't like to leave you alone, I offered to sit with you awhile, in case you might want a drink, or anything. The doctor was here to-day, and left this for you to take when you woke up. You'll do nicely now that the headache has gone off."

She spoke in such an easy, matter-of-course way, and her manner of offering the medicine was so free from concern, that Mrs. Paull swallowed it without remark upon the physician's visit, or his prescription. She closed her eyes, and dozed for twenty minutes under the influence of the sedative; then they opened, and the perplexities dreaded by doctors and watchers under such circumstances crept darkly into their depths. She was beginning to piece together straggling thoughts, and to call memory to her help.

"Where are the children?"

"Gone to school as good as kittens, bless their hearts! That is, the boys have. The baby was carried off by Mrs. Lanier, who wanted her to spend the day with her little girl. I heard something about Central Park, so I think there is a frolic on foot."

"Has anybody been ill except myself?"

"Nobody at all. Why should they be? Headaches — even such bad ones as yours — are not catching. And you must n't think of yourself as ill now. You're a bit tired and weak, and must lie still and eat all the nourishing food the doctor will let you have, and take all the rest the law allows. You'll be astonished to find how soon you'll be up and around."

The homely commonplaces and the smooth, leisurely enunciation of them lulled the listener temporarily. It seemed altogether proper that this comfortable-looking stranger should be there and her custodian while Elspeth bustled about downstairs. The blackened lips relaxed into something like a smile.

"You are very kind. I am much obliged to you."

The drowsy intonation promised well, but, as before, her mind rebelled against the inertia of the body. Her brows were knitted; the lids contracted like those of a short-sighted person. The next query showed that recollections were tardy in adjusting themselves.

"Have any letters come from Mr. Paull while I was ill?"

"I have n't heard them say. 'T was n't likely I should, being a comparative stranger, although a neighbor and a well-wisher, as all neighbors ought to be, according to my way of thinking. And Mendebras Avenue has the name of being real sociable, especially when there's sickness or the like. But there! I always say there is n't a truer word in the Bible than that 'a man that hath friends must show himself friendly.'"

She had reduced the knack of talking her patients to sleep to an art. But the pleasant monotone, almost lengthening into a drawl, the non-exciting utterances strung upon a silken string and slipped along at equal distances, failed now of their usual effect.

"Do you know whether or not my brother ordered that picture to be taken down?"

The nurse laughed, a good-humored gurgle of innocent amusement that made her incipient double chin quiver.

"I know for certain that he did n't! He does n't even know that it is down. There never was a kinder, lovinger, attentiver brother in all the world; that I'll testify to. He's been over every day, so they tell me, to see how you are, and if there's anything you'd like to have, and all that. A great many men have n't but one idea in the world about sick people, and that's, 'What'll they have to eat?' And he'd give you all of Washin'ton Market, and Fulton thrown into the bargain, if your room would hold it, and Elspeth would let you have 'em. But he'd no more to do with taking down that picture than the king o' the Canary Islands, wheresomever they may be. 'T was Elspeth and me that were all the time brushing up against the frame, and shouldering of it crooked, being neither of us willows, so to speak, — no, nor yet *syllups*. Soon's you get strong enough to set up, you shall have it back. It's only in the other room, — safe's can be."

She contrived to give this monologue the effect of dropping water, and had the satisfaction of seeing Mrs. Paull's eyelids fall slowly and remain closed; the plait between the brows was smoothed out. Another half-hour went by. Mrs. Williams was immovable, — a study of charity in gray stone, after the realistic school, abundant in curves, and wise with the tender sagacity of years. Before she dared change her position, the eyes, misty with sleep, opened a little way.

"Ernest would n't like it, I am sure," she murmured. "He gave it to me one Christmas; ten years ago, maybe twelve. He hung it there, where

I could see it the first thing in the morning. He said it would be — the spirit of love — keeping — watch — over — me."

The last syllables were barely audible. The watcher did not move until the soft respiration assured her that slumber had again interposed a merciful screen between the spent nervous forces and the glare of truth.

With all her natural aptitude for her calling, her tact, and her skill, she was not a trained nurse. That is, she had not been graduated from a "Training School," with a diploma that gave her the right to wear kerchief and coif; to snub "unprofessionals," and awe the families of patients. She was stout in her objections to the uniform of the order, maintaining that the apparition of a hired nurse to the vision of an ill and nervous person was in itself alarming. She would rather be taken for what she accounted herself to be — the volunteer neighbor of the sufferer — until the feeling of strangerhood wore off.

Without going to the length of equivocating to Mrs. Paull, she had succeeded in evading her catechism as to the causes for removing the portrait. It was literally true that she and Elspeth, in tending the sick mistress and making the bed, had once and again come in contact with the corners of the elaborately carved and gilded frame, and that both had exclaimed at the discomfort of having it there. But, on the eleventh day of her illness, Mrs. Paull had conceived a sudden and violent dread of the handsome visage smiling down upon her. She hid herself shudderingly under the bed-clothes, declaring that the eyes hurt her, that the lips said cruel, mocking things; and, worst of all, that the face of a woman sneered at her over her husband's shoulder. Nor would she uncover her eyes until assured by servant and nurse that the picture was no longer there.

Marie had witnessed all this with a horror-stricken countenance, and followed Mrs. Williams as she carried the portrait into the back chamber. When it was deposited carefully upon a table, the back propped by the wall, the girl threw herself upon her knees in front of it, kissed the pictured face over and over, and laid her cheek against it, the tears raining from her eyes.

"Poor, dear papa! It would break his heart if he knew of this. Oh, Mrs. Williams, what does it all mean? Did you hear her say that he was trying to drag her heart out by the roots? He, — the gentlest, kindest, most affectionate of human beings, who could never bear to see anything suffer!"

"It's oftener this way than otherwise, dear, when people's wits have been sent away by fever or anything of that sort. It's a very common thing for them to turn against the very ones they love the best. Wait until your mother is herself again, and you'll see that she'll be the first one to insist upon our bringing the portrait back. She will not have the least recollection of what has happened to-day, and we must take care that she never knows it. It would grieve her more than it does you."

The demeanor of the patient upon her return to consciousness fully justified this prediction, but to the nurse's surprise, she made no further reference to the portrait upon her second awakening. Her eyes wandered over the blank space it had once filled as listlessly as over other parts of the room.

To Mrs. Williams's proposal to Elspeth that they would better restore it to its place, the Scotchwoman replied curtly, "Bide a wee! When she asks for it again, it wull be time eno' to fetch it."

That time did not come. Mrs. Paull asked for her children, smiled faintly into their awed faces, let them kiss her, and hoped, in the changed voice that frightened them into decorum, that they would be "good, and not give Elspeth too much trouble,"— then wearily turned away and seemed to sleep. She was composed in appearance when her brother was admitted, and calmly affectionate with her sister-in-law, thanking both for their kindness to the children and herself, but evidently indisposed to converse upon any subject whatsoever. The dull apathy that had taken the place of her natural vivacity increased as time passed, instead of wearing away with the increase of strength. When left alone with the nurse, she would lie for hours together, staring at the ceiling, her wasted hands laid, one upon the other, over her breast, never speaking unless directly questioned, and answering in the fewest possible words. But for the settled gloom of the dark eyes, she might have been thought to be in a trance.

Finding and leaving her thus one afternoon, Mr. Lanier signalled to Mrs. Williams to accompany him when he went downstairs.

"This is an unnatural, and to me an alarming

state of things," he said, in strong emotion. "Surely something can and ought to be done to break it up. Will you ask Dr. Bacon if he would like to have Dr. Jaynes or Dr. Steele over again? What does he think of her? What would you suggest?"

She answered the last question first, — a safe rule when the dialogue lies between a calm person and one who is laboring under powerful excitement.

"I have seen other cases, and worse, that came out straight in time. There 's nothing to be done but to wait patiently for what good nursing and tonics will do. So Dr. Bacon says, and the other doctors would agree with him. High-ups must be followed by low-downs, you see, before one gets to a healthy everidge. Mrs. Paull has a fine constitution, and then she has her children to get well for. It 's a good sign, — her noticing them."

"That is the doctor's opinion, you say. Do you think as he does? I would rather have the judgment of a really competent nurse than that of a whole college of physicians. You have watched Mrs. Paull closely now for nearly three weeks. Has anything occurred to you as likely to be helpful to her? If she goes on as she is now for a week longer, she will die, or become insane."

"Shall I speak out plain, sir? You 'd maybe think me too free."

"I have asked you to speak, have n't I? Excuse me if I seem irritable, but I am greatly worried by all this, — more than you or any one else can imagine. I am tormented by the dread that my sister may never rally. I see no signs of convalescence other than were perceptible a week ago, and — " falteringly — " we have been much to each other, — Alice and I. Next to my wife and children, she is the dearest thing alive to me."

The honest face before him expressed sincere and respectful sympathy. His soul must have been moved to the depths before he could admit a stranger to his confidence. She spoke simply and gravely, —

"I think, Mr. Lanier, if I may be so bold, that a letter or a message from her husband would do Mrs. Paull more good than all the medicine in the drug stores in New York and Brooklyn mixed in one tonic. There's a spring broken or a band slipped off the wheel somewhere, that doctors and nurses have n't touched, and can't touch. If Mr. Paull could arrange his business matters so as to hurry home, or if he would write oftener, — some men are thoughtless about such things, — you'd soon see a blessed change in her."

Something so hot and bitter burst from the lips of the stately gentleman that she actually recoiled. It sounded like "Despicable hound!" but she could not be sure as to the wording of the epithet, gathering the purport more from his emphasis and countenance. He walked up and down the parlors, went into the hall, opened the front door, and stood bareheaded in the frosty air for perhaps two minutes. Then he came back.

"Again I must beg you to excuse me if I appear unreasonably irritable. There are some things which it is difficult to discuss with anybody. Family secrets ought not to be shared with any one except blood relations. And, as a family, we are disposed to be reserved; perhaps we are proud. If so, pride is likely to catch a hard fall."

He had said this pacing the room restlessly. Now he stopped, facing her.

"You are a widow, I believe, Mrs. Williams?"

"No, sir. That is, not by death."

The response was so direct and unlooked-for that he was abashed. Her mournful firmness had a touch of the heroic. He felt convicted of wanton cruelty.

"I beg a thousand pardons. I had supposed —"

"Most people do, sir!" interposing to save him further embarrassment. "When asked direct, I can say but the one thing, of course. But, as you say, there are sore spots in every family and every heart that it's best to keep well covered up. Now, sir, as to Mrs. Paull, — if there's anything you can think of that I can do to help her —"

He came to an abrupt determination.

"You are a Christian, Mrs. Williams, and a brave, God-fearing, tender-hearted woman, with great refinement of feeling. You are prudent, too, and, I believe, discreet beyond the average of your sex."

Excited as he was, he could not but note that she listened as if he were praising somebody else than herself.

"I will be frank with you throughout our discussion of this miserable business," continued Mr. Lanier. "Mr. Paull will never come back to his home, and my sister knows it. He has disgraced his children with himself, and deserted a faithful, devoted wife. I brought this news to her on the day she was taken ill. What has happened since then is in consequence of what I was obliged to tell her. You know the whole story now. You see what you meant, without comprehending why it was, when you talked of broken springs and ungeared wheels."

She had borne herself thus far with such equanimity, and she looked so strong and steady, that he was utterly unprepared to see her sit down as if her knees had given way, and lifting her apron to her eyes begin to sob hysterically.

"The poor dear! the poor suffering dear! Oh, Mr. Lanier! how can any man be so cruel? God forgive him for bringing such sorrow upon her and her innocent babies!"

Roger Lanier did not say "Amen!" to that. His face hardened, not relented, at the prayer. His eyes were sternly unmerciful.

The nurse got hold of herself almost immediately.

"It is n't often I give way like that, sir," she pleaded, in her quaintly respectful way. "But I 've had a pretty hard strain lately, you know, and this caught me by surprise. I 'm obliged to you for telling me the truth, and proud and thankful that you feel to trust me to hold my tongue. What you 've said makes me a grain less hopeful. I won't deny that. But it will move me to great boldness in carrying the dear lady and her grief to the Great Physician, now that I really understand how much she needs Him. There 's nothing impossible with Him, Mr. Lanier, and He is very pitiful and of great mercy to His children. Our extremity is

His best opportunity. That's a blessed saying, — 'most good enough to be in the Bible itself."

Elspeth, supposing her mistress to be asleep, had slipped away to attend to her domestic duties, leaving the chamber-door ajar. Mrs. Williams entered soundlessly, cast a glance at the bed, and seeing the occupant quiet, took a seat out of range should she stir, and buried her face in her hands.

This woman, to whom she had been sent to minister, high-born and delicately nurtured, carried a cross of like form and weight with hers. With home and kindred and wealth at her call, she had been swept out to sea by waves as rough as those that had overwhelmed herself years ago; had fallen, fainting with thirst, beside the fountain of Marah. Widely separated as the two might be by education and social position, they were sisters in the sorest sorrow that can visit a woman's heart.

God must have meant much in directing her feet to this house. His ways were always wise, and always full of meaning to those who cared to study them. He did nothing idly, and He made no mistakes.

She whispered under her breath one of the proverbs, of which she had an exhaustless store, —

"Whoso will observe the wonderful providences of God, shall have wonderful providences to observe."

She must move warily, for life and death might hang upon her efforts to pour balm into that wounded heart, and to raise the fallen spirit. In all the narrow and critical passes through which she had been mercifully guided, she had known few more perplexing than this.

"And, like a blind, conceited bat, I had it in my mind to hang up that picture to-night, after she was sound asleep, that her eyes might light on it the first thing in the morning, as she said her husband meant they should when he gave it to her. I was that pleased with the idea of giving her something pleasant to think of, that I could hardly wait for night to come. What risky things we short-sighted creatures are let to do, when we get to priding ourselves upon our own smartness! I do declare, I've no respect for Mary Williams, if she does set herself up as a 'nurse, etc.,' when I catch her in such conceited ways. Talk of the mercies of the Lord being from everlasting to everlasting! They ain't a circumstance compared with His patience with our foolishness! That's just everlastingest."

A restless movement upon the bed called her to her feet. The gas was low, and she raised it to a cheerful flame, on perceiving through the obscurity that Mrs. Paull was looking about her.

"You've had a good sleep, ma'am!" cheerily congratulatory. "In my humble opinion, there's no better time o' the day for dozing than twilight. Seems if 't was made a-purpose for us to catch our breath in after the day's work is done, and before 'the evening shades prevail,' as the hymn says. Do you feel equal to sitting up in bed while you eat your supper?"

"If I must eat it," said the listless voice, "wouldn't it be less trouble to take it as I am? Less fatiguing for you and for me?"

"Oh, as to me, no way you could contrive would

fatigue my tough bones and sinews. But I think appetite comes easier when one is n't flat on her back, as if 't was n't intended that human creatures should eat in that shiftless, lazy way. And, come to think of it," — with her jolly little gurgle, — "I don't know of any animal that prefers to take his victuals in that position, without 't is a shark. They do say he has to turn over on his back before he can catch holt of his prey, and that many a swimmer has been saved on account of his being made that way.

"There now! Is that comfortable? Don't say 'yes,' without it is entirely right. It will amuse me to keep on trying till I get them so as to suit you. There's as many ways of fixing pillows as there are people to lie upon them. They ought to fit into all the tired hollows, and support every bone, and give into every joint, or they are not just as they ought to be."

"They are very comfortable, thank you." Mrs. Paull lay back, with a sigh, in the downy nest arranged by the deft hands. "What time is it?"

"I heard the whistles blow for six a few minutes ago. I thought maybe that was what woke you."

"Only six! I thought it much later. The night is all to come."

"Time will go twice as fast when once you're up and dressed," said the nurse, blithely, over her shoulder, in going into the adjoining room.

CHAPTER VII.

Be sure that if you do your very best in that which is laid upon you daily, you will not be left without sufficient help when some mightier occasion arises.

J. N. GROU.

Why should I start at the plough of my Lord, that maketh deep furrows on my soul? I know He is no idle husbandman. He purposeth a crop.

SAMUEL RUTHERFORD.

CHAPTER VII.

UPON a table in the room that had been the guest-chamber of the house, Mrs. Williams had arranged medicines, glasses, spirit-lamp, and kettle, and other appliances of her profession, and the specific work she had on hand. She never dropped or measured or mixed a dose in the patient's sight or hearing, or arranged a tray, or cut up food in her presence. Aladdin's slaves were not better drilled in making an appearance all ready for waiting or action, in the precise nick of time, than the born New Englander, who had not known the discipline of regulation "training."

To protect the polished top of the table from stain or hot liquid, she had covered it with a folded newspaper, and this with a napkin. The latter was spotted in several places, she noticed now, and having administered Mrs. Paull's tonic and lighted the lamp under the vessel containing beef-tea, the neat-handed attendant took the moment of leisure for removing the soiled, and spreading in its place clean linen. A like instinct of orderliness caused her to reverse the newspaper. It was a secular sheet of manifold pages, and a Sunday issue. Accordingly two columns of the least conspicuous page were devoted to religious intelligence and moral selections. Right in the middle of one of these columns was an extract headed *Good Advice.*

"If I don't need that at this identical minute, — good measure, shaken down, pressed together and a-running over, — nobody does!" reflected the nurse, and, forthwith and then and there, proceeded to make it her own, standing under the gas-burner, one eye and both ears attent upon the warming beef-tea.

Having gone through it twice, she picked up a pair of scissors, cut out the paragraph, and tucked it for future reference into her Bible, that lay on the mantel.

"If that ain't a ' find '!" she ejaculated softly.

The contents of the sauce-pan were simmering. With a look of unwonted abstraction, she poured the liquid into a cup, put with it upon a tray a strip of toast, and took it into the other room. When she brought back the cup and plate, she could not resist the temptation to read the "find" over again.

Acquire the habit of living by the minute. Take care of this moment now while you have it, the next when it comes, and you will not then neglect any. You can live this minute without sin. Is it not so? Do it, then. Never mind what is before you. Do not sin now. When each successive minute comes, do likewise. If you will do this, — if you will observe this simple rule, — you will not fail, you will not sin at all. Days are made up of minutes; if each one is sinless, the day will be so. Now try this. Nothing is easier, nothing is wiser. Live by the minute. Carry on your business, trade, labor, study, and plan for the future by the minute. Trust in God now; do God's will now; do not offend God now. — *Bishop Foster.*

"Wouldn't that go straight to Mr. Stevens's heart?" she said, inly, to her edified self. "I'll send it to Mrs. Barnes, and when she's got her share of honey out of it, I'll mail it to him. I wonder if Bishop Foster is alive or dead? I'd go far to thank him for this brook by the way. It's made me lift up my head — and my heart. There's another of the blessed ones, whose feet are set in the Royal Road. Pretty soon they will be a great multitude that no man can number. To come upon this right in the heart of one of them Sunday papers, is like finding a pearl in a stale oyster. It's a lesson in charity, too, if I take it in the right way. There's some good in everything, and after this I'll never say that the Sunday paper mayn't be the means of saving a soul.

"The question for this one of my minutes is why I was led to light upon this at this particular time, when my whole soul is going out in prayer, and longing to hit upon some way of comforting her. Nothing happens by chance. Mr. Stevens says the day is as full of guide-posts to duty as a paling fence is of pickets. Is this one of them?"

She took the cutting into the front chamber with her, holding it in her left hand, while the right brushed a minute crumb from the counterpane.

In her eyes, and lingering about the corners of her mouth, was a happy smile.

Mrs. Paull's languid regards passed from the printed slip to her attendant's face; and an instinct of politeness, rather than curiosity, prompted a question, —

"Is that something that you would like me to see?"

"I suppose you wonder why I am carrying it about with me, like the woman in the Bible, with the piece of silver she found by lighting the candle and sweeping out the corners," she said, the happy laugh mellowing yet more the voice already so soothing to the ear. "I made up my mind, a great while ago, that the pleasantness and misery of this world are made up of many littles, and that those are the best off who make much of the day and hour of small things. We all know that whatever God sends has a meaning, and will accomplish that whereunto it is sent; and that if we keep our eyes and ears open all the time, we may come to see a great deal more of what He does mean than we're apt to believe, if we haven't tried that plan of living. We've fallen so much into the habit of saying, ' What He does we can't know here, but we shall know Hereafter,' that most of us think it is a religious duty to wait for everything until that Hereafter."

"But those were Christ's own words."

A tiny ray of satisfaction kindled at the back of the nurse's eyes.

"If I can once arouse her to argue with me, it will be a sign she's waking up!" she thought.

"Yes; but He said them to Peter, and about an altogether different matter, reproving the poor rash fellow for over-inquisitiveness. He blames nobody for considering His ways, and being guided by them. Now, it seems to me, and I'm sure the Bible backs me up in it, — not in so many words, of course, but in the spirit of it, — 't seems to me that that way of taking life is a good deal like a cake with all the fruit settled at the bottom. 'T ain't nice, nor yet wholesome. It's better cooking and better religion to flour the raisins and citron and currants, and mix 'em well through the batter, so they won't sink into one heavy streak."

Her prattle was so ingenuous in style, and so brightly delivered, that her auditor was beguiled into the reality of listening. For the first time Mrs. Williams saw the perfect teeth gleam in a spontaneous smile.

"And is that" — looking at the cutting — "a new recipe for insuring success in fruit-cake making?"

Nurse Williams laughed outright.

"You've no idea what a clever guess you've made, ma'am! If it wouldn't bore you to hear me read it, you'd be ready to laugh yourself, to see how exactly you've hit it. I'll hang this banner-screen on the gas-burner to keep the light from your eyes before I begin."

While making arrangements for the other's comfort, she twittered gently on, —

"It came about in what some folks would consider an odd way. The oddest things are often the most natural, if we see them in the right light. I was in the brownest sort of a study when I happened upon this cutting. 'T was just as though an angel poked it right under my eyes, and said, 'How is it that you have no faith? Here's what you need.' There's no doubt that such things do happen. And why not, to be sure? He gives them charge to see that we don't stub our toes in our daily walk. I heard a minister say once that passage meant in the language — Hebrew, I think it was — it was first written in, ' Lest thou touch thy foot against a very little stone.' A pebble, I suppose, and there's different sizes of pebbles.

"But here's my recipe for mixing the fruit even all through the cake."

She read better than could have been expected from a woman of her limited education, giving each syllable due consideration, and was heedful of punctuation points.

"Some sick folks — mostly men — like to be amused by having the newspapers read," she used to say; "and children can be kept still any length of time with nice little stories; and it's surprising what an effect reading the Psalms — the comforting, promising ones — has upon nervous and low-spirited invaleeds. As for the Gospels, they suit all kinds, I find."

When the article was finished, she saw that Mrs. Paull had turned upon her side, and slipped her hand under her cheek. The gleam of the sunken eyes was dimmed, not quenched. It was something that she had shifted her position voluntarily, but her tone was not encouraging, —

"I know just what manner of man wrote that," she said, a slight flavor of scorn in the feeble voice. "A pious, easy-going soul, who never had deep experience of any kind. Life had gone upon velvet for him, and he judged other people's trials and temptations by his own."

"Do you think so?" said the nurse, looking at the reverse side of the clipping, as if hoping there to discover whether or not the criticism were correct. "Now, I was hoping that he had studied the lesson out for himself, and found it so useful that he could n't help but recommend it to us, who had been tried and tempted, and had suffered in the same way. It reads to me like, ' Oh, taste and see.'"

She read the extract over again silently to herself before resuming her talk.

"I know lots of people who have learned to live by the day, and even hour; but this minute business is spandy new to me. And it does seem to me to fit in splendid with the hairs-of-your-head and the falling-sparrow and the grass-of-the-field and the young-ravens-when-they-cry doctrine."

"But nobody takes such figures of speech literally. It would be childish to pretend to live in that way in a practical age. An intelligent man or woman must plan and provide for — and dread — the unknown future. With at least one-half of those who know the uncertainties and terrors of life, it is a fearful looking-forward, — a fearful looking-forward!"

The scorn was sadder, the intonations were desolate. She moved uneasily among her pillows. The probe had found the ball. Mrs. Williams had assisted at too many operations not to understand what the flinch meant.

"That fearful looking-forward is a part of the doom of the impenitent," she said, quietly. "When the beloved of the Lord are permitted to look ahead, they are commanded to lift their heads and look up. That's the only use they have for far-sighted eyes.

"'*I will lift up mine eyes unto the hills, from whence cometh my help.*'

"'*Look unto Me, and be ye saved.*'

"From Genesis to Revelations it is 'Up! up!' It's the only safe and sensible thing to do when you're travelling in dizzy places, whether it's with our bodily feet or in spirit. The dear Lord blindfolds us when the road is very dangerous, then lays tight hold of our hands, and His voice — not behind us, but close beside us, oh, so close and so sweet! — says: '*This is the way! Walk ye in it!*' And '*I will lead them in paths they have not known.*' The sheep know His voice, and ask nothing better than to follow Him. 'T would be the foolishest thing in nature to try to pull off the bandage. Yet that is what the best of us are apt to do."

The conversation was stayed at that for a long while. Mrs. Williams took up her knitting, — a shawl of cream-white Saxony wool, intended, although nobody but herself knew this, for a Christmas present to Mrs. Paull. Her needles did not click, and the fluffy fabric harmonized with her personality in some mysterious way.

"I don't think I took in the full meaning of what you said just now," came at last from her companion. "Existence would be a tame affair if all ordered their thoughts according to your rule. We might as well have been born short-sighted in soul and mind."

"'T would have been more comfortable if this was all the life we are to have. My eyes are uncommon strong for a woman of fifty-three, but a year ago this month something or other ailed 'em. When I'd hold a book or my work down this way, I'd see a shadow of a line just above the real one. 'T was a sort of double sight, and it bothered me no end. So I went to an okkerlist. My pastor gave me a letter to him. He flashed a light way down to the bottom of my eyeballs, and went through all manner of tests with 'em, and then, says he, ' What have you been doing to strain your optic muscle? Have you been reading in bed or anything like that, when you were n't in your usual health?'

"So I had to confess that, being laid up for a couple of weeks with influenzy, I had read in bed the whole enduring time, seeing I so seldom get a chance to indulge myself that way, and being awful fond of books. He said when I did that, the angle of vision was n't right. So I paid for my foolishness and ignorance by being unable to wear civilized people's glasses, but must have a pair ground slanting-like to suit the sight I'd twisted from the uprightness in which the Almighty had created it. Now, 't seems to me that's about what we do when we go against God's law of spiritual sight. He gives us one day at a time, and tells us to make the best of it. And we are continually peeping 'round or under or over it, in a fease to see what's coming next, at an angle He never intended us to use. It's no wonder we get cross-eyed and what not, and lose our clear views of life, and can't see heaven straight without we have gospel glasses, ground expressly to suit what we've made ourselves to be."

Mrs. Paull looked unaffectedly amused, yet thoughtful.

"Still you say there are people who have trained themselves not to look beyond the day. How do they begin the work?"

"By receiving the kingdom of heaven and all belonging to it as little children. When God says a thing, they just simply believe it. That's the whole secret. They believe it as babies believe in their mothers, — take Him at His word as Gladys takes all you say for gospel truth. If you were to say to her in a thunder-storm, ' Mamma will keep you safe, dear,' she'd not have another fear."

"Yes, because she sees and hears me. We have no guarantee that God has any especial message for the individual human soul. I am still in the dark as to the first lesson of your faith and practice. Where do you get your certified orders?"

"He says, ' When ye pray, say our Father, who art in heaven,' and so on. When you get to ' give us this day,' — or, as the New Version puts it in the margin, ' day by day our daily bread,' — stop and ask yourself if He hasn't some merciful reason for repeating that ' daily ' idea so often. It is a kind of fence He has built about to-day.

"You've got nothing to do with what is going on outside; He says to you by that form of prayer: ' To-day is your business, and there's enough to do to keep you busy. To-morrow belongs to me.'

"I've got a piece of poetry at home I'll have copied off for you some time, if you don't mind, that says how ' from the coming ages ' we must ' reverent take the virgin day.' That's the idea! A new day, a clean day, — something made just purposely for each of us, that nobody has ever had in all eternity past until this very morning; something to be improved and enjoyed with all our heart, soul, and strength, before it is sealed up and laid away with all the yesterdays that have been since creation, and labelled along with God's eternal years."

She wrought industriously at the creamy shawl, knitting one needle out and another in, then looked up smilingly, —

"I shall never forget when I first got hold of that beautiful idea, and what a lovely thing the fresh day seemed to me! Not a thumb-mark, not a spot or wrinkle, or any such thing. I saw a thousand pleasant things to be happy for, and to wonder at, as the hours went by, that I would have missed if I had been thinking about what might happen tomorrow; and knowing it's all I am sure of, I make so much more of little things," unmindful, in her enthusiasm, of the change in her tenses. "By bedtime, when you come to say your prayers, —" mixing up persons in like happy confusion, — "you are actually afraid of wearying the Lord, if that could be (which it is n't!), with your thanksgivings. And, when you lay your head upon your pillow, you fall asleep like a well baby in its mother's arms. That day is done with, — shut and wrapped up carefully and put into God's safe hands."

"Nevertheless, I should think you would find life monotonous, — a very tame affair, as I said just now; just the same story over and over and over to the end of time. The hope that to-morrow may bring a change in their condition is all that keeps miserable people from despair."

"You would swap hope off for faith. I'd better say, perhaps, you would run the two into one grace. 'What man has done, man may do again,' is a saying that people find no difficulty in believing. What God has done in the way of goodness and mercy, God will do again, and keep on doing to all eternity. If He took care of me all day yesterday, and every other yesterday I have ever lived; and forgave my sins and granted me the joy of His countenance, and healed my sorrows, and strengthened me to do His holy will, — He's bound to do as much for me to-day. Why, it's for to-day He promises strength and grace, and our Saviour positively forbids us to worry about to-morrow. Our minister's wife made a real helpful talk on this subject at our last woman's prayer-meeting. In it she told how some good man — John Newton, I think — had said that each day of life is like a stick of wood given us to carry, and how we are promised strength to be able to do it. But, he said, when we lay atop of that to-morrow's stick, and day after to-morrow's and next week's, it's no wonder that we break down. We are abusing God's long-suffering, and not keeping ourselves back from presumptuous sins. He holds fast to His word. The trouble is we have n't obeyed orders. 'For,' as she said, ' there is nowhere in God's word the promise of grace for fagots.'

"But there! I ain't going to preach any longer. Dr. Bacon makes lots of fun about that very thing.

He says my tongue runs like a mill-race when I get started upon the Royal Road."

"I am not tired, — except of myself and my own thoughts!"

The last words escaped her unguardedly. She tossed her hands out restlessly upon the coverlet.

"It is good in you to talk to me of something else. It all sounds as if it ought to hold a world of comfort, if we only had the key. I can understand" — with a sort of sorrowful archness — "why you have been so patient with me all these dreary days. You took me by the day. Go on with your story. What is this Royal Road at which Dr. Bacon laughs?"

"That's Mr. Stevens's name for it. In the first sermon I ever heard him preach, he said, as near as I can recollect, —

"'We were told when we were little tots of children, and were so foolish as to think that we could read right off, without learning our A, B, C's, that there is no Royal Road to learning. That is a fact there is no getting around. It's just as truly a fact, and a far more glorious one, that there *is* a Royal Road to happiness. That's what all the men and women that have lived for the last six thousand years have been trying to find, — the certain way to be happy.' Then he went on to describe the hundreds of ways they'd taken, the blood that had been shed, the money that had been wasted, the hearts that had been broken, the souls that had been lost in searching for happiness along the wrong roads. There are as many of them, he told us, as there are stars in the

Milky Way, and folks are all the time opening and laying out new ones.

"At last he said if we'd all come again next Sunday night, he'd tell us how to find, and how to keep in the Royal Road to happiness. And with that, he gave out a hymn, and pronounced the benediction, and sent us home, not knowing whether to laugh or be provoked, but all of a mind about coming again next Sunday night.

"He's all the time doing that sort of thing. Folks call him 'eccentric' and 'sensational,' and harder names than those; but he knows how to 'fetch' the common people. Come to look at his ways, they may n't, after all, be very different from what Saint Paul meant by catching his hearers by guile. I should n't wonder if the scribes and Pharisees brought some such railing accusations against the Saviour when they found Him telling stories to the multitude about Prodigal Sons and Unjust Stewards and Houses built on the Sand, and Rich Men and Beggars, and calling their attention to lilies of the field and red sunrises.

"Well, you may be sure, we were all on hand next Sunday evening, and it looked like every one of us had fetched his own brother and his own sister to boot. There was n't room to move, and hardly air enough to breathe, with the people packed into the seats and standing in the aisle.

"It's time for your drops again, I see! They're pleasanter than the last, ain't they?" when the medicine had been taken. "They're beginning to take hold of you, too, I can see. Your color is better, and strength is coming into your body. I've faith in Dr. Bacon, if he does enjoy making game of me."

She broke off at the sound of a tap at the door.

"It's the little ones on their way to their supper," she said tenderly.

CHAPTER VIII.

'T is easy to be gentle when
    Death's silence shames our clamor,
And easy to discern the best
    Through memory's mystic glamour;
But wise it were for thee and me,
    Ere love is past forgiving,
To take the tender lesson home, —
    Be patient with the living!

                    MARGARET E. SANGSTER.

CHAPTER VIII.

MARIE brought in the three children.
It was Friday afternoon, and she had arrived at four o'clock to pass the Sabbath at home. After sitting for half an hour with her mother, she had volunteered to look after the children, while Elspeth was busy below-stairs. Since Mrs. Williams had been put in charge of the sick-room, a sullen change had gradually stolen over the girl's face and demeanor, unperceived, apparently, by the mother, but painful to Elspeth, and perplexing to the hired nurse.

From her birth this daughter had been the father's favorite child. Latterly, the tie between them had been the romantic element in her young life. He had laughed to himself slyly sometimes, at certain indications that her devotion to him went to the length of being jealous of the loverly attentions he liked to pay his wife when the fancy seized him to act the exemplary husband. From the time the child could run alone, she used to declare that she intended to marry papa when she was grown. Her seat was next his at table, and she was oftenest selected as his companion in drive or walk. Her vivacious chatter amused the world-weary man. He liked to lie upon the lounge, his head in Marie's lap, her fingers toying with curls from which her own had caught their sunshine, while his wife played plaintive nocturnes and brilliant sonatas for his delectation. Mrs. Paull did not interfere with the display of injudicious favoritism. Whatever helped to keep Ernest at home, and bind him to the children, must be for good. While Marie remained dutiful and affectionate to herself, she found no fault with her greater fondness for her father. It was better that she should idealize him than to learn prematurely to know him for what he was.

Following what he knew would be his sister's wishes on this head, Roger Lanier had told the girl that troublesome business had called her father abroad for an indefinite period, and enjoined upon her the necessity of avoiding allusions to him in her mother's presence while she remained ill.

"You are old enough to understand, Marie, that there are unpleasant complications in business life, and that some of these would deprive a man of his good name, in the estimation of some people," he added, awkwardly enough, for the fixed gaze of the blue eyes challenged the correctness of his tale. "I cannot enter into particulars at present. You must try to believe that I am acting for the best, and be very patient with your mother until she is strong enough to take control of her own affairs."

"I can be patient with her, but not with any one who insinuates that my father is guilty of anything that could injure his reputation if the whole truth were known," Marie answered, with the haughtiness of an offended princess. "Of course, I shall tell the children, as you advise, that their dear papa will not be home for a long time, — just that, and nothing more. And you may depend upon me never to introduce his name in conversation with mamma. Further than this, I promise nothing."

Angry, compassionate, yet somewhat amused by what he considered her "ridiculous high-tragedy airs," the uncle next sought an interview with his eldest nephew, who bore the family name and his mother's face. Him he took into fuller confidence. Lanier was over seventeen, a lad of singular sense and discretion, and a Freshman in Yale College. His uncle admitted to him, by tactful degrees, that his father had misapplied trust-funds, intending, no doubt, to put them back into the hands of their lawful owners, when he had made his profit out of them. The failure of a speculation that had promised well would compel him to remain out of the country until the matter could be adjusted or should be forgotten.

The young face flushed darkly; the features were set hard in pain and mortification.

"Can there be no mistake, Uncle Roger? Have you looked into the affair for yourself?"

"My boy! could I rest a day without going to the bottom of it? All that I have told you is unfortunately, fatally true. Your mother, I need not remind so good a son as yourself, Lanier, is the person most seriously affected by your father's error. You are now her mainstay. Care for her as a loving, sorrowing wife should be cared for. It is a sacred charge."

The most shameful part of the story was kept back

from all of Ernest Paull's children. It was not a tale for young ears.

Lanier wrote daily to his mother, when she was well enough to read his letters, fondly, and with tenderest solicitude, striving to cheer her without betraying his knowledge of the extent of her grief and need. The brightest hour in the twenty-four for her was that in which she received and read his love-notes, yet Mrs. Williams had marvelled within herself that the effect produced by them was transitory.

Mrs. Paull held out her hand to the babyest of the quartette, as they tiptoed up to the bed.

"Lift her up, please, Marie!" she said, motioning to the place enclosed by her arm.

When the rosy cheek touched hers upon the pillow, she asked, —

"What has my little Gladys been doing this afternoon?"

Marie's attempt to catch the child's eye, unseen by the mother or Gladys, did not escape Mrs. Williams.

"Marie has been dressing my doll, and talking to us of dear papa," chirped the baby. "I wish he would come home!" heaving a sigh. "We cried two times this evening — Marie and me, both — for him."

"*We* didn't!" protested the boys, stoutly, nine-year-old Tom adding, "All the same, we want to see him awfully."

Mrs. Paull pressed her hand over her eyes. The lower part of her face was so ghastly that the nurse came to the front.

"Now, my chickens, your supper is all ready for you downstairs. When I was in the kitchen awhile ago, I was sure that I smelled cookies; or it may have been gingerbread. Your mother hopes to sit up in her easy-chair a little while to-morrow, if we don't tire her too much to-night. I should n't be a mite surprised if she should be strong enough to hold Gladys in her lap in a week. People get well fast after they begin to sit up."

She swung Gladys from the bed, and tossed her up at the full length of her robust arms, kissed her cheek as she set her upon the floor, and opening the door, bustled the laughing party into the hall.

"If you eat a good supper and don't get your faces and hands sticky, you can peep in at mamma again to say ' Good-night,' " she sent down the stairs after them.

Marie darted a ray of indignant contempt at her, drew up her slight figure, and from her stand at the foot of the bed, surveyed her mother silently, evidently waiting for her to uncover her eyes.

"If I believed in shaking people, I should be disposed to try it on her," was the nurse's first thought, superseded by a kinder second, after a glance at the pale misery of the girl's face. Something must be done before Mrs. Paull met the meaning gaze. She began in desperate cheerfulness, —

"You have no idea, Miss Marie, what a difference your coming home makes to us all. I believe those children begin to count the days from the time you leave us on Monday morning, until you are to be with us again; and I had to laugh to-day, to hear

Elspeth singing, 'There's nae luck aboot th' house,' while she was making up your bed."

"She didn't sing the next line, I suppose, being under orders?" struck in Marie, unexpectedly, a sardonic gleam playing over her face. "Can I speak to you in the other room, Mrs. Williams?"

Mr. Paull's portrait was there still, set carefully upon the table, but in a corner out of the reach of possible harm. Marie closed the inner door behind them, and confronted the nurse, head up and nostrils quivering.

"I am forbidden, by my uncle, Mr. Lanier, to speak to my mother upon the subject that lies nearest my heart," she said frigidly. "It is evident that you, also, are acting under orders. Perhaps you may be authorized to transact business in his absence? It is a singular state of things when a daughter, who has been honored all her life long with the confidence of both parents, must use a comparative stranger as a medium of communication with her mother."

She became more stilted in speech as she went on, bent as she was, in her girlish arrogance, upon crushing the presumptuous intruder. She completed the absurdity by a wave of the hand, which, had Mrs. Williams ever known Ernest Paull, would have brought him to her mind.

"But let that pass. My object in asking for a few minutes of your valuable time — for which, I suppose, my uncle remunerates you — is to inquire if I may take that picture up to my own room. It is but so much rubbish on this floor. Have you the liberty to tell me if my mother has expressed any desire to have it back in the old place, — the place my father meant it to hold when he gave it to her?"

"Not yet, Miss Marie. She is, as you can see, extremely weak and nervous; not at all herself, in fact —"

Another wave of the hand, intended to be majestic, but merely impatient.

"I do not care to enter upon the subject of my mother's nerves — or notions. Mrs. Williams, Dr. Bacon, and Mr. Lanier are the committee upon them. I have, however, I am proud to say, some claim upon my father. Will you discover, at your earliest convenience, if I may be allowed the slight consolation in his absence, of having his portrait? At least until his wife's nervous system recovers tone, and she can bear the sight of it."

Mrs. Williams was the picture of unruffled benevolence, unconscious of her figurative annihilation at the hands of Ernest Paull's champion.

"There can be no earthly objection to your having the picture whenever you like, I am sure, my dear, and hanging it wherever you think best. Next to your mother's, yours is the best right. I will carry it up for you while you are at supper."

"I want no supper! And I will take it up myself and now, before the permission is withdrawn."

It was a bulky burden for the slender arms; but, with her unfailing tact, Mrs. Williams restrained the impulse to offer assistance beyond holding the door open for her to pass out with the coveted treasure. The habit of close, silent observation showed her that the girl's heart swelled and that she bit her lips in mounting the stairs.

"She is game to the backbone, but she is nothing but a child," she reflected, her throat swelling in sympathy. "He is her idol. There's depths of mercy even for the unthankful and the evil, and that man may yet see the error of his ways."

Mrs. Paull asked no questions when her custodian returned. If she was cognizant of the interview, and gave it a thought, she imagined that Marie had wished to consult Mrs. Williams upon some matter of household economy. She had fallen back into her old attitude, — her hands clasped below her chin, her eyes resting upon the ceiling. The nurse resumed her chair and her knitting, and neither spoke until the children looked in for their "Good-night" kiss.

Elspeth was directly behind them. She brought up half of a broiled quail, a bunch of purple hothouse grapes, and a cluster of La France roses, all of which she set out in order upon a bedside stand.

"Mr. Lanier sent the bonnie bird; Mrs. Lanier sent the grapes. The roses are from a leddy who says she was at school with ye lang syne."

The card she presented with the flowers was engraved with the name of "*Mrs. William C. Barnes, 106 Wyandotte Avenue.*" Upon the other side was pencilled, "*Have you forgotten Annie Meredith? She sends these, with dear love and prayers for your speedy recovery.*"

"Annie Meredith!" repeated the sick woman, wonderingly. "Am I in her part of Brooklyn?"

"Why, that's our minister's wife! And I was talking about her to you only this evening!" cried Mrs. Williams. "Here is something to give you an appetite. I always insist there's no sauce like an agreeable piece of news. I met Dr. Barnes right by your door last night when I ran around to the druggist's, and stopped to tell him that I was nursing you, and that you were getting on comfortably, with never an idea that you knew his wife. I s'pose she put it all together when he got home and spoke of seeing me. Ah! but she is one of the blessed among women, I can tell you!

"You're another, Elspeth, for cooking this quail to perfection. No!" seeing Mrs. Paull about to speak, "I can't answer a single question about your old friend, — 'though there's lots and lots to tell — until you've done justice to your supper and to Elspeth."

The Scotchwoman's dry smile was somewhat forced. One of her nurslings was missing; and as soon as she could get them out of the room, she marshalled the boys, and, with Gladys in her arms, mounted to the upper story.

The front chamber immediately over Mrs. Paull's was Marie's. The hall bedroom adjoining was shared by Tom and Edwin; Elspeth had slept in the nursery with Gladys's crib beside her bed since Mrs. Paull fell ill. She undressed the child, and put her to bed before looking up the absent and fasting member of her flock. Marie's door was locked on the inside, and half-a-dozen guarded knocks upon the panels were unanswered. Elspeth stooped to put her lips to the key-hole.

"Me bairnie! winna ye open to yer auld nurse?"

Still there was an irresolute pause before the key was turned, and Marie appeared, her eyes swollen and cheeks discolored with crying.

"Cannot even you leave me alone, Elspeth? I would not have let anybody else in."

"That's partly why I cam'. Ye'll be ill if ye tak' neither bit nor sup the night."

"I want nothing! I could not eat a mouthful."

The stiff pose and defiant tone gave way before the sweep of childish emotion. She threw herself sobbing into the Scotchwoman's arms.

"Elspeth! my heart is breaking for my father! Where is he? What terrible thing has driven him from home and lost him everybody's love but mine? Why am I to ask no questions, and why does my mother shudder at the sound of his name as if he were something evil and hateful? He has been gone over three weeks, and not a word has come from him. Is he dead, — and Uncle Roger will not let me know?"

"Save and bless the child! what could put that into your bit head? No, my puir bairnie, no! never that I've been told. Mr. Lanier, he but said to me that Mr. Paull had gone over the sea to furren pairts on business, and it wad likely be quite a while before we'd hear from him. But there's nae sic thing as ye spoke of, my bonnie lassie. Not nearly so close to it as she that lies downstairs, that's been to the very gate of the dark valley, and is still as like to gae through the one door as th' ither, if the truth were known. It's your mother I'm on the knees of me heart for, all the day long. Yer father's a man, — and healthy and strong, for all ony of us ken to the contrary, and able to fend for himself."

Marie raised her head from the broad shoulder, and pushed herself away from the would-be comforter.

"You are like all the rest of them! He is an angel on earth or in heaven! And there is not one of all those whom he has befriended, or whom he loves, who cares whether he be alive or dead, but only myself. But I'll never forsake him, — never! never! Do you see that?"

She pointed to the portrait hung over against the bed, as it had hung by her mother's. Upon a stand below it, she had arranged her Bible and several devotional books, and directly under the pictured face was a vase of clouded glass, — a "tear vase," as it is called, — with a spray of heliotrope.

"It was his favorite flower. Do you recollect how he would come to me every morning for a sprig from my heliotrope bush, and how he always kissed me after I had pinned it upon his coat? I'll say my prayers right there, night and morning, when I'm at home, — if the house where he is forgotten and his very name blotted out can be called ' home.' Wherever I go, he is my patron saint."

"Humph!" Had her life depended upon her silence, Elspeth could hardly have repressed the homely sniff. "I'm thinking ye'll mak' but a puir Papist if fasting for a matter of sax hours has made ye daft. It's to be hoped the mother will surely get well. The children wad fare ill if they'd nought but a feather-headed bit like ye to look to for clothes and common sense. I've nae time to waste chattering an' havering here aboot heliotropes and patron saints, when there's a living Christian in need of nursing. Ye'll either come down to yer tea like a sane body, or I'll send it to ye by the hand of Mrs. Williams, and mysel' step around to Dr. Bacon for ye. I doobt but he'll clap a blister on the back o' yer heid. Ye're not a' right there or somewheers else!"

She looked, and as Marie knew, was altogether capable of carrying out the threat. Dumb with useless wrath, the defeated girl chose the lesser evil of sitting down to the cream-toast and broiled ham prepared for her by the tyrant who waited upon her as if nothing had occurred to mar their friendly relations.

Sentimentality, which may be defined as fatty degeneration of naturally healthy sympathies, met with no toleration from Elspeth. Just now she was too much engrossed by actual and pressing anxieties to waste thought upon imaginary or over-wrought grief.

Her tone had a more hopeful ring, but care still sat visibly upon her brow when she met Mr. Lanier at his visit on Saturday forenoon.

"She's sitting up the day, sir," in response to his queries. "She will have it that she is better, and her heart is set upon having a talk with yoursel'. She tell't me awhile ago that there was important business must be looked after, and she had put it off over long a'ready. I'm wistful to be putting a word into yer ear, sir, upon another matter before you see her. Saving your presence, Miss Marie will come to grief unless her mind is made easier the one way or the other."

In fewer words than any other of five hundred women would have used, she narrated the incident of the portrait.

Roger Lanier's clear-cut features were marble as he listened. He had never liked Ernest Paull, when the latter was at his best. At his worst, he detested him as cordially as a Christian man can detest an unrepentant sinner. Marie's impassioned loyalty was but another trail of the serpent over the stirred nest. Elspeth was not supersensitive, but she lost courage to plead the cause she had in mind when she began her story, at sight of his stony visage. Her voice shook a little in concluding with an appeal.

"If she might but write to her father, say once a month, sir, — he's that, you know, sir, and unco' fond o' her, — 't wad mak' her the more content, and wad, mayhap, be blest to his guid —"

Discovering here that she was drifting into her vernacular, and standing always in awe of her mistress's dignified kinsman, she lapsed into silence.

Mr. Lanier raised his eyes abruptly from a seemingly minute scrutiny of his patent-leather boots.

"You have been with Mrs. Paull a long time, Elspeth?" he said mildly, although his face was not softened.

"Sin' five years before she was married, sir."

"You are so well acquainted with our family affairs, it is but just I should take you into full confidence now," — two odd white dents deepening about the nostrils as he talked. "In my judgment, it would be better if the two elder children, at least, were given plainly to understand that Mr. Paull is no longer to be considered their father, or their mother's husband. In all human probability, he will never return to America. Not to disguise an ugly truth, he is passing off another woman as his wife and travelling companion. I beg your pardon for speaking so plainly!" — for the upright Scotchwoman uttered a low, horrified cry, — "but it had to be said. Their mother will not consent that the children shall hear the facts in the case. She thinks that they will gradually forget one whom they never see, and whose name is seldom mentioned. I have paid to his employers the money he stole, and have seen to it that the wretched story did not find its way into the newspapers. I stand prepared to keep my sister above the chance of want, and to help educate her children. All this I have written to Ernest Paull. He is, I have discovered through agents I have on the other side of the Atlantic, living in Nice, France, under the name of 'Mr. Paul Morgan,' and that he and his companion are already known in that town as gambling adventurers. I have furthermore notified him that if he ever shows his face in this country again, I will give him up to the law; as I shall, were he doubly my brother-in-law. He has destroyed my sister's happiness. He shall not hang upon her life like a foul growth that would draw all the strength and sweetness out of it!"

"Does she know — what you have told me, sir?"

The question was whispered. The rugged features were wrung out of their grim impassiveness by the revolting revelation.

"She does. I had to break the news to her in the first place, and three days ago she sent the nurse out of the room, and would know what I had heard since she was struck down by that blow. I had to tell her."

"The wonder is that she is n't dead outright, sir, — her that fairly worshipped the very print of his feet in the dust."

She raised a corner of her apron to her eyes.

"If she had not sprung from genuine Lanier stock, — if she were one degree less spirited, — she would have died," said the brother. "As to Miss Marie, — she is an especial pet of yours, I am aware, Elspeth, — but she is her father's daughter, within and without. All this rubbish about making a patron saint of a man who is not worthy to black her mother's shoes, — this keeping flowers under his portrait, and praying to it —"

"Na! na! Mr. Lanier! I dinna say that; on'y that she was minded to kneel down before it when she prayed."

In the depth of her honest distress, she could not have her nursling misrepresented.

Mr. Lanier smiled in indulgent amusement.

"It amounts to about the same thing. Marie would be a nice girl but for her likeness in character and face to her father. She may come to something better now that she will be left entirely to her mother's management. But she is a Paull, and must be watched carefully. I shall urge my sister to-day to tell her everything, young as she is, but I have little hope of succeeding in making her mother see that she owes it to herself to do this. It will be just like the silly little sentimentalist that Marie is to nurse her fancied sorrows, and go on idolizing the rascal, who would, by now, be lodged behind prison bars if he had not happened to marry Alice Lanier eighteen years ago, — more's the pity! It would be just like Marie, I say, to add to her mother's trials by disrespectful behavior and cruel questions, even if she does not defy her authority altogether."

"She'll not do that, sir. She's been too weel reared, and she has too good a heart."

He almost laughed now at the anxious deprecation in word and accent.

"I am willing to hope so, if only because she is your favorite, my sister's eldest daughter, and my mother's namesake. All depends upon our success in getting the Paull out of her nature, and the Lanier in. I shall, as I remarked, try to change her mother's mind with respect to the wisdom of telling Lanier and Marie the truth, the whole truth, and nothing but the truth. Is she ready to see me now?"

When their footsteps sounded upon the floor of the upper hall, the folds of the half-drawn portière hanging in the doorway between the parlor and dining room moved, and Marie stepped into sight.

She was studying in the front parlor when Elspeth

answered the door bell the young girl had not heard. At the sound of her uncle's voice, she ran behind the curtain, supposing that he would, as was his custom, go directly upstairs. Disappointed in this expectation, she saw no impropriety in remaining in her hiding place while the talk ran upon her mother's health. He would, undoubtedly, go to see his sister as soon as he had satisfied himself on this point. He had not taken a seat, and the interview would be brief and unimportant. When Elspeth introduced her own (Marie's) name, and entered upon her description of the portrait-scene, anger and shame paralyzed the eavesdropper. Each instant made it more difficult to discover herself; presently she ceased to think of doing it.

They were conspirators, plotting against her happiness, — slanderers of him whom she revered and loved beyond all other created things. Self-preservation, and, yet more, jealousy for her father's honor and fair fame, incited her to get all the information she could collect, by any means, of their dastardly scheme. In asserting that she was Ernest Paull's own child in character as in features, her uncle had not specified among the traits they held in common a vanity so sensitive that the mother had often been sick at heart in recognizing the offshoot of a stock too deeply rooted in the father ever to be killed out. Mr. Lanier's criticisms of herself, so much more disdainful than if he had revealed her faults to her mother, or spoken to herself of them, stung her like spatters of boiling oil. She would have flouted hotly the insinuation that a large proportion of the resentment that carried her beyond the bounds of reason and natural affection for the mother who bore her, was not so much generous indignation over her father's wrongs as the smart of scarified self-esteem.

She had never been fond of her Uncle Roger, reflecting, while yet a child, her father's sentiments toward his upright and stately brother-in-law. As she gained in age and intelligence, her father and she exchanged views as to her mother's best-beloved relative, and she sympathized warmly with his wounded pride — he named it "feeling" — when the terms of her grandfather's will were known. Ernest Paull was always consciously or mechanically posing for effect in one character or another. As an affectionate husband, ready and glad to expend his worldly substance for his family, he doubtless sometimes imposed upon himself. Marie's belief in him was absolute. Roger Lanier was sorely tried that day, and spoke with more warmth than was habitual with him, even under strong provocation. Judgment and language would have been more charitable had he been given more time in which to digest the information sprung upon him by the serving-woman. As it was, he carried a more temperate spirit into his sister's presence. Before the stairhead was reached he would, if appealed to, have modified the sentence hastily pronounced upon a young, passionate creature, whose chief fault in his eyes was the resemblance, for which she was not responsible, to the man he abhorred.

She stood, trembling like an aspen, her palms

pressed hard upon her temples, her eyes wild, her face livid from the storm that raged in her soul.

"I don't believe it! It is a lie, an abominable, wicked, wicked lie!" she hissed through locked teeth.

Then, hearing Mrs. Williams coming up the kitchen stairs, she dashed up to her room, bolted the door, and flung herself, face downward, upon the floor, clutching fiercely at the carpet until her nails fastened themselves in the threads.

"Papa, papa, my wronged, insulted, persecuted darling!" she moaned. "Oh, I could kill them! I could *kill* them!"

At three o'clock that afternoon she entered the post-office, a mile and more from her home, and asked for "a French stamp."

"I beg pardon, miss!" said the clerk.

"I want to send a letter to Nice, in France," she answered, coloring as she felt that another customer standing beside her turned toward her at the words.

"Ah!" Without explanation of her blunder, the servant employed by his master, the Public, to discharge his nominal duties with the slightest possible outlay of language and courtesy, passed over a five-cent stamp.

"Do you think that will take my letter all right?" faltered the novice, doubtfully.

"Take it anywhere on the globe."

She affixed it, without further remark, laying the envelope on the counter to do it, the address in bold black characters, uppermost, and dropped it into the slit over the letter-basket.

She was overtaken at the outer door by a bright-faced, dark-eyed personage, whose apparel and speech bespoke the lady.

"I beg you to excuse the seeming impertinence, but am I mistaken in supposing you to be Miss Paull?"

"That is my name," civilly curt.

Just now she was disposed to aggressiveness, with or without provocation.

"Your voice is so like your mother's that it startled me, but you have your father's face," resumed the stranger. "Your mother was my schoolmate and dear friend. I am Mrs. Barnes. I heard yesterday, for the first time, and then through apparent accident, that she is living in Brooklyn, quite near us, and that she is ill. I could not resist the temptation to follow you when I heard you speak just now, and caught a glimpse of your face. Will you tell me exactly how she is to-day, and if there is any way in which I can be of service to her?"

CHAPTER IX.

For patience, — when the rough winds blow ;

For patience, — when our hopes are fading;
When visible things all backward go,

And nowhere seems the power of aiding, —
God still enfolds thee with His viewless hand
And leads thee surely to the fatherland.

From the German.

CHAPTER IX.

HE who knows the Pequod New Jersey of to-day has but an imperfect idea of what Pequod township was at the date of which I am writing.

Beautiful for situation it must ever have been, since the hills settled upon their foundations, and the waters found their level at the foot of the range of hills. Right in the centre of the valley lies a lakelet, three miles in length, and less than one mile in breadth at the widest part. The shores are notched boldly by headlands, and curved graciously by meadows, and grooved at intervals by reedy creeks, and brown brisk brooks racing down from the mountains to see for themselves what the greater open world is like. Back of the lake, and on all sides of it, are the hills, — mountains, the New Jersey folk call them, — proving the correctness of the nomenclature by reference to the map of the United States, whereupon they figure as faintly outlined spurs of the far-stretching Blue Ridge, which forms the ribs upon the right side of our continent. With over-lapping declivities, these eminences encircled Pequod Lake, an Old Guard of honor.

They are friendly mountains, and socially-minded toward the valley they environ. In benignant swells and dips they lie against the sky, looming through mists, and sinking to sleep under the stars. At the date of this humble chronicle, they were the boundary of this sparse settlement bearing the same name as the lake and township.

There were not more than fifteen dwellings within sight of a young girl, who sat one June forenoon upon the steps of a church set well toward the base of the tallest wall of the amphitheatre of hills. The building antedated the Revolutionary War, and, although modern vandalism under the disguise of improvement had done its best, or worst, to spoil it by daubing with white paint bricks redbrown with age, it was still a creditable specimen of colonial architecture. It stood about twenty yards away from the highway, — "street," by courtesy, and by virtue of definite, if unpaved sidewalks. Behind the church was the burying-ground, better kept than the majority of rural cemeteries, and across the side-street to the left the "Academy," *alias* the district schoolhouse, the junior by fifty years of the sanctuary. The broad thoroughfare was lined with spreading elms, and, sweeping by the church and the white parsonage, nestled confidingly under the venerable eaves, divided the church property from the grandest house in the township, — erected by a retired city merchant, — crossed a bridge and rolled along a hundred-yard level, ran over a second bridge built above one of the racing brooks aforesaid, then past another homestead inferior in size, and superior in age to the former, and, swerving slightly to the left, had an easy time of it until it gained a third bridge, which carried it into "the village," situated nearly a measured mile from the church. A woollen mill made the village, and the same corporation ran "the store" and post-office.

The girl, who had let herself down wearily in the shade cast by the elms upon the broad low step of the church, was Marie Paull. As she took off her straw hat and fanned herself with it, one could see that she was slighter in figure and more ethereal of visage than she had been six months before. The lines of cheek and chin were fine to delicacy; the blue eyes were larger and deeper; the corners of the mouth had a dispirited droop. Sanguine observers foretold that she would pick up flesh when she stopped growing. She had "run up like a mullein-stalk or a hop-vine. By-and-by she would get all her perpendicular inches, and go to work to make bone and flesh."

Pessimistic well-wishers asked solicitously if there were consumption in any branch of the family, and "only hoped that she might weather the next three years. So many girls went out, like the wick of an empty lamp, between seventeen and twenty-one."

The change in her appearance, and her failure in vigor and appetite, together with the hacking cough that wore upon Mrs. Paull's vital forces after she was convalescent from fever, were the alleged causes of the removal of the family to the country in April. Roger Lanier had come into possession, in the way of an exchange of property, of an old-fashioned farmstead in a retired neighborhood of Northern New Jersey. He offered it to his sister, rent free, for as long a time as she chose to occupy it, having, as he said, no use for it himself, and preferring to put a good care-taker into it to troubling himself with a farmer-tenant. The location was healthy. It was, by stage and railway, within two hours of New York City. For some years to come, the three younger children would be better off in the country.

Mrs. Paull was not hoodwinked by the dry, business-like details of the scheme as propounded by her brother. She was too familiar with his style of conferring benefits to embarrass him by voluble gratitude; but when he had gone, she secluded herself in her chamber for an hour before she could trust countenance or voice to make known the purport of Roger's visit to Marie.

She would consult the child, first of all, in the momentous matter of a change of home. It was a golden opportunity for breaking down the thickening wall of reserve, of which she had become conscious by the time she left her bed, and endeavored to take her old place in the household. Indeed, the change in the once merry, affectionate daughter, whose graceful development she had watched with maternal pride, was the means of awakening her from the strange numbness of brain and heart considered by physician and nurse the gravest symptom of her malady.

Marie's very features were altering into premature sedateness. She was alternately petulant and moodily reserved when she was not feverishly gay, and as the weeks wore on, had an air of nervous expectancy unaccounted for by any clew of information or of suspicion at the mother's command until Elspeth offered one.

"The bairnie is mayhap fretting for her father," she felt constrained to say to her mistress, lest she might discover the secret by other and less gentle means. "His name never passes her lips, and I 'm thinking that 's a sign she thinks of him the mair."

Marie was in her third-story room, where she spent at least two-thirds of her time when she was at home. The door was locked. Elspeth could have told her how common an occurrence this was, but her mother was surprised when her knock was answered by the turn of the key.

"Why do you lock yourself in, my love?" she asked. "I hope the children do not annoy you by running in and out? I have charged them not to disturb you when you are busy with your studies."

"Oh, no! they are good little things, and never come unless they are called. But it is cosier to sit on the right side of a locked door."

The flippant tone and studied indifference of behavior continued while her mother unfolded the particulars of the news she had brought, until, out of the fulness of her gratitude, she dwelt upon her brother's generosity.

"He intends, he says, to put the house in perfect repair, to have a furnace built in the cellar, and a bath-room in the second story, and hot and cold water throughout the house. All this, he would have me believe, is not contingent upon our removal to Pequod, but I know better. There will not be another dwelling in the region so luxuriously appointed. That is Uncle Roger's way. He dreads being thanked as much as ever Mr. Jarndyce could have dreaded acknowledgments. I anticipate your scruples in this matter, my darling. You feel with me that we are already under such heavy obligations to your uncle — surely the noblest, tenderest counsellor ever given to a woman in the hour of need! — that you hesitate to make further draughts upon his goodness."

Marie smiled sarcastically.

"On the contrary, mother, I have no scruples on that score. You have read me wrong for once. Uncle Roger is a pattern of truthfulness, as of liberality. When he declares that he is spending some thousands of the money he does not know what to do with upon a new toy for his own personal gratification, without a thought of pauperizing us, we are bound to believe him. As to our share in his project, I cannot understand why you should go through the form of consulting me. While I am a minor and dependent upon you, — and Uncle Roger, — I am at your disposal, to come or to go, or to stay, as you shall decide. One place is as good as another to me, since we cannot go back to New York to live. I cannot dislike this country place with an Indian name more than I dislike Brooklyn. I suppose we cannot go into society anywhere. So what difference does it make what I say or think or feel, when you and Elspeth and Uncle Roger are adequate to manage everything?"

"You misjudge me and your uncle," returned Mrs. Paull, with no sign of the cruel pain this reception of her story had cost her. "If I did not believe that your health would be improved by the removal to higher, drier air, and by the outdoor life you could enjoy in Pequod, all the other considerations you have named would have no weight with me. As to my advisers, we will leave our faithful Elspeth out of the question entirely. She does not deserve to be introduced into such a connection. While I depend upon your uncle in business affairs, as he has given me abundant reason for doing, I am strong enough to trust to my own judgment in whatever concerns my children and my home and theirs. You ought not to require me to assure you of that."

Marie was cold and still; her eyes were downcast; her lips were a straight, stubborn line.

The mother's voice changed from argument to entreaty.

"What has come between us lately, my daughter? We used to be dear and intimate friends, who believed in each other's affection, and trusted each other's motives. What have I done to grieve or to alienate you?"

Another long dumb interval, growing more oppressive as the seconds ticked themselves into minutes upon the tiny clock upon the desk. Marie had wheeled her chair around to receive her mother, and sat under her father's portrait. The tear-vase, with its spray of purple heliotrope, was in its place, lightly perfuming the air of the room. A pale purple scarf of soft silk, given to Marie at Christmas, was knotted across one corner of the gilded frame.

Suddenly the girl raised her eyes abruptly, light in them that confounded her companion as they blazed into hers, then passed to the portrait hanging between them.

The handsome, sunny face, with the crowning curls and golden chestnut mustache, and half-smile of content with himself and good-will toward his fellow-men that won his way everywhere, — the lover of Alice Lanier's gloriously happy girlhood, the husband she had idolized, now the banned refugee from her, and home, and native land!

Without the utterance of a syllable, the daughter arraigned one parent for irreparable wrong done to the other.

"You affect ignorance of your offence against me!" said feature and gesture. "Can you answer to me, his child and yours, for what you have done to *him?*"

For an instant Mrs. Paull was deathly white. Her features were sharpened, and the dull, hopeless misery was again in her eyes. The next, she rallied her native powers, and her glance followed Marie's to the pictured face.

"I will not pretend to misunderstand you, although I could have wished that the charge had been brought out in a different way. You would accuse me of injustice to your father, and unkindness to you, because I do not talk of him to you and the children, or give you any news of him. Perhaps I have erred in my silence. My brother thinks so. Had I been led as blindly by him as you intimate, you would have had the whole story before this; but I hoped that you had faith in your mother's love. I wished to spare you pain, and there are things which it is not easy for me to say to any one. Your father loved you very dearly —"

"If it gives you pain to tell me that, you may leave it unsaid!" interrupted harsh, husky accents. "I know it better, — a thousand times better than you can ever tell me. He said to me, — and I would believe him in opposition to all the canting uncles in Christendom, — he said the last time I saw him that I was the dearest thing to him on earth or in heaven. How that would shock Uncle Roger! I never told you; I shall never tell your brother that my father came to see me that Thursday evening and said 'Good-by' to me. He expected then to go to New Orleans the next day on business, — business that worried him exceedingly. He took me in his arms and kissed me twenty times, and asked me never to believe anything his enemies might bring up against him when he was not here to defend himself. He had battled a long time with them, he said, and they might get the better of him for a while, but I was never to doubt his innocence or his love for me, never! never!"

Her vehemence did not lessen the fond compassion with which her mother looked at her defiant face.

"You say that this was on Thursday, — the 21st of November?"

"It was. I came home on Saturday, my heart so full of grief and wonder that I would have rushed up to tell you all and cry myself quiet in your arms, and found you ill."

"He said that he was setting out for New Orleans?"

"He did. He was dressed for travelling then."

"Yet his passage was already taken for Havre. Have you ever thought to compare statement and fact?"

"No. I had his word, which was absolute truth to me. Something unforeseen changed his plans. I suppose you know what. His passage must—it *was* taken after he saw me. He said — oh, so sadly, mamma! — that you often misjudged him, and undervalued his love; that the day would come when you would see that you were mistaken, and maybe regret the devotion you had thrown away. He longed to know that he had the love of one true heart, and so came to me; I would never desert him. I promised solemnly, my arms about his neck, his dear cheek (there were tears on it, mamma!) against mine, that I would always love him and believe in him, and no cunning slanders that other people may persuade you into crediting will ever make me break my word. If he were to send for me to-morrow to come to him at the ends of the earth, I would go, if I had to steal the money to take me there. I would rather starve with him than live in luxury upon Uncle Roger's money!" cried the child, terrible, dry sobs breaking up the torrent of confession.

She sat erect, her fingers interlocked upon the desk, and talked fast, blood and brain at fever heat.

"My poor, loyal darling!" With tears running down her own cheeks, Mrs. Paull would have drawn her child to her, but Marie eluded the embrace by setting her chair further away. "My love! do you imagine that what you have said can make your mother love you less? If anything could draw a man to his home and hold him there, it would be such devotion and such faith as yours. Wherever your father may be, — and Marie, you must believe me when I say that I have not had one line from him since he wrote to your uncle on the day he sailed from America, saying that he was obliged by business misfortunes to go abroad, — wherever and whatever he may be —"

"He is the purest and noblest of men, always and everywhere!"

"I do not contradict it, dear. I was about to say that I hope and pray he may always remember how his daughter loves him. For myself, I have no complaint to make in his children's ears. I have insisted upon this to your uncle —"

"My uncle!" broke in Marie, fiercely. "My uncle, who is rich enough to rectify any ' business misfortunes ' my father could have met with, without feeling it, the purse-proud Pharisee who cheats him out of the first place in his wife's affections —"

"My daughter!"

"I mean it; every word of it! And drives him out of the country that he may the better blacken his good name. The high-bred gentleman, who stoops to gossip with sympathizing servant-women over the ruin he has caused. Oh, how I loathe that man's very name, and his sneering smile and plausible lies!"

"Marie! shame!"

She raved on.

"Shame! yes! to him for saying such things, and

to Elspeth for listening to him, and to you for not turning both of them out of your house, instead of believing their horrible slanders! No, mother! you have complained of my reserve, and I shall leave you without excuse for finding any such fault again with me. I am a Paull, through and through, and there is no hypocrisy in that strain. If I knew in what vein of mine runs the Lanier blood, I would cut it this minute, and let the false black drops out, — here, before the blessed angel's picture! It would be a sweet savor in his nostrils if he could know that I had done it!"

She laughed wildly, as the listener, aghast, raised her hands imploringly. There was unholy triumph in the mirth. In the defenceless woman before her she saw the impersonation of the evil influences that had ruined and exiled her father.

"Don't stare and gasp as if you believed me crazy! I have my father's head, and I can think out things without Mr. Roger Lanier's assistance. I know just how it all happened. My father, always generous and trusting to his own hurt, wanted to borrow money of his rich brother-in-law, who had prevailed upon his father (and yours) to leave all your property in your dear brother's hands; and the immaculate Roger would not lend him a dollar, although aware how cruelly crippled were his finances, and hunted him into exile. Or perhaps he was obliged to go away from unmerciful creditors; and when he was gone, Mr. Millionnaire Lanier, to cover up his own crooked dealings and inhumanity, fabricated a story which I would not believe if all the Laniers who ever lived were to swear to it on a pile of Bibles as high as the Brooklyn Bridge!"

"God give me patience!" murmured the unhappy mother, rising so feebly that had not her child been half-frenzied, she must have been moved to pity.

Instead, the perverse devil that was driving her onward prompted a final thrust. She became all at once apparently as cool as she had been hot.

"So, you see, mother," also rising, and assuming a judicial air that pierced the wife with a new sense of familiarity, so faithfully was it copied from her father, "you are wasting your time and strength in trying to bring me around to my dear relative's ways of thinking in anything. If he has set his heart upon hiding his poor relations in the country where they will not disgrace him and his fine-lady wife, why, he will do it. Where is the use of my opposing him? On the side of the oppressor, there is power. I am amazed at discovering that he has a vulnerable place left in his conscience, and can be made uncomfortable by the sight of his victims. I am glad that my face reminds him of the man he has injured.

"We need never go all over this ground again, mother, now that we have had it all out. By all means, let Uncle Roger salve his conscience with furnaces and water-works, and all the other luxuries he may choose to put into his farmhouse. Unless my father should send for me, or gives me other orders, I must, for propriety's sake, live in your house until I can support myself, which will be in a couple of years at the farthest. I had a talk with Mrs. Marcy yesterday, in which she promised that she would make a place for me in the primary department by the time I am graduated."

There are but two classes of beings in civilized society whom one may maltreat with a refinement of barbarity without fear of reprisals. These are mothers and wives. Ernest Paull had discovered for himself this cardinal truth. The instinct of heredity had revealed it to his daughter, and his teachings emboldened her to avail herself of it. When anger had burned down, she could create sparkles among the ashes by reminding herself that he was partially avenged.

Decidedly, Alice Paull had enough pressing upon her shoulders and spirit to drive her into her grave, or into a mad-house, by April 15, the day on which she turned the key for the last time in No. 363 Mendebras Avenue, and departed with Elspeth and the two boys, — Gladys being left with Mrs. Lanier, — to unpack and settle her household goods in the rambling homestead, red-brick in front and back, rough, hewn stone at the gable ends, upon the western bank of Pequod Lake.

Marie's vacation had begun a week before the long walk that stranded her upon the church steps.

Elspeth would have it that she had studied herself pale and thin, and built many hopes upon the system of feeding and general bracing that must go into effect, now that books were laid aside for two months and a half. The "puir bairnie" must walk, row, and drive abroad in air which the Highland-born woman sniffed eagerly as "a'maist as sweet and strang" as that of her native heaths. Accordingly, errands were manufactured for her by the score. There were wild strawberries to be gathered, wild flowers to be transplanted into the garden, and fish to be caught for the table. Mrs. Paull had found in the stable, upon her arrival, a stout roadster, young enough to be lively and good-looking, and old enough to be well-broken and safe, and a neat, light carriage; and after Marie's arrival, she was elected charioteer-in-chief.

She listened with a smile — always joyless, sometimes sadder than tears — to the various schemes for luring back light and color to her thin face. She was willing to try them all, she said obediently, but proposed none of her own accord, with a single exception.

She walked, unbidden, every morning down the two hills grading the half-mile slope lying between the hillside farmhouse and the village post-office. She had to-day taken quite a batch of letters with other mail from the freckled hand of the social young clerk, who inquired, in giving it, if her folks kept pretty well. She sorted the "mail" hastily in the long porch of the "store."

Three letters for her mother, — one in Uncle Roger's handwriting; one with a New York grocer's letter-head upon the envelope for Elspeth; one for herself from Lanier, and one other, which she tore open hastily.

Four pages were covered with the fiercely pronounced chirography peculiar to some fifty thousand-and-odd young women of the modern school, and which, until this fact is recognized, leaves one unprepared for the very small beer of ladylike correspondence.

Marie did not pause to read it. A glance showed her that the envelope contained nothing besides this epistle from Carrie Storrs, her bosom friend and classmate at Mrs. Marcy's school. She tucked it back into the cover, dropped it with the rest of the letters, the daily paper and a magazine, into the flat satchel on her arm, and instead of going home, set off at a swift gait across the bridge and up the broad highway beyond. It was shadeless for a quarter of a mile, but the city-bred girl did not raise her parasol. The air breathed freely over acres of hay-meadows and corn-fields, and there were no brick walls to absorb and radiate heat.

She did not heed or care whither her brisk pace would take her.

CHAPTER X.

The humblest occupation has in it materials of discipline for the highest heaven. — F. W. ROBERTSON.

> Dear Comforter! Eternal Love!
> If thou wilt stay with me,
> Of lowly thoughts and simple ways
> I'll build a nest for thee.
> FABER.

CHAPTER X.

CARRIE STORRS was the one confidante of the tremendous secret that Marie Paull had been trying, since the middle of last December, to open communication with her father. She had easily convinced her friend that Ernest Paull was foully maligned by his enemies, and persecuted by his relations-in-law. In each of the letters Marie had despatched, at first hopefully, of late desperately, to "Mr. Paul Morgan, Nice, France," she had instructed her father to reply under cover to Carrie, whose parents were too well disciplined, according to free American ethics, to inquire into their daughter's correspondence. Not a line had rewarded her filial fidelity; yet the sight of Carrie's handwriting upon the outside of an envelope would set her pulses to galloping and check her breath until inspection of the contents brought a sickening revulsion of feeling.

As she had walked down the hemlock-and-cedar-shaded road to the post-office, twenty minutes ago, — the lake on one side, the woods upon the other, the plunge of the waters at the lower end of the pretty sheet over a thirty-feet-high dam, booming upon the rocks that threshed them into clouds of fleecy spray, — an inspiration, as refreshing as the cool breath of the falls and the spicy incense of the evergreens, had stolen into her soul.

She recalled bitterly in her wayside musings the stages of her lapse from exaltation to despondency. For one quarter of an hour she had permitted herself to feel sure that to-day's mail would yield up for her the news from a far country for which she really believed she was slowly pining to death. While she waited in the dark, low-browed "store," redolent with soap, cheese, brown sugar and molasses, new shoes, new woollen and new ginghams, — watching, with interest that flattered the clerk, the freckled fingers that manipulated the contents of the mail-bag, — the hope assumed the proportions of certainty. The clerk was airily arrayed in dust-colored corduroy trousers and a loose linen coat of indescribable hue; his hair would have been exactly the color of ground ginger had it been less heavily greased. It hung straight behind, and was parted so low upon the left side that the comb laying out the line must have grazed the hem of his prominent red ear. His hands were red, too, where the great brown freckles let out glimpses of the background; his fingers were stubby, with square tips and flat nails edged with black.

She noticed all these things as senses, overstrained by excitement, become sensitized plates for the repetition of the minutest particular of environment. She recollected that she had prayed with especial fervor, at rising that morning, for the coming of the letter. For one second her fingers tingled prophetically in closing upon Carrie's envelope.

It was all over now! As she forged up the shadeless turnpike, she registered a mental vow never to let herself be sanguine again in expectation of the coveted good. It was a daily death. By the time she reached the elm-shadowed portion of the road, she had arrived at the conclusion that it would be folly to commit any more bread to the waste of unknown waters. If her father had cared to hear from her, why had not he, ready-witted as he was, devised some method of communication? Could there be a minute grain of truth in the version of his flight so coarsely retailed by Uncle Roger to Elspeth?

This, the first doubt of him that had ever assailed her, fairly beat the breath out of her lungs, the light out of her eyes. She felt herself grow sick and giddy, — a leaf in a whirlwind of horror and despair. Then it was that she groped, rather than saw her way to the broad stone step, and sank down.

She sat there so still that the phœbe-birds, whose forbears had for many generations built mud nests in the church tower, hopped upon the stones within arm's-length of her to peck the crumbs dropped yesterday by the school-children who had come across from the academy at recess to eat their lunch in the shade.

She sat there so long that a child, playing in the parsonage garden, after staring at her, himself unperceived, until his nose took the impress of the two palings between which it had protruded, ran in to report to his mother upon the pretty lady who had gone to sleep upon the church steps.

She moved stiffly at last; her head was light; her

tongue had a queer, rough taste, as if she had been dosed with calisaya or quassia. Automatically she fumbled in her satchel for Lanier's letter. She was not nearly rested yet. When she should be she must go home. It was getting on toward noon. She would not think any longer. Thinking only made her pain the harder to bear and did no good. For six months one idea had been the centre about which thought, affection, desire, and hope had revolved. She had fixed her eyes upon it until, when she tried to force them away, she saw nothing but whirling darkness everywhere else. Yet she had resolved to hope and expect no longer. In very idleness of misery she would see what Lanier had to say. She loved her brother, but there was little sympathy between them nowadays. She had not seen him since Christmas, and then he was as plainly averse to speaking of the altered conditions of their home as even Uncle Roger could desire. All his thought seemed to be centred in their mother. He had not remarked upon his sister's dejection and reserve; probably he had not observed them. That was another debt she owed to Uncle Roger. But he wrote entertaining letters, — full of college news.

Instead of drawing out a sealed envelope, she had lighted again upon Carrie's. She opened it indifferently. Carrie's affluence of spirits jarred upon her friend occasionally. She carried no cross of personal sorrow and others' misfortunes.

The opening paragraph of the unfolded letter set her teeth together as might the scratch of a pin upon glass.

My Mary-bud, — Open your pretty eyes and read what a transcendently delightful, and yet comical, happening has come to me. I cannot wait a minute longer without calling upon you to admire the cleverness of your usually-ever-so-much-less-bright-than-yourself friend and admirer.

Mr. Maynard, a friend of papa's, dined here this evening, and he and papa were speaking of the appointment of "Dick Oliver" as United States Consul at Nice. Of course I pricked up my ears, and when there was a gap in the talk, I put in an oar.

"Papa, what are the duties of a consul?"

"To see that national interests are protected in foreign towns, Puss."

"What, for instance, could Mr. Oliver do for me if I were in Nice?" was my next advance.

"If you got into any trouble, or needed any information, he would help you out."

"Suppose, then, I had run away from home, and was living in Nice, and calling myself 'Sarah Jane Johnson,' and you wanted to ferret me out, could he find me for you?"

Well, they all laughed, and papa said I was a goose; but in the end I found out what I wanted to know. The thing for you to do is to direct your next foreign letter in care of "Mr. Richard Hurst Oliver, U. S. Consul, Nice, France," and put in it a note to Mr. Oliver, asking him to see that it reaches the person to whom it is addressed, etc., etc.

When both these letters are written, enclose them to me, and let me mail them in New York. Country postmasters are the veriest gossips everywhere, and the official at Pequod (horrid name! why is n't it Avondale, or Rosemont, or Cedar Gorge?) will have it all over the neighborhood that "that eldest girl o' the Paulls sent off a furren letter to-day." Of course the reply (you'll be sure to get it now, my beauty!) will be enclosed to me.

I rush this off that you may get it by to-morrow's mail. Ever and forever yours,

CARRIE.

"Excuse me, but can I be of any service to you?"

Marie had sat motionless for ten rapturous minutes, her elbows upon her knees, her forehead upon her hands, tears, of which she was unconscious, falling upon the letter in her lap. She flushed rosily at the query, uttered in a pleasant, manly voice, her startled eyes, large with happy dew, were lifted to the countenance of a man in a strait-breasted black coat, who had approached unheard across the turf. It was a genial visage, with regular, refined features, and she knew him for a clergyman before he added:

"I am Mr. Morse, the pastor of this church. My wife saw you sitting here, and feared that you were ill, or that you had lost your way. Will you step into the parsonage and rest, or, as I am just going out in my buggy, will you allow me to take you home?"

Marie arose, self-possessed and ladylike. In her lately-born happiness she showed at her best, and she had inherited much of her father's magnetic charm of manner.

"You are very kind, but I am quite rested now. I have walked a little too far in the hot sun, I think. I am Marie Paull, the daughter of Mrs. Paull, who has taken the house on the other side of the lake. She has had the pleasure of hearing you preach several times, I think. I have just come home from my school in New York."

The frank reply pleased and attracted him. He held out his hand, and removed his hat.

"I am happy to meet you, and esteem it a fortunate coincidence that I was just setting out to call upon Mrs. Paull. Will it be convenient for her to receive a visit in the forenoon?"

"She will be glad to see you at any hour of the day, Mr. Morse, and I accept gratefully the offer of a seat in your carriage, if you are really going to call upon my mother."

She was like the Marie Paull of bygone days in the radiance and warmth of her new hope.

"A thorough little lady from crown to toe!" Mr. Morse informed his wife when he went around to the side-door of the parsonage for his carriage and horse, Marie preferring to await his return at the church. "Judging from her behavior and from the mother's appearance, the family will be an acquisition to the church and to the neighborhood."

Mrs. Paull had held long and weighty counsel with Elspeth while Marie was absent that morning.

To not more than one housewife in one hundred thousand is it appointed to be served as long and faithfully as this woman was by the sturdy Highlander. Without demur, or so much as the deepening of a furrow in a forehead criss-crossed by years of care-taking for others, she had gathered up such "stuff" as she could call her own, and followed the family into a region as unknown to her as the promised land to Abraham. Country housekeeping was a vastly different matter then than in this era, when hot and cold water, stationary tubs, bath-rooms, and gasoline are insisted upon as essentials of "our girls'" existence, in rural districts as in the city.

Elspeth's kitchen occupied, with her chamber overhead, a whole wing of the old farmstead. By Mr. Lanier's orders, a modern range was set into the wide fireplace, but the brick oven still yawned in the wall to the right of this, and in the rafters ridging the ceiling were hooks where festoons of onions, dried apples, and peppers used to hang. A wooden floor was laid upon the bricks worn by the tread of four generations of busy Marthas, and another window, let in at the back, made the room lighter and sweeter. The building was substantial and weather-tight; the walls of solid stone kept it warm in winter and cool in summer; a hipped Dutch roof gave the upper rooms a loftier pitch than would have been afforded by a story-and-a-half frontage, had the decline from combing to eaves been unbroken. There were seven bed-chambers above-stairs, and four spacious rooms on the ground-floor, exclusive of the kitchen and store-closets. A dry cellar underran the whole house.

The consultation between mistress and maid was held in the long porch on the lakeward side. The flooring of this was of brick; white columns, small and frequent, upheld the roof, and honeysuckles of the old-fashioned varieties, hardy, and prodigal of bloom and scent, curtained this open-air sitting-room of the present inmates. Clumps of such roses as our mothers loved to plant and tend, — red and white damask, and many-flowering cinnamon, now a mass of pink fragrance, — grew lushily upon the lawn. To the left of Mrs. Paull, as she sat beside her basket work-stand, were garden and orchard; to her right, a row of tall pines broke the northern winds in winter. Beyond, and right in front of her, were the lake and the wooded hills she was learning to love, — calm, restful, and full of hopeful uplifting, — abiding forever.

Elspeth was shelling peas into a brown bowl, sitting as straight as a ramrod upon her kitchen chair. The three children were at play in the grove of native woods, — oak, hickory, and tulip-poplar, — that separated the house by several hundred yards from the high road.

"I feel virtue enter into me day by day," Mrs. Paull had written to her brother the night before. "I am like a shipwrecked man, who, thrown upon a friendly shore, sits in the shade, gathering his forces, and recounting over to himself how much he has for which to thank God."

In like strain she had opened the dialogue with Elspeth. Nevertheless, there were certain matters that gave her serious and perplexing thought, she said.

"To begin with, I cannot let Mr. Lanier do anything more for us. Under his management, my income ought to support the children and myself. He is rich, and he is generous to a fault; but he has a family of his own, and you will understand me when I say that we cannot afford — nobody can afford — to be paupers."

Elspeth nodded in grim sympathy. She seldom spoke until a case was laid fully before her.

"We cannot get along without a horse and carriage, but I propose, when Lanier's vacation begins, to dismiss Aleck Sands, and let my big boy learn how to take care of a horse. He will have to make his way in the world, and the experience will be of service to him. One day's work from Aleck in each week will keep the garden in order, with such weeding as Tom and Edwin must be taught to do. The two cows in your hands will supply us with milk and butter, and the poultry-yard will be my affair. I shall enjoy the open-air life and diversion it will give me.

"Elspeth!" — coming to the point of the discourse, — "we must, in one way or another, manage to live upon nine hundred dollars a year, — the children's schooling and all. I know that I can depend upon you to help me do it."

"Ye may."

Whatever might be the spring of her mistress's earnestness, she answered her as the helm the pilot's grasp.

She had, in early life, subsisted and thriven upon oatmeal porridge and milk, bannocks and tough cheese, and was not now to be terrified by talk of hardship.

"'T wull likely come hard upon Master Lanier and the bit laddies for a while," she subjoined, tentatively.

"Lanier will understand. He has become a man in the last few months, and is not ashamed to do a

man's work. I shall keep nothing back from him.
I know what his answer will be."

She folded the pair of Tom's socks she had
mended, picked up one of Gladys's stockings, ran
her hand into the toe, and, detecting a thin spot,
threaded her needle. The rattle of the shelled peas
falling from Elspeth's fingers, the singing of the
birds in the grove, and the distant voices of the children
made a summer song to the murmured accompaniment
of the breeze in the pines. Elspeth did not
steal so much as a glimpse at the face which, she
divined, took on a graver thoughtfulness before the
mistress spoke again.

"Nor do I intend to conceal from you why we
must work hard and save all we can by simple living.
There was a debt of three thousand dollars which
Mr. Paull could not pay before he went abroad. Mr.
Lanier paid it. While I live, the interest upon that
money must be met regularly by me, or by my children,
whatever Mr. Lanier may say to the contrary.
My husband had no claim upon him. I have made
my will. It orders, that, before my property is
divided among my heirs, the sum of three thousand
dollars shall be paid to Mr. Roger Lanier, or his
heirs. It is a debt of honor and of conscience."

Again Elspeth gave her confirmatory nod.

"Three thousand dollars! The interest on that
wad be one hunder' an' eighty."

"At six per cent — yes."

"Where there's a wull there's a way, barring the
interfairence o' Providence, which ye have nae call
to expect. What I have on my mind now goes to

show that the leaning o' Providence is quite in the contrairy direction."

She plunged both bony hands into the basket of peas at her side, brought up a bounteous supply, which she bestowed in her aproned lap, and, eyes intent upon her task, proceeded to empty her budget.

She had spent a day in the city a week ago, and lunched with an old friend and fellow-countrywoman whose husband kept a grocery upon Sixth Avenue. In conversation with him at dinner, she had learned that he would pay fifteen cents apiece for half-pint tumblers of currant jelly of really excellent quality, and stood prepared to take all she could send to market. He would pay fourteen cents per glass for grape, and the same for quince jelly; twelve cents for marmalade and for nice preserves; for chow-chow, picklette, and good mixed pickles, a dollar a gallon; twelve cents a pint for catsup and chilli sauce of the best quality.

At this point of the narrative, Elspeth brought from her pocket a paper on which the same long-headed Scot had computed the cost of jars, glasses, and bottles, at wholesale, and the freight to New York, delivered at the dock. He would do the hauling uptown with his own wagons.

"I've put down in me own figures the wholesale price o' sugar, vinegar, spice, and the like," added Elspeth. "The fruit ye have on yer own land for the picking. Thanks to Mr. Lanier, there's wood in the shed over yonder to last a full year: so there's no expense of fuel. If me figures are correct, ye should clear eight cent a glass on the jellies, eight cents on the jam, and eight on the preserves; ye can buy butter-tubs from the grocers for yer pickles for fifteen cents apiece, and new ones wholesale for thirty cents. Ye suld mak' on a' evveredge from fifty to sixty cents a gallon, and eight on every bottle of catsup. There's no nicer pickles in America than yours, and self-praise gaes leetle ways, I know, but the mither wha' tached me to mak' marmalade wad not hae been fashed had she heard that hers was on the Queen's table."

Mrs. Paull's hands, with stocking, darning-ball, and needle, had fallen upon her lap; she stared bewildered at her lieutenant, as she returned the paper to her pocket and dived for another double handful of peas.

"You take my breath away!" the lady found the strength to ejaculate, at length. "Do you really believe that you and I could make and send enough of such things to market to make it worth our while to undertake the work? With all the rest that you have to do?"

"We could put up enough in a year by working three days of each week in the summer to more than half-pay yer interest money," declared the parent of the astounding scheme. "We'd mak' that our work. Just as a man goes into carpentering or blacksmithing or whatnot-ing, or " — her mouth twitching — "making marmalade for his leeving. I've had a-many serious thought o' late months ma'am. We've passed through that that sets folks' wits to working. And it's come to me — 1 don't believe from the de'il either — that one o' God's ways o' helping us when we are sair put aboot, and cast down in spirit, is to give us some one particular thing that we must do. Not to leave us to our own devices, with leeberty to pick a bit at this duty an' a wee bit at that, as suits our notions.

"I can't but believe the needcessity of working day by day, because that one peticklar thing has to be done, and done then, would do more for you than all the doctors on baith sides o' the sea, or even the sweet air of these blessed hills. There's all the differ betwixt this sort of work-a-day living, and that done by most ladies, that there was betwixt the ploughing done once upon a time by my twa brothers. Jem had his eyne on the ground, on the sky, or anywhere, and Rab took tent o' one tree at the other end of the field, and never took his eyne off of it. One furrow was like the wriggle of a snake, and the other straight as a bow-string."

"There is a great deal of truth in what you have said. The same thought has been with me often lately. I have found my mind swinging back to what I most wish to forget, as soon as I sit down quietly to my sewing, and, now and then, when I awake early in the morning, the old question comes in upon my mind, — 'Is life worth getting up for?'"

She was looking across the lake at a certain obtuse peak in the second range of hills. It had reminded her, when she first saw it, she could not have told why or how — of the "Old Hoaryhead" of Jacob Abbott's ever-delightful book of that name. Into the midst of thoughts excited by what they had been talking of, recurred to her now the proposition by

Gilbert's mother on the evening of the day in which they had heard that they could not have the house they had hoped to buy: —

"Cannot we do something to keep us from thinking about it?"

Gilbert had answered, "We might make maple candy."

While they were busied in the manufacture of the maple candy, came the news that the home they desired was to be theirs after all.

A sharp pain caught and sobered the dawning smile with which she recalled the story. Nothing could reverse the current of her life. Streams diverted from their course by earthquakes do not flow back into the old channels. The river-beds are themselves riven and upheaved.

Yet Elspeth was wise in her generation. There is wisdom in every age in the pursuit of a specific line of labor as a balm for bruised hearts and bleeding sensibilities. "Something to take our thoughts off of ourselves" is the homely phrase for the conditions in which work is most truly God's medicine for his smitten ones.

"The idea gains upon me," she continued, after a thoughtful pause. "We are a colony in ourselves, — a community with few ties to that which lies about us. Why not establish an industry of our own? be a hive of working-bees, and not drones or butterflies?"

Elspeth caught at one word: —

"I had thought of bees for Miss Marie, — after a while, when her schooling is done. There's acres of white clover, and buckwheat, and linden-trees yon by the lake. If she could fasten so much as one thought upon something near her home, it would be mair halesome for her. Mr. Cameron had his word to say aboot bees, as well as the preserves and pickles. He tellt me of one man who spent twenty-five dollars in hives and bees, and the very next year he gathered fifteen hunder' punds of honey. Bees are friendly, lovin' creatures, and if Miss Marie wad hearken to the notion, she 'd tak' kindly to them at the end. But, it's not to be gainsaid that she is a very determined lassie."

Did the loving nurse suspect how "determined," or the deadly sinking of the mother's heart at the mention of the wilful child, who, of all her brood, held her eyes waking into the far watches of the night? — vigils in which one query was rung like a warning knell through the chambers of thought, — "What will be the end of it all?" Labor for a definite and desired end might bring temporary relief from the wearing burden, but the cross would settle back into its place as soon as she let herself think of her love for her girl, and the gulf that gaped between them more widely every day.

"A determined lassie!" Her repetition of the words was an inward groan.

CHAPTER XI.

It is the duty of all to be firm in that which they certainly know is right for them to do.

JOHN WOOLMAN.

He often acts unjustly who does not do a certain thing; not only he who does a certain thing.

MARCUS ANTONINUS.

Evil, once manfully fronted, ceases to be evil. There is generous battle-hope in place of dead, passive misery. The evil itself has become a kind of good.

THOMAS CARLYLE.

CHAPTER XI.

MR. MORSE was a model country pastor, whom the appellation, always respectful, sometimes affectionate, of "Dominie," fitted as naturally as his skin. His sermons, as Mrs. Paull had already discovered, would never be brilliant, or striking in originality. They would never be dull, or devoid of spiritual instruction. Out of the pulpit, he was leader, teacher, and brother. All this his people knew and appreciated, without a glimmer of a suspicion that he was (for their good it is true) as very an autocrat in the hill township as was ever a Leo or a Gregory in his papal see.

He met Mrs. Paull, introduced by her daughter, with the easy freemasonry of one who had been at home in the world she had left. A reader of men, rather than of books, he had many acquaintances in New York, and he had kept step mentally with the advanced line of workers in church and letters. Of the Laniers, father and son, he had heard through those who were his personal friends and theirs. He asked not one word of her husband, a circumstance that might be significant or unimportant. He might imagine that she was a widow; it was possible that, through some of these same personal friends, he had become cognizant of what she had hoped to leave behind her when she had quitted the city. In either case he was a gentleman, and spared her needless pain.

"You have come into a quiet, orderly, God-fearing and kindly neighborhood," Mr. Morse was saying when she shook herself free from the haunting thought. "Primitive in their mode of living, and, you may think, narrow in many ways, but should you ever be in trouble, they will show themselves to be made of the right stuff. I have lived among them for ten years, happily, and I hope not uselessly. They are a peculiar people in some respects, — these New Jersey farming folk. The New England yeoman is not more sturdy in his independence and pride of ancestry. Many of them live upon the very lands granted to their forefathers by the English crown; yet there was not a Tory in the Pequod Valley when Washington pitched his camp upon the beetling cliff you see over there. More than one bloody skirmish took place upon the road on which I found this young lady to-day," — smiling at Marie.

He and she were friends already. Mrs. Paull was surprised and gratified that the smile was brightly returned, and yet more when the girl joined in the talk, asking questions as to local traditions, the names of their nearer neighbors, and the make-up of families, and engaging readily to take a class in the Sunday school, should her services be needed during her vacation. It was plain that she had taken an unusual liking to the frank-faced clergyman, and that his society, or the walk or drive, had aroused her out of the morose apathy that had enwrapped her for so long.

Yet when he took leave, she was flying off to her own room, without word or sign to her mother.

"Marie, love, come and sit out here with me!" called the latter from the porch. "I have something which I wish to talk over with you."

Feigning not to observe the partial scowl upon the fair young face, she pulled a chair close to her own, and motioned her daughter into it.

"Elspeth has broached an extraordinary scheme to me this morning," she went on to say. "Since your co-operation will be an important factor in our plans, I am impatient to see how it will impress you."

Elspeth, passing from kitchen to dining-room in preparation for the early country dinner, marvelled secretly at the mixture of wisdom and simplicity in the manner of the mother's communication. That which had commended the novel undertaking to the wife must be withheld from the defaulter's daughter, and in the place of reimbursement of the stolen funds, the hope of retrieving in some degree the fallen fortunes of the family must be made much of.

"We shall never be rich, dear," said the refined tones, wondrously gentle and cordial in the ear of one who had seen the speaker held persistently at arm's-length during the period when physical infirmity and heartache should have commended her to her child's tenderest sympathy. "While we live in this retired quarter of the world we cannot expect to be 'society people.' But we can be a busy, happy, self-supporting community, working harmoniously together for one and the same end. There is a sort of Swiss Family Robinsonish flavor in the scheme that makes it inviting to me. I see already, in imagination, that long storeroom on the north side of the dining-room filled with jars and glasses ready to be shipped to market. Doesn't that sound important? There are literally bushels of currants, red, white, and black, in the garden, that will be ripe in a week or so; raspberries, wild and cultivated, will be ready for picking by the time the strawberries are gone; the quince-hedge at the bottom of the orchard is loaded with fruit, and there are four large Siberian crab-trees, not to speak of other apple and pear-trees — oh! and plenty of grapes in the garden and woods, for jelly. The fruit on this place would seem to have been a hobby with the former owner. Elspeth sees a special providence in this."

Her manner was the livelier for the effort she was compelled to make to ignore the forbidding silence with which her remarks were received, and not to betray the failure in courage it caused. She was by temperament, and in practice, brave beyond the average of her sex, but she had discovered lately that she was actually afraid of Marie.

In nearly every household where there are several members, there is to be found almost invariably one who has a Temper (with a capital T); as invariably, this member is the object of more consideration than any or all of the rest. Let temper take on what guise it may, it demands, expects, and receives, solicitous conciliation. The owner may be "sensitive," and her tender-heartedness express itself in tears as softly-abundant as the flow of Sweet Afton. It may choose to be classed as Moods, many, and varying in intensity and duration. There is the Dynamite Mood, around which friends and kindred step with stockinged feet and cautious respiration. It may be the Slow Combustion Mood, lurid and dull, like ignited subterranean coal-beds, betrayed only by a puff of smoke through an occasional fissure, until, all at once, everything gives way before the heat, and lives are wrecked in an abyss of vindictiveness. In all phases these are Temper (with a capital T); — not necessarily the child of the devil, — rather like fire, a good servant, but the worst of masters. Finally, I may observe that the most effectual way of nursing it into masterful proportions is by showing it the respect I have alluded to as the practice of many Christian folk who have to do with it.

In nine times out of ten, sinful temporizing with Temper (with a capital T) begins when the offenders are no older than our cherubic would-be tyrants. It is easier, argue mistaken parents and friends, to go around a hill than over it; it is easier to fill up valleys than to tunnel mountains; yet shrewd engineers drive rocks to their adamantine hearts, and run their roads right through them. Peace is dear to the mother's soul, but it is dearly bought by the sacrifice of lawful authority and the subversion of the rights of those whose claim to consideration is as worthy of respect as that of the Temper's owner. The chief sufferer, however, from this system of amiable or cowardly truckling to the leashed wolf of the home, is he whose own the beast is. For a while the creature may follow meekly at heel, or stalk with red eyes and dripping tusks at his master's side, ready to rend at his command. In the end, he is sure to spring at his leader's throat.

Mrs. Paull was a good woman, and, as a rule, judicious in the management of her children. That Marie was spoiled to some extent by her father, she had seen from the girl's babyhood, and that certain inherited traits made her spiritual education a more arduous undertaking than that of her brother. In the excess of compassionate tenderness that overflowed her heart in the discovery of the girl's morbid wretchedness and exaggerated loyalty to her absent parent, began the course of treatment which the mother would have characterized as mischievous and short-sighted in another. She had helped to nurse discontented fancies and preposterous conceits of sublime self-devotion. In constituting herself her father's champion against his traducers, the daughter had arrayed her powers against the foes in his own household. Refusing blindly to credit one item in her uncle's indictment of the embezzler and bigamist, she virtually accused the wife of weakness, or open want of fealty to her husband. In the creed of the youthful judge, Ernest Paull's lightest word should have outweighed any accumulation of evidence brought by others. The lofty generosity that made Alice Paull submit to censure of herself, and accept the lowered place in her child's esteem, sooner than break the idol of gilded clay which the misguided votary adored as pure gold, told incalculably against her. The patient ingenuity of love that strove to beguile the wilful mourner into healthier lines of thought was misread as the mean-spiritedness of a woman who knew herself to be in fault, and would cast dust in the penetrating eyes of her accuser.

In a word, the whole policy of forbearance with the girl's perverse imaginings was the surest conceivable method of confirming her errors and vitiating what was noble in her nature. She had grown into the habit of viewing Marie Paull as the most important and interesting personage in her small world, — which she gradually contracted by this persuasion. A stubborn, fanciful, passionate child, she was elevated into a heroine by self-love and the mother's ill-judged indulgence.

The story is not pleasant in the telling, or in the hearing. It would be more tolerable were it not the repetition of the history of hundreds of other homes in which the eldest daughter — green in years and in judgment — is promoted to the dictatorship in family councils. While the mother lives in the possession of a moderate degree of bodily health, and such intellect as the Lord has given her, and which was hers when her husband endowed her with all his worldly goods, her abdication in favor of the wisest, discreetest, and best of daughters is violence done to natural law. She is queen-regnant until death or disease wrests the sceptre from her nerveless hand.

Marie sat in the chair to which her mother had directed her, the sweet summer air fluttering the rings of golden hair above her forehead, the goodly panorama of velvet lawn, laughing waters, and the wooded heights rising toward the ineffable blue of the June heavens, spread before blank eyes that saw them not. The very fact that appeal was made to her to ratify the scheme sketched by Elspeth and seconded by her mother, settled her belief in the value of her opinion, and predisposed her to dissent. These two women knew themselves to be so far wrong, and her so entirely right in the main question at issue between her and themselves, that they were afraid of her. Her word was fast becoming law in the household; her adverse vote would have the force of a veto. Her mother had artfully seized upon the moment when the meeting with a sensible man who could appreciate a young woman of parts had, as the elder woman supposed, put her into a sunny humor, to spring the absurd proposition upon her. It was of a piece with the transparent wheedling of which she was continually the disdainful subject when in her nominal home.

She meant that her face should harden as she listened; she did not know that it was likewise supercilious.

"Well?" she said, as her mother ceased, with what she designed as a haughty cadence, and which was provokingly pert.

Elspeth stopped stock-still in the kitchen door, a wrathful glare in her eyes that her petted nursling had never beheld there.

The patient parent made yet another effort to propitiate her auditor.

"You will, I am sure, agree with me, my love,

that we ought not to draw further upon — resources that are not our own. Yet our expenses cannot be lessened to any considerable extent for some years to come. Lanier has still three years at college, and you two more at school, and while I can and shall continue to teach the little ones at home for some time to come, the boys must, after a while, go to school. I am thankful for the prospect so unexpectedly opened of adding to a non-elastic income. As to what may be said of our new industry, we can certainly afford to be independent of popular opinion, especially in this out-of-the-way quarter of the world, even if there were any reason why we should be ashamed of honest labor. If I were an artist, or a famous author," — with a sickly attempt at playfulness, — "I should glory in exercising my talents for the sake of making money. If I have a taste — 'talent' may be too dignified a word — for jellies, pickles, and catsups, why not improve it to the same honorable end? You recollect how Miss Dunstable, in 'Framley Parsonage,' prided herself upon the fortune made by the hereditary 'Ointment'? We will think up a telling name for our place here, and have some labels lettered with it, or, perhaps, when our reputation is made, may go to the length of having it blown in the glass. Think of it! Who knows but my name may go down to a grateful posterity along with Mrs. Rundle's and Mrs. Glasse's?"

"If that is your ambition, I hope that you will use 'Lanier,' and not 'Paull,'" retorted Marie, in a tone as offensive as the words. "As my father's representative, I have the right to say that much."

Observing the pale surprise in her mother's face, she went on inexorably : —

"You should not have asked my opinion, if you did not want it, mother. I know that this whole enterprise, as you call it, born, you would have me believe, in the brains of Elspeth and her Scotch grocer, would be abominable in his sight. However little we may care about maintaining our position as ladies among those with whom we have been accustomed to associate, I hold that something is due to his reputation as a gentleman. He would feel outraged and disgraced forever were he to hear that a jam-and-pickle factory was established in his house. In his name, and for his honor, I shall fight the detestable plan to the end."

"I aye thocht" — came in grating accents and Elspeth's broadest Scotch from the kitchen door — "I aye thocht, being a fule body wha fears God and honors her betters, and is gr-r-ratfu' to them wha hae loaded her wi' benefeets — that it war Meester-r-r Lanier's hoose wha keepit oot th' rain o' heaven an' the heat o' simmer, an' wull shelter their bairnies an' their mither frae th' winter's cauld."

Marie sprang to her feet, and wheeled upon her, eyes blazing and face dark with anger.

"How dare you interfere between my mother and myself? How dare you remind me that I am obliged to live under that man's roof, and to eat the bread of his charity ? — the man who, if you two would tell the truth, is at the bottom of this degrading plan for pulling my father's children down to the level of factory-operatives and hucksters ! Oh," — wringing her hands and bursting into a storm of passionate tears, — "if he were here, we should soon see who is master, — he, or Roger Lanier, whose puppets you two are!"

Mrs. Paull arose from her seat, deliberately, and with calm severity. The likeness to her brother was marked as she confronted the mad creature, putting a firm hand upon each quivering shoulder.

"Elspeth," to the thunder-stricken servant, "please leave us! Marie, stop crying, and listen to me! Your coarse violence has forced me to say what I had not intended to have pass my lips, at this, or any time. But for him of whom you speak, there would be no necessity for the work which I propose to carry on without further consultation with you; and until you can treat your mother with something like the respect due to her age and position, I forbid you to mention him again in this, your uncle's house. Now go to your room, and come down at dinner-time in a more reasonable frame of mind."

"I am not to be treated like a child!" sobbed the insulted heroine.

"Then do not behave like one," said Mrs. Paull, coolly. "Gladys, dear, it is time for your music lesson."

The muffled scales and exercises run by the small fingers under the gentle tuition of her mother, arose through the flooring on which heroic Marie stretched herself to have her cry out. When the baby sister tapped at her door to say that dinner was on the table, there was no response.

"She may be asleep," remarked the mistress of

the house, composedly, when this report was made. "We will not disturb her."

The sun had set, and supper was eaten, before the young lady of the house appeared below stairs. Mrs. Paull was writing at a table in the shade of the honeysuckles. Marie passed her with level chin and proud step, went out to the barn, thence to the poultry-yard, in search of the man-of-all-work, returning presently, unsuccessful.

"Aleck has gone to the village, my dear," her mother remarked pleasantly, glancing at the bulky envelope in her daughter's hand. "Your letter is too late for the evening mail, but Elspeth will take it when she goes to the city to-morrow."

She resumed her writing, which the discomfited heroine could not help seeing was a long memorandum.

Elspeth's errand was then the purchase of machinery for the abhorrent jam-and-jelly manufacture!

Her mother looked up again, seemingly unobservant of the sodden complexion and drooping eyelids that told their tale of the afternoon's experiences.

"Elspeth is keeping your supper hot for you, my daughter. You would better get it now."

With the mortifying reminiscence fresh in her mind of Elspeth's summary measures upon the occasion of a former refusal to partake of the food prepared for her, Marie deemed it best to obey the recommendation. After which she betook herself again unchallenged to her locked chamber, and tore off the envelopes of two letters to add a postscript to one: —

"Will you not let me come to you, darling papa? I would rather starve at your side than live anywhere else away from you. And I am very, very miserable here! Nobody sympathizes with, or understands me. I feel, as never before, that you are the one being upon earth who ever entered into my finer feelings. How well I recollect hearing you once repeat some lines beginning, —

'The frigid and unfeeling thrive the best!'

"Your little 'song-bird' has her breast against the thorn now!"

CHAPTER XII.

It is not by regretting what is irreparable that true work is to be done, but by making the best of what we are. It is not by complaining that we have not the right tools, but by using well the tools we have.

F. W. ROBERTSON.

In just that very place of His
Where he hath put and keepeth you,
God hath no other thing to do.

ADELINE D. T. WHITNEY.

CHAPTER XII.

LANIER PAULL did not come home at the close of the college term. He wrote, instead, to communicate a proposal made by the wealthy father of a classmate, that Lanier should accompany his son to the family country-seat, near Keene, N. H., to "coach" the lad in mathematics during the vacation. Young Paull, although not yet nineteen, stood high in his classes for scholarship and steadiness, and had gained an influence over the decidedly indolent and somewhat wild boy which the father wished to strengthen. For four hours' work a day, and a general supervision of his friend's associations and pursuits, Lanier would receive two hundred and fifty dollars a month, his board and lodgings.

"I cannot afford to let the offer slip through my fingers, mother darling," said the letter. "Uncle Roger, who came up to Commencement, agrees with me, but begs me to run down to New Jersey for a peep at you. As Mr. Bradley and his son leave to-morrow for Keene, and would like to have me go with them, this cannot be, even if there were no question of expense in the way — and there is. We are one, you and I (when were we otherwise?) in sentiment as to further drains upon the purse of the noblest, most open-hearted and open-handed man that ever lived. I am thankful for this opportunity to pay my way through college next term, and to relieve your dear, over-full hands of the weight."

Until the news came, the mother had not confessed to her own heart how hungrily she longed for the presence of her first-born,— the tall, broad-shouldered fellow, who was in person and character so much more the man than his years warranted. In the poignancy of her disappointment at Marie's undutiful behavior, she turned with fonder desire to him with whom she was ever at one in thought and purpose.

The letter was received just one week after the fruit-preserving industry was resolved upon. With the recollection of the terrible scene with his sister sore in her mind, she had determined to wait until she could explain details face-to-face, before taking him into her counsel. The necessity of setting it down upon paper, with no opportunity of softening this feature of the work and emphasizing that, was, in itself, a tax upon her nerves. By return mail she had a long reply, full of encouragement, and admiration of the "pluckiest of all plucky women," tempered by loving concern lest she should overtax her bodily powers. From her brother she kept the whole matter secret, as yet. Sensible and high-minded as he was, she could not be sure that he might not shrink from the suggestion of manual labor and trading for her, and insist upon increasing her income in some other way Should he suspect the specific purpose for which she was to work, he would undoubtedly put down the enterprise with the strong hand few could resist.

So it came to pass that in the initial stages of the task, Elspeth was her only coadjutor. She it was who insisted upon going to the city to buy gallipots, glasses, firkins, and bottles, with such groceries as would be needed, driving bargains that opened her mistress's eyes with amazement upon the energetic thrift of the Scotch character, and stirred with amusement the lines of a mouth that was forming into pathetic curves sadly unlike the spirited bow of earlier years.

With wise decision, for which Elspeth was not prepared, Mrs. Paull assigned to Marie a stated round of domestic cares, in order that her mother and the tireless maid-of-all-work might have more time for the duties of the season. While careful that the girl should not become a household drudge, the mother gave her to understand that she was responsible for the condition of her own and Gladys's clothing, for the cleanliness and order of her bedroom and the parlor, and for the tasteful array of the table at each meal. If the girl's performance of the allotted duties was lifeless and perfunctory, the service of a slave, who could not gainsay her taskmistress, Mrs. Paull gave no sign of perceiving it. Nor did she wince visibly in the sight of daughter or servant, at the distant respect with which the former addressed her, and the studious literalness of her obedience to orders.

The little boys threw themselves eagerly into fruit-gathering, each dropping daily into his savings-bank the pennies paid to them for so many quarts of strawberries, currants, and raspberries measured by

Elspeth. Even the baby had her harvest and her hoard.

"They say that bairnies' work is more plague than profit," said the serving-woman, one hot July day, as she extracted from the heap of "black-caps" upon a broad platter, green caps and fragments of stems and leaves, indicative of juvenile industry. "I dare say that 's true, if all that the work is worth is what grown people gain from it."

Her eyes strayed affectionately to the trio, who were having an afternoon tea-party of bread and butter, berries and milk, upon a flat rock in the shadow of a bushy lilac.

"I 'm thinking, though, that they are mair content for believing that they are helping along the wark o' the warld. I 'm minded, in watching them, o' th' laddie who, when the men could not get the vessel off the stocks, ran and pushed with all his wee might against the hull. 'For,' says he, 'I can push a pound.' The tale goes that the great ship slipped right down into the water. All the force of the men who were straining to launch her happened to fall short of just that one pund. I have me doubts o' that pairt o' th' tale, but that does n't alter the moral. It 's the old parable o' th' talents all the way through. The main thing for all is the good the helping does to him that gives it. If it 's only going through th' motions, it 's somehow healthy for the soul. I mind when I first cam' to this country, and lived for a year in Quebec, I used to see the garrison drilling night and morning as careful as if the enemy was in sight of the walls. 'T was the drill made soldiers of them mair than the fighting, which, it's likely, some o' them never gat. I've known lads to enlist, and live to be old men, and never smell powder that had a ball at the front of it."

Mrs. Paull's eyes followed Elspeth to the sturdy urchins and their pretty little sister, the queen of the feast, all as brown as buns, from the country breezes, and glowing with health.

"Our children are certainly happier for thinking that we cannot do without them, — which is true. Now that they are out of hearing, and are quiet for a little while, I wish to consult you, Elspeth, about a letter Mr. Morse brought to me from the post-office this forenoon. He very thoughtfully stopped at the store on his way up, supposing, as he said, that I should not like to send Marie down the hill on such a warm day. He is a kind, good neighbor and friend."

She was unfolding a double sheet, closely written.

"Mrs. Barnes would like to find a boarding-place for a month, for herself and Harry. He is just Gladys's age, you know. Elizabeth has gone abroad with her father, and Will is at his grandmother's in the neighborhood of Newburyport, Mass. Mrs. Barnes thinks the mountain air will be better for her, as a change from the seashore. She wishes to live very quietly, somewhere near us.

"She says: 'I should be willing to take care of my own room; and as to fare, with good country bread and butter, fresh milk and eggs and vegetables, we shall be satisfied, even if meats are indifferent and desserts uneatable.'

"I know little of farm-fare hereabouts, but that

little makes me doubt if she will not find more soda-biscuit than good home-made bread, or if any vegetables except potatoes and cabbages are frequent visitors to our neighbors' tables. Yet it would be an unspeakable comfort to have my dear old friend near me just now for a few weeks."

"The sight o' her bonnie face would be gude for sair een," responded Scotch Elspeth, briefly. "We must speir around a bit for a comfortable nest for her."

The subject was not brought up again until the berries were boiled into jam of jelly-like consistency, sealed up in the gallipots, which Elspeth had been at great pains to procure, because they "'minded" her of those in which the Dundee marmalade is preserved, and the jars had joined the hundred-and-fifty glasses of currant jelly gleaming redly upon the long shelves of the store-room.

"Ten dozen of the marmalade," said Elspeth, shutting the door of the treasure-chamber. "An' warranted to keep till the Day o' Judgment, when, as I tak' it, — 'though there 'll be neither jelly nor jelly-making, — the deeds o' all men and women will be made known, whether they've done good, or whether they've done evil. There's religion in jam-making, as well as in preaching and praying. To scant the sugar and th' time o' b'iling is eenee-quity, according to the Auld Testament, and to th' New."

The jars had not been packed away until they were perfectly cold. It was now nearly eight o'clock. The children were in their beds; Mrs. Morse had come by in the afternoon to invite Marie to go home with her, her young sister and her brother from Philadelphia having arrived unexpectedly the preceding day. Mrs. Paull gave her consent with grateful alacrity. Ungracious as Marie had proved herself of late, the mother-heart yearned over her in unspoken pity. A week before, she had proposed to the lonely girl to invite Carrie Storrs to spend a month with them, a suggestion contemptuously negatived.

"I should be ashamed to invite her, or any of the other girls to visit me here," her nostrils curling, as the odor of boiling sweets saluted them. "No! tradespeople should associate with tradespeople. I do not complain of my solitude."

Nevertheless, she had gone off blithely with the clergyman's wife, with whom she was always friendly. The ring of the happy laugh borne back to the house from the receding carriage had wandered drearily through the listener's memory ever since. It was the echo of a departed joy, music once as familiar as the sight of the radiant face, and the strain about the mother's neck of arms that never rested there now.

This thought it was, and not physical weariness, that moved her to the sigh with which she sank into her accustomed seat on the piazza, and looked out toward the fading glories of the late sunset.

Pink and gold were changing into the purple bloom of the June twilight that does not grow cold until an hour before the morrow's dawn. In the heart of the grove beyond the orchard the thrushes prolonged their evening service; the mountains were stretching themselves out to sleep, wrapped in robes that had the rich blue of a ripe plum; the rising dew was freighted with the perfume of honeysuckle and cinnamon roses, thyme, bergamot, and lavender. Elspeth's kitchen was "redd up" so thoroughly that all traces of the day's business were purged from the air. Her range shone blackly; the sweet dampness of newly scrubbed boards softened the dry heat; brasses and tins glimmered through the duskiness of the side most remote from the door. Comfort, cleanliness, and rest abode within-doors; without, beauty and peace. As the twilight spread and mounted, the young moon, a frail sickle of tender light, with one brilliant planet so near and so directly under the lower tip that one could have fancied it pendent from it by a viewless chain, appeared above the broad band of vapor, brownish-dun below, dull crimson on the upper edge, that lay behind the hills.

Elspeth had another simile for the crescent and the star.

"A foolish body that knew naught o' the ways o' the heavenly bodies might think the moon had melted a bit, and a drop had caught on summat, instead o' coming all the way to the earth."

She had donned a clean gingham (she was fond of pronounced plaids) and a white apron; a starched kerchief was crossed stiffly over her flat chest. Her sleeves were buttoned at the wrist in token that her day's work was accomplished. Except while she waited at table, they had been pinned up to her shoulders ever since she arose with the sun, and revealed arms as muscular as a prize-fighter's. She had taken up her stand against one of the small numerous pillars upbearing the far-projecting roof, her knitting in hand. She never needed to look at her needles while shaping a stocking. She wore none but those of her own fashioning, and kept the chubby legs of the boys similarly clad up to the hems of their knickerbockers.

Giving a nervous pull to the ball in her apron pocket, she continued, —

"I dare say, now, ma'am, that Mrs. Barnes could paint all that into a braw picture."

"Hardly, I think, Elspeth. Nor could any artist. Colors such as those are not to be bought."

"I'm thinking that ye may be right, ma'am. But she could, no doubt, come as nigh to it as any of them. She's a clever one, is Mrs. Barnes, and that knows how to use her fingers as well as her tongue, and, ye might say, her head better than either hands or tongue. I wish she war here the night, ma'am, to help ye enjoy what ye are seeing this minute."

"You enjoy it with me, Elspeth."

"Not with the liking ye and the likes o' ye have for it, ma'am. It's no good for ye to have none o' yer kind aboot ye. Blood is blood " (she pronounced it like "good"), "and education aye opens the door o' the lips the one to the other, and the understanding also. If Mrs. Barnes were sitting there beside ye, there wad, mayhap, less be said than is spake now. But ye'd feel in yersel' what she war thinking, and she the same with you. It is n't just now that the thought has taken tent o' me. Mony's the time when I'm fair daft wi' wondering how to clear some o' the thorns out o' yer road."

Tears seldom seen there welled to Mrs. Paull's eyes.

In no external manifestation of inward discipline is the difference between vulgarity and refinement more apparent than in the habit of restraining or of giving way to watery grief. The weak woman yields to the selfish tide if she break a tea-cup or tear a gown; the underbred hireling wails aloud if she has a tooth drawn, or cuts her finger. She who has studied from her cradle to be mistress of herself, smiles under the knife that separates bone from flesh and joint from marrow.

The spray she saw her mistress brush furtively from her lashes, before she smiled up at her, was a token to the servant of how deep was the hold her heroic fidelity had taken upon the lady's heart.

"No one has removed more thorns and stones than yourself, my dear, faithful friend. God has given me no stronger arm than yours to lean upon. If I do not tell you this oftener, it is not that I do not feel it continually, and do not thank Him upon every remembrance of you. You have continued with me in my temptation, Elspeth. He who knows the bitterness of my trial will reward you. I never can."

Across the charmed silence of the summer night that lay between them — solemnly placid now that the thrushes had ceased their hymning — struck a queer muffled sound like the whirring of a snapping clock-spring. In another minute, Elspeth had cleared her throat, spoke as usual, — even a little more dryly: —

"I'm aye awkward at threshing aboot the bush, ma'am, as ye know fu' well. What I've had in me mind to say since ye tellt me of Mrs. Barnes's letter was to ask ye why we can't give her and the wee laddie the north chamber yon," — jerking her head sidewards and backwards at the same time, — "and let this be the farmhouse where she'll get board. She'll not be lacking bread and the milk, the butter and vegetables, and all the rest of it, in peace and plenty. The laddie will be content wi' ours, and there's no sweeter air this side o' the New Jerusalem. Of that she may be sure. And for the two of ye, ma'am, it wad be going back to the lang syne she spake of when she first sent you the box of bonnie roses — d' ye mind?"

She had her reward in part for the new proof of unselfish devotion to her idolized mistress in the animation with which the plan was discussed and finally adopted.

A letter went off to Brooklyn next day.

In four days thereafter the old school-fellows slept under the farmstead roof, and Harry was joyfully adopted into the family of lesser folk.

From the moment she alighted from the carriage that had brought her from the market-town of Peddlington, nine miles away, and where was the nearest railway station to Pequod, Mrs. Barnes was an integral part of the modest establishment; her light, swift touches infused new spirit into everything. She made the boys happy by sketching them in their berrying-clothes, — clever portraits that anybody would have known at a glance or two. Each boy rapturously identified his own berry-basket and broad-brimmed straw hat, although these last were exactly alike when bought at the store week before last, and Tom had only since then lost the band from his, while Edwin had left his on the lawn one day, where a hungry calf had found it and chewed a great piece out of the brim.

She was the inspiring genius of the famous picnic to the Big Patch, four miles away, a common of forty acres, claimed by nobody since it had settled down bodily, thirty years ago, into some subterranean cave or bog, and now lay six feet below the level of the surrounding country, overrun with "high bush" blackberries. The Morses and Paulls joined forces in the expedition, Dr. and Miss Lyell, Mrs. Morse's brother and sister, being still the guests of the parsonage household. Two big open wagons, each one drawn by a pair of horses, were packed with people and baskets, great and small. Nobody was left at home by the Paull party except the big mastiff "Duke," who kept house all day upon the lakeward porch. The whole affair was an immense success; the abundant luncheon was eaten in the shade beside a running stream from which Dr. Lyell and Mr. Morse drew a dozen beautiful trout just before they left the Big Patch for home, and the harvesting was six bushel baskets of great ripe berries, the finest any of the party had ever seen.

Mrs. Barnes it was who furnished the incomparable recipe for spiced blackberry cordial, which, in the hands of a druggist recommended by her, took rank with the medical profession as a specific in a certain class of disorders, and had a large sale throughout New York and New Jersey. She it was who triumphed over Elspeth's prejudice against attempting to put up blackberry jelly, because, as she alleged, "it was like many folk, ower dead-sweet ever to set into any shape whatever." Under Mrs. Barnes's directions juice and sugar were put together after the former came, boiling hot and clear, from the fire, then were poured into glasses and set daily in the hottest glare of the sun until firm, and luscious with the aromatic spiciness brought by the fruit from the wilderness where it had companied with juniper, angelica, and sweet fern.

As for blackberry vinegar and jam, and the blackberries canned for pies, and blackberry sweet pickles, — and all the other ways she propounded of carrying the wholesome dainty over into the winter, — is not their fame perpetuated in many a farmstead in the Pequod Valley?

I saw the other day, in a catalogue of small fruits, the "Barnes Blackberry" in a place of honor, and smiled to think how direct was its lineage from the roots brought that same autumn from the Big Patch, and set out by Mr. Morse in the very shadow of the century-old church. The Dominie was a skilful horticulturist, and in a few seasons brought the wild fruit to a size and flavor that did honor to her for whom it was named.

The Paull purse was the heavier by many dollars for Mrs. Barnes's visit, and the Paull hearts lighter for the every-day ministrations of the practical "all-around woman." So far from pitying her friend for the fall in her fortunes, and bewailing the necessity of engaging in "business," she bade her "God speed" in the cheeriest of tones, wished that every woman in the land had a profession, the independence to engage in the actual duties of the same, and the skill to make her handiwork excellent in itself.

"Not appealing to the public because she chanced to be born a woman, and therefore an object of charity!" protested the latter-day prophetess. "When the world acknowledges that it is more honorable to make capital pickles than to paint pictures which are only tolerable because a woman 'executed' them; better worthy of an intelligent creature to bring bread-making to perfection than to hawk poor prose and worse verse from publisher to publisher; nobler to cultivate strawberries well than to go into the teacher's office for a piece of bread, — the real Woman's Age will be here."

For Marie, Mrs. Barnes had several new books and half a dozen pieces of music, — among them three duets which the donor and her daughter Elizabeth had practised together. They liked them so well that Marie, who was a far better performer than either of them, must learn them. She could play them with Mrs. Barnes while the latter was at Pinehurst. (At Mrs. Paull's request the guest found a name for the place before she had been there three hours.) After her return to Brooklyn, Marie could practise with her mother. Incited by her praise and bright-heartedness, Marie aroused herself into a passable show of interest in passing events and her present.

She actually opened the piano of her own accord, and played, alone and in the dark, passages from oratorios and other sacred compositions on the second Sunday evening of Mrs. Barnes's stay at Pinehurst. Her touch was exquisite, and her rendering of the numbers full of taste and feeling.

"I cannot thank you as I would for the good work you have begun in her," said her mother to her friend. "I have been sadly disheartened about her for a long time. I seem to have lost touch with her since my illness last winter. Until then, we were every whit as intimate as you and Elizabeth. My heart sinks in looking forward to what may be the outcome of the estrangement. Estrangement! Annie! can you conceive what pain it costs a mother to use that word with reference to her very own child?"

CHAPTER XIII.

Build a little fence of trust
  Around to-day;
Fill the space with loving work,
  And therein stay.
Look not through the sheltering bars
  Upon to-morrow;
God will help thee bear what comes
  Of joy or sorrow.

M. F. Butts.

CHAPTER XIII.

THE two women were sitting upon the honey-suckled porch; Elspeth had drawn her chair to the kitchen-door; her hands were folded in Sabbath quiet upon her snowy apron.

"Why do you look forward?" said Mrs. Barnes, quietly.

Mrs. Paull gave a surprised little laugh.

"Because I cannot help it. My tendency has always been to borrow trouble."

"Yet I don't know an honester woman. You would be wretched if you had to live upon borrowed capital."

"This is altogether different."

"Yes; you would borrow money from your fellow-men. You try to negotiate a loan of to-morrow and next year from Him who has made you an ample allowance for to-day, and forbidden you to anticipate supplies."

"Ah-h-h!" a light breaking in upon the speaker's mind. "I had forgotten that you belong to Nurse Williams's school of what the dear old soul calls 'The Royal Roaders.' She began once to explain their creed, but we were interrupted, and other things pressed it out of my mind. As nearly as I can recall it, her system of belief is predestination, simple and severe,—the persuasion that 'what is to be will be,' no matter what we do or say. I call that downright fatalism,—the blind faith of the Mussulman, not the rational belief of the Christian."

"At its baldest, it is more rational than the other extreme, of 'what is to be may not come to pass.' Mrs. Williams got the phrase 'The Royal Road' from Mr. Stevens, the New York evangelist of whom you have heard me speak so often. I went with her to his church on the evening set by him for telling his congregation how to find and to keep in 'The Royal Road to Happiness.'

"What a congregation that was!" she resumed, musingly. "I had been a pastor's wife for fifteen years, and thought myself fairly well versed in varieties of human nature; but I was in a different sphere from the law-and-order orbit in which I had previously revolved. There were men and women in good clothes about me, most of them evidently belonging to the laboring classes; but there were men who were ragged and dirty. Shop-girls were there in cheap finery and imitation jewelry, and close beside them women in black stuff gowns and black shawls pinned bias across their bosoms, and bonnets that were meant for mourning, and cotton mitts upon hands that were hardened by the wash-board. There are unsuspected saints among working-women of that type, and their Sunday clothes are always mourning suits. Mixed in with these respectable folk were others with handkerchiefs tied over their heads and knotted under their chins, and gowns stiff with dirt, that were falling apart by their own weight, and faces that seemed never to have known soap, or even a 'dry-wash,'—faces seamed by sin and trouble and weary waiting for the good time which they were sure, by now, would never come to them. Men skulked in corners who, you could not help thinking, would skulk into corners in Paradise from the force of habit, if they ever got there,—a species of human fungi that shuns the light, and fattens in the dark, and upon rotten things; and bolder-faced men, who stood conspicuously in the aisles, and crowded up near the pulpit, at sight of whom you couldn't help feeling for your pocket-book, and were surprised that it was still there.

"Such a 'mix' of all classes and conditions of humanity I had never beheld before; yet there wasn't a policeman to be seen, and there was no confusion, beyond what was inseparable from the massing of so many and such various sorts of people in a limited space. There was, it is true, the buzzing of whispering, and the indescribable sound of clothing rubbing against the seats and against other clothing, but it stopped all at once when the preacher walked upon the platform. He is not tall, and he is somewhat thick-set in figure, with a kind, honest face. It beamed with benignity in looking over the motley audience. Without invocation or preface, he began somewhat in this fashion:—

"'There must be five,—maybe there are six kinds of politics represented here to-night,—Democrats, and Republicans, and Mugwumps, and Prohibitionists, and Anarchists, and Home Rulists,—and the great party of Look-out-for-Number-One-ists. I am not here to find fault with any one of these parties. Saint Paul once preached in a town where they worshipped thirty thousand gods. In fact there were so many that a law had been passed against inventing any more idols. But in case any of the heathen gods should have been overlooked, they had put up an altar with this inscription on it: "To the Unknown God."

"'That was something like what you ward politicians would call "hedging"— eh?'

"Of course everybody laughed, and there was some clapping, and a cheer from one corner. He got them quiet with one gesture of his uplifted hand. Then he went on:—

"'Saint Paul was a long-headed man, who had been a lawyer before he was a preacher. Yes! and a tent-maker to boot. He paid his own salary in one town by working at his trade. So he preached to this idol-ridden people that this Unknown God "whom," he said, "ye ignorantly worship," was the Lord whom they were feeling after, and had not found.

"'This brings me to what I am here to say to you this evening. God, that made the world and all things that are therein, He is the Lord of heaven and earth, the Lord of lords and King of kings; and He so loved the world,— this sinful, fallen, soiled, and sorrowing world of which you, my brother, and you, my sister, and I who speak to you, are a part,— that He came, Himself, in the person of His Son, to die for us! I want all of you, each one here present, whether he has any ear or not, any voice or none,— whether he ever sang before in his life or not, — to join me now in singing, —

"All hail the power of Jesus' name!"'

"Alice! you never heard such singing! How they kept the tune and time I do not know; but they did, and carried the hymn clear through with a rush and a shout. When the old woman on my left — who must have been a rag-picker, if one might judge by the dirt on her worsted hood and the grime on her hooked fingers — joined her cracked screech to the rounded sweetness of dear Nurse Williams on my right, in, —

'Oh that with yonder sacred throng
We at His feet may fall!
Join in the everlasting song,
And crown Him Lord of all!'

I just got my face between my two hands, and cried harder than I ever let any baby of mine cry. It was wonderful."

She was excited in the telling. Into the eloquent interval dividing the two parts of the narrative, Mrs. Paull's voice stole, sweet and thrilling: —

"*And I heard, as it were, the voice of a great multitude, and as the voice of many waters, and as the voice of mighty thunderings, saying: 'Hallelujah! for the Lord God Omnipotent reigneth! and let us be glad and rejoice, and give honor to Him!'*"

"Nurse Williams thought of that, for she whispered to me, before I dared show my face again, —

"'Ain't it, for all the world, like a chapter right out of the Book of Revelation?'

"The prayer came next. I had been afraid of something approximating irreverence, but I need not have feared it. It was not like other people's prayers, of course, but his tone and language showed that he knew in whose presence he stood. He told the Lord that all of us, small and great, were seeking one and the same thing, — happiness, here and hereafter, — and entreated Him to help ' the weak, unworthy speaker ' to direct us into the right way, — the plain path, — the Royal Road.

"There was another hymn, ' Come, thou Fount of every Blessing,' and then he took his text: —

"' *Your Heavenly Father knoweth that ye have need of these things.*

"'Yes!' he blurted out, ' knows so much better what things we need and how much we need them, that we may well be ashamed of ourselves, fretful, babyish fools that we are, for presuming to give Him any information. It's sillier and more impudent than if the boy who peddles peanuts on Water Street should stop Jay Gould's carriage as he is hurrying up-town to deposit a cool million in the bank, and give him his opinion as to the best way of making money. It is not in any mortal to be as disrespectful and officious to another mortal, not even to king or president, as it would be for the wisest saint in earth or in heaven to dictate to the Almighty. Ask Him what you like, but put it in spirit, if not in speech, into four words, — "Thy will be done!"

"'That is to say: "if what I want isn't good for me, please, O Lord, read my foolish prayer backwards, and don't give it to me!"'

"He gave incident after incident, proving what mistakes we make in praying for what God in His wisdom and mercy refuses to let us have, and how we blunder into wrong and dangerous ways, screaming and kicking at this bolted door, and trying to pick the lock of that, and to blow the door of another off the hinges, and the folly of it all, and the love ' that saves us from the consequences of ourselves ' (that was his phrase), and at last he got to the sure prescription for securing peace of mind here and blessedness hereafter. It was to throw ourselves upon Christ for salvation, and let Him have us entirely for His own, and to lease our time, as God means and commands us to do, for one day only, and to recollect that it *is* a lease, and that the Landlord holds the insurance, pays the taxes, and keeps the premises in repair.

"' Trust Him with your soul, and then with the life that now is. The smartest man in the world cannot manage more than one day at a time, and the man who lived a hundred years never owned two days at once.

"' You may say, "Since I cannot help myself, I 'll make a virtue of necessity, and not worry about to-morrow." That was the trick of fools who lived three thousand years ago. "Let us eat and drink, for to-morrow we die." They did n't know how much that day was worth. Just as your baby would as lief chuck a five-dollar gold-piece into the gutter as a cent.

"' A day! oh, my brother! take the beautiful new thing into your hand and look at it! Fresh from God's mint, stamped with His image and superscription, His present to you, and to you alone, made expressly for you, and not another like it in all the universe, or in eternity, past or present. Hold it with both hands, and get all the good you can out of it. You may never have another day. Another thing, — Every day that is counted out to you is registered in His Book of Remembrance, and when you have had the last one, the ledger will be shown to you. "*Thomas Smith. One New Day,*" with the date set opposite to it, and a memorandum of the condition it was in when it got back to the Book. For it's bound to go back! You can't melt it down, nor tear it up, nor "sweat" it, nor burn it. Whatever God makes and stamps is immortal.'

"He gave us thirty minutes of such talk, and nobody moved to go out. I can convey a very faint idea of his style, and none of his manner of saying these things. He concluded by asking each one of us to begin to walk in the Royal Road the very next morning.

"' Monday is a tough day for it, I know,' he said. ' It does seem sometimes as if the devil were bound for a season over Sunday, and got out of limbo with a leap and a howl, like a giant maddened by Jersey lightning, before honest folks are out of bed Monday morning. There's all the more reason why you should choke him off at the start. Now, listen! as soon as you, my sister,' — and his eyes seemed to take in Mrs. Williams, my rag-picker, and myself, —' wake up to-morrow, say your prayers. They need not be long. A great English preacher, Rowland Hill by name, used to say that he liked very short prayers, such as are jerked out of a man when sorrow or temptation grabs him all of a sudden. He said they reached heaven before the devil got a chance at them. You can get yours over in a minute or less. "Give me this day my daily bread," will do, if you mean all you say,— food for the soul, food for the heart, food for the mind, and, last and least, food for the body. Don't sit down to cry over the mistakes you made yesterday. Don't pipe your eye over what you are afraid is coming to-morrow. You may never see to-morrow, and if you do, it will be to-day by the time it gets here; and God — who has never broken a promise, and never will break one — promises that you shall have strength given for that day. A man told me, when I was a little shaver, that all the fortune he cared to have was one little pocket in which he could always find a sixpence. All the fortune of time that you need — and this your Heavenly Father knows — is just one little day.

"'Trim your day clean at both ends, and don't waste a scrap of it. If you are a housekeeper, Monday is washing-day. You would n't mind washing-day so much if it was n't for the thought of how much longer it takes to iron than to wash clothes. You 've got nothing to do with Tuesday until Tuesday comes. Put it out of your mind. Say, "I won't think of it!" and keep your word. You 'll be surprised to find how much more strength you 'll have for to-day, if you don't fritter it away worrying over to-morrow. When Tuesday comes, take hold of it, too, with a brave heart, and clean, empty hands, that have none of Monday's mud sticking to them.'

"But, Alice, I am talking you into the Land of Nod! I, who have scruples against evening services in hot weather! You know my tongue of old, and that you have the magic art of drawing me out and on."

"You cannot stop there!" said Mrs. Paull, with sportive decision. "The sermon is incomplete without the application. Oh, Annie, talk is so easy and so cheap! You will think me a reprobate for saying that I distrust many people whose business it is to preach and to teach religion. They all fall into one rut, — 'Do this, and live! Do that, and die!' Half of the time they say it with the professional side of them, and live their own lives out just as other fallible mortals live out theirs. I should like to know something of your evangelist's six-days-in-the-week walk and conversation. While I am trenching upon irreverent talk of the profession which is above every other, I may as well be frank. Is his the Squeersian principle of first spelling a word, and then going out and doing it?"

Her forced lightness did not cheat her companion into forgetfulness of the significant truth that Ernest Paull was, for years, the popular superintendent of a Sunday-school and a telling speaker in Sabbath-school conventions, also a notable worker in other departments of church enterprise. Her answer was grave and direct: —

"He does the thing before he spells it. He gives away more than half his income yearly, and gives himself wholly to what he considers ' the reasonable service of every saved soul.' His capacious lungs are full of oxygen, and his bodily health is perfect, notwithstanding the tremendous labors of a day that begins at five o'clock in the morning. He rises then to go to a breakfast-room furnished and supported by himself for tramps and newsboys. He asks God's blessing upon a substantial meal, and, when it is over, talks to the five or six hundred men and lads there assembled of the duties and temptations of the day, and of God's love and care, and of His expectation that they will love and serve Him, and carry everywhere with them the thought that God's eye is upon them. His parish comprises, as he once said, everybody who needs him. He is constantly on the alert for the opportunity to do ' little deeds of kindness.' Somebody has found fault with him that he is always ' on the side of the under dog.' His sympathies go out most quickly to those whose cry is, ' No man careth for my soul.' He would as readily run up five flights of stairs to pray with a sick man or woman at the top of a tenement house, as to enter a church to electrify an audience with his sound common sense, his all-pervading spirituality, and the spirit of consecration that is manifest in every word and look. It matters nothing that people call him an unpractical enthusiast and a fanatic. He knows that every-day practice is the very foundation of his doctrine and action. His private life is the best possible commentary upon his teachings."

"Elspeth!" called Mrs. Paull, over her shoulder,

"move your chair out here. Mrs. Barnes is talking of the Royal Road."

Something in the aspect of the upright figure filling up the kitchen door suggested to the mistress the isolation of the follower who had forsaken all other friends for her, and with it arose a misgiving lest, in her own satisfaction in the society of her early friend, she had left the faithful creature too much to herself of late. With the instinct of true gentlehood that never deserted her, Mrs. Barnes turned her chair slightly towards Elspeth as she joined the ladies, still at a respectful distance.

"I was about to tell Mrs. Paull how, after hearing Nurse Williams's Mr. Stevens, I went home determined to try for myself his rule of living by the day. Mrs. Williams left me to my own thoughts during most of the journey back to Brooklyn. She saw that my mind and heart were full, and, as she has told me since, contented herself with praying for me. My husband was not at home, and I had several hours to myself. As soon as I laid off my hat, I got out my Bible. I would take nothing upon man's word without appeal to the Law and the Testimony.

"I had said over to myself times without number, 'Take no thought for to-morrow,' very much as a Roman Catholic wears a scapular, and a pagan a charm against the Evil Eye. Now, when I sat down with the one desire to take God at his word, the text took on a new meaning. By the way, the Revised Version puts it yet more clearly and strongly than the Old. It says: —

"'Be not therefore anxious for the morrow, for the morrow will be anxious for itself. Sufficient unto the day is the evil thereof.'

"That was the first verse I looked up. On the same page I read, as if I had never seen it until then:

"'Be not anxious for your life, what ye shall eat, or what ye shall drink, nor yet for your body, what ye shall put on. Behold the birds of the heaven, that they sow not, neither do they reap, or gather into barns; and your heavenly Father feedeth them. Are ye not of much more value than they?

"'Consider the lilies of the field, how they grow. They toil not, neither do they spin. Yet I say unto you that Solomon in all his glory was not arrayed like one of these.'

"I stopped there to read those last words over again. All that man's wealth and wisdom and skill could accomplish — the tribute of Tarshish and the isles, the gifts of Sheba and Seba — could not array this mightiest monarch of the earth like one of these wild flowers. I took the little preacher in imagination between my fingers, gazed into the glowing cup, and touched the velvet petals reverently, my heart well-nigh breaking with love and penitence.

"The rest followed naturally: —

"'If God so clothed the grass of the field, which to-day is, and to-morrow is cast into the oven, shall He not much more clothe you?'

"You, Annie Barnes! whose life He has thus far crowned with goodness and mercy; whose cup overflows with blessings; you who are His dear child, whose name is graven upon his hands; you for whom

Christ died that you might live and reign with Him forever. By this time I was prepared for the tender reproach,—

"'*O ye of little faith!*'

"Why, Alice Paull! I told Him then and there upon my knees, between my sobs, that I had never had one atom of real faith, and asked Him to give me just one more trial. Still on my knees, I turned the leaves of my Testament.

"'*If ye then, being evil, know how to give good gifts unto your children, how much more shall your Father in heaven give good things to them that ask Him.*'

"'*Come unto Me, all ye that labor and are heavy-laden, and I will give you rest. And ye shall find rest to your souls. For My yoke is easy, and My burden is light.*'

"That is, when He is taken utterly, simply, and joyfully at His word.

"And after the miracle of the loaves and fishes, — really no more of a miracle than happens often and often in the lives of those who are on the alert to interpret his wonderful providences,—

"'*O ye of little faith! Why reason ye among yourselves because ye have no bread? Do ye not perceive, neither remember the five loaves of the five thousand, and how many baskets ye took up?*'

"'*Whoso shall humble himself as this little child*' — believe that I mean what I say, and that every jot and tittle of my Word shall come to pass — '*is the greatest in the kingdom of heaven.*'

"'*All things whatsoever ye shall ask in prayer,— believing,— ye shall receive.*'

"' *The very hairs of your head are numbered.*'

"' *Ye are of more value than many sparrows.*'

"' *Boast not thyself of to-morrow.*'

"' *They that seek the Lord shall not want any good thing.*'

"' *Casting all your care upon Him, for He careth for you.*'

"But you and Elspeth know them all, and could recall a hundred more, one and all bearing the same message to the simple of heart: ' Trust Me to do what is right and best for you, and I will be your refuge. Underneath you are the Everlasting Arms. Lie peacefully and happily within them.' Reading them in the new white light that streamed upon the page, I was as one who had found great treasure.

"Marie! dear child!" holding out her hand as a light step fell upon the floor behind her. "Mrs. Morse approached me with a petition, after church this morning, which she dared not prefer to you. The young man who officiates as organist goes away this week for a month's vacation. She says that if you will take his place for that time you will gratify Mr. Morse and herself, and delight the congregation. I could not answer for you, of course."

"Certainly not."

Marie spoke in a lifeless tone, and did not return the pressure of the firm fingers enfolding hers. She stood perfectly still, one hand on the back of Mrs. Barnes's chair. The impulse that sent her to the piano had exhausted itself in her long practising.

"Would you like to take the position, my love?" her mother queried.

"That is for you to say, mother."

It was always "mother" nowadays; never "mamma."

"I do not wish to force your inclinations. I thought you might desire to oblige Mr. and Mrs. Morse, who are so kind to you."

"Very well, then. I will do it," as passively as she had spoken before.

Mrs. Barnes was not easily put down. A wet blanket had no appreciable effect upon her spirits; nothing short of a deluge drowned her energies. She pressed the small limp hand to her warm cheek, smooth as a sixteen-year-old girl's.

"These same deft fingers will serve you well, should you ever care to become an organist in a city church. I know a woman who plays very little better who gets a salary of one thousand dollars a year."

She felt an electric quiver in the fingers she praised, and heard the irregular breathing that went with the girl's exclamation,—

"One thousand dollars! Oh, Mrs. Barnes, do you really think I could ever get half of that?"

"Easily, should there occur a vacancy in a city organ-loft. When you have left school, if you still wish it, we must see about it."

Marie was mute for a minute, then spoke dreamily, but with suppressed passion that startled her companions:—

"I wish I could earn some money! I wish I could earn five hundred dollars! It is a dreadful thing to be a woman, — in any circumstances. It is intolerable to be poor as well. Good-night, Mrs. Barnes. Good-night, mother. I am tired almost to death!"

She went off without offering to kiss either of them. Elspeth arose and followed her silently. Coldness and ingratitude could not weaken her attachment.

"And you blame me for looking forward anxiously to her future!" sighed Mrs. Paull. "She is more of an enigma to me every day. A mother should know her daughter."

"A girl of seventeen does not know herself. Yours is forcing her way single-handed through the debatable ground, trying to ford the current 'where the brook and river meet.' A majority of girls take to misanthropy and mysticism and melancholy during the transition period, catch it from one another, or inhale the bacteria of that miasmatic region as they caught measles and whooping-cough when babies. The worst thing that could happen to Marie would be to fall heiress to a million dollars to-morrow. I am well content that she should not have the five hundred for a year or two. Alice, darling," dropping the jesting strain, "take your first step in the Royal Road by committing that precious creature entirely for this one night into the hands of Him who careth for her as for you."

"I will try!" The answer was low and not prompt.

"Say 'I will,' dear heart! That is the Bible phrase.

"'*I will praise the Lord while I have my being.*'

"'*As for me and my house, we will serve the Lord.*'

"'I will abide in thy tabernacle forever.'

"' Therefore, will we not fear, though the earth be removed, and the mountains be carried into the midst of the sea.'"

"I will!"

The lips of the friends met in a mute seal upon the covenant.

The holy calm of the summer night rested upon the waters and field and mountain, and upon the troubled sea of human thought, like a Sabbath benediction. Puffs of perfume, now warm, now cool, were the welcome of the pines to the visits of the breezes wandering down from loftier heights by way of the northern gorge through which the lake escaped to the valley.

"'*As the mountains are round about Jerusalem, so the Lord is round about His people, from henceforth, even forever!*'" said Mrs. Barnes, by and by. "That is the oratorio of your hills. It came to me when I saw the amphitheatre of the valley from the top of Baldmount, on my way from Peddlington, and I hear it continually. Henceforth, even forever! Never off guard! There is another proof-text for you."

CHAPTER XIV.

Any child of God, who, in any adequate way, believes that he can partake of the divine nature, knows that he has strength enough for any business that looks the right way; that is, which helps to bring God's kingdom into the world. If you are working with Aladdin's lamp, or with Monte Cristo's treasures, you are not apt to think you will fail. Far less will you think that you will fail if you are working with the omnipotence of the Lord God behind you. — EDWARD EVERETT HALE.

CHAPTER XIV.

TWO years had flown since Ernest Paull passed from the sight and ken of his family and the friends of his better days. Since the vessel that bore him, under his false name, left New York Harbor, no more word or token of his existence had come to his wife than if he had fallen at night into mid-ocean, unseen, and never been missed by his fellow-voyagers. In the business world, where he used to consider himself a personage of note, he was missed as little as would have been a pebble thrown into a lake a hundred years ago. His disappearance had created wonderfully little sensation at the time, so little that his brother-in-law — to whose promptness and energy was due the fact that few knew of the elopement, and fewer of the embezzlement until the scandal was desiccated by time into odorlessness — smiled sometimes to himself in reflecting that the queer combination we know as self-love would have smarted had the criminal suspected the truth.

It would mortify many and console none of us to comprehend the absolute insignificance of the human unit in the sum of the ages.

Mrs. Paull's removal from city to country helped to keep the disgraceful story quiet, and her infrequent appearance in scenes where she had once been prominent completed the effacement of herself and her affairs from the minds of mere acquaintances. Tom and Edwin, sturdy and happy in the free spaciousness of the Pinehurst woods and orchard, gradually ceased to think of the absent parent, whose image had faded entirely from Gladys's memory. Their mother was their teacher, co-worker, and playmate, and the sun of the domestic system. Her country neighbors nodded and smiled in cordial good fellowship in meeting her upon the highway, or, as happened oftener, in mountain passes, where the grass grew high and flowers bloomed between the wheel tracks, — stepping lightly, head erect and cheeks glowing, — a son on each side. Sometimes all three carried baskets for nuts or berries, or for roots to be transplanted in the garden that was the talk of the region for beauty and variety.

In church she sat in her own pew, her children about her, earnest and devout, a chastened serenity in eyes and upon lip that was a wonder to those who had gleaned fragments of her history and pitied the forsaken wife and toiling mother. Her hair had gathered frost during the terrible winter of two years agone, while the face, beneath the abundant locks rolled back from her forehead, gained placidity and almost youthful bloom.

"I know now why the hoary head is said to be a crown of glory," said Lanier, one September evening, as he lay at her feet, his head in her lap. "Your hair is a veritable diadem, and sheds a sort of radiance over your face, such as falls from the nimbus about saints' heads in the pictures of the old masters. It is mysterious, but beautiful. Yet" — raising a hand to the head bent above his — "it gives me a heartache. Mother, you are the bravest woman I ever knew! This" — stroking the silvered coil — "is the only tell-tale."

"It is the habit of the Laniers to turn gray early in life," said Mrs. Paull, in cheerful evasion. "Since this is so, I should be thankful that it is becoming. I don't want to be frightful in my children's eyes."

"That could never be, had you small-pox, complicated by leprosy. I wonder sometimes if you are as happy as you look."

"Happier — often. The heart knows its deepest bliss no less than its own bitterness. God has been — He *is* so loving-kind to me that I have no excuse for gloomy thoughts. Every day is crowned with goodness, and He never lets me doubt that all my steps are ordered by Him. How could I be discontented?"

The boy lay looking into the heart of the fire built of pine cones, of which a great basketful stood at the corner of the hearth. The night was rainy, the clouds rushing down the valley before a strong northeast wind. The ceaseless moan of the pines was blent with the surf-like roar of the grove of oaks and hickories behind the house. Mother and son had the room, dusky-red with firelight, to themselves.

Lanier's "coaching" engagement had been renewed during each of the vacations that had passed since his first visit to Keene. He had, nevertheless, contrived to visit his mother in the September of both years, besides spending two Christmases at Pinehurst. He had arrived this afternoon upon a three days' furlough, and her soul basked in his presence with grateful delight.

As her firstborn grew in knowledge of books and of men, the tie knitting the heart of the man she had gotten from the Lord to the heart of the mother strengthened and shortened. He was very like her in feature and manner, — a resemblance peculiarly striking to-night in the ruddy half-light that colored both faces alike.

"He is lover, friend, and son, all in one," she had said to Mrs. Barnes, in one of the impetuous bursts of confidence that were rarer with her now than of yore. "Pulse of my pulses, core of my heart!"

In the close folding of his left hand in hers now, the yearning fondness of the regards bent upon the lineaments she thought so handsome, the ring and thrill of her voice as she addressed him, one read all this and more. Sometimes, while she talked of him, or listened to others' praise of her eldest son, she blushed like a girl at mention of her lover's name, and laughed at her own sweet folly. Maternal love of this peculiar quality and power is seldom seen in wives whose hearts rest in full satisfaction in their husbands' affection. God gives in this life no richer compensation for disappointment in the dearest hope of a woman's heart than is to be found in the chivalric fondness of her sons.

"You do not weary of your Royal Road, then?" resumed Lanier, at length, smiling thoughtfully.

"Who does, who has found it?"

"It has been the path of peace to you, evidently,

mother dear. I suspect, nevertheless, that few are willing to walk in it until more attractive avenues are closed. Without hope and ambition, youth would have no dreams; and what is youth without dreams?"

"Hope! ambition! do you mean that we leave them behind us when we set our feet upon the King's highway? My darling, then begins the only hope worthy of the name, — sure and blessed, — an anchor that never drags.

"*'For I am persuaded,'* says Paul, *'that neither death, nor life, nor angels, nor principalities, nor things present, nor things to come, nor powers, nor height, nor depth, nor any other creature shall be able to separate us from the love of God which is in Christ Jesus our Lord.'* And *'Shall He not also with Him freely give us all things?'* And again, *'All things work together for good to them that love God, who are the called according to His purpose.'*

"The beloved disciple, whose head rested upon the Master's heart while He said His parting words to his disciples, asserts, as one who knows whereof he speaks, —

"*'And this is the boldness which we have towards Him, that if we ask anything according to His will, He heareth us.'* Can hope be grounded upon a firmer rock?"

"Abstractly considered — no! All of us, who hope that we are Christians, yield intellectual assent to these things. The trouble is that the promises seem vague, and fulfilment afar off, when the question is of a note to be met next week, or bread to be bought to-morrow, when there is no money in hand with which to buy it. Steadfast souls — women's souls — can fix their thoughts and concentrate their energies upon to-day's tasks and interests; but what of a man's duty to provide for those of his own household?"

"Provision for to-morrow may be, it often is, a part of to-day's duty — "

"Aha!"

"You interrupted me! I said 'provision' — not anxiety. Not to make intelligent provision for what experience and common sense tell us must be met, is fatuous and childish.

"Tom and Edwin had their little gardens laid out, last spring, side by side, and I gave each the same quantity and kind of seeds. Tom got all his in on Monday; and on Wednesday, Thursday, Friday, and Saturday, scratched open the rows to see if they were sprouting and likely to come up. Edwin let his alone. It is useless to say which has the better show of vegetables by this time. I try to keep one text continually before the eyes of my heart, — '*And having done all, to stand.*' Some err in stopping short of doing with their might whatsoever their hands find to do, not working while the day lasts. The hard task for me is to 'stand' when I see nothing else that my hands can do just now. As to next week's note, make the best arrangements to meet it that your judgment and ingenuity can devise; then stand still, and see what great things God will work. So with to-morrow's bread. Look narrowly at the work laid to your hand for to-day, to see if this may not include getting together cents enough to buy a loaf for to-morrow's breakfast. Perhaps — God knows whether or not this is to be, and what good end is to be gained by it — you are to suffer protest and loss of credit, and to go hungry. If so, you can rest submissively in the belief — which is the substance of things hoped for — that the day's strength will come with the day's trial. Oh, my boy, this is not a rainbow theory with me, but a tower, tried and found steadfast, into which I have run and been safe."

Lanier pressed first one, then the other, of her hands to his lips.

"Precious mother!" he murmured in strong emotion. "The sight of your practice goes leagues upon leagues further to convert me than your texts and your sermon. Where is there another woman who would make such a bright, beneficent life out of such poor material?"

"Poor material! Don't say that!" a hasty terror in her tone. "Not while I have my children — and work to do for God and man. Dear! have you noticed that blasted oak on the hillside up there, — just where a gap in the woods gives you the first glimpse of Pinehurst, and the lake, and the mountains? Your uncle spoke of cutting it down, but I would not let him do it. It is an object-lesson to me, a symbol, a likeness of myself."

"My pretty, graceful mother! that I will not listen to!"

"Hush!" laughingly pulling her face away from the hand he would have laid upon her mouth. "It was struck by lightning eight or ten years ago, — that tree, which is not so old as one might think, — and the bark stripped from one side. At least half of the trunk is bare. All the same, it bears leaves and acorns, and carries aloft a branchy crown all summer long, and you ought to have seen its foliage last fall. Rich purplish crimson, that, as the snows and cold rains came, gathered, as it were, gray ashes upon the upper surface of the leaves, before they changed to a comfortable sober brown they held all winter long, and until the young buds pushed them off in April. The edges of the torn bark have healed healthily, making a long lip against the flayed trunk; all the sap necessary for the life of the tree is carried up through that strip. I have stood by that tree with my hand laid upon the bark, until I could be sure that I felt it throb sympathetically."

Her voice had fallen, as she went on; the words were uttered more and more slowly, until she ceased. Lanier drew himself to her side, wound his arm about her, and laid his head against her shoulder. Verbal response was impossible, and needless.

"I told you that I saw Marie this morning," was his next remark.

"Yes, and that she is looking well."

"Well and handsome. She will be a splendid woman soon. She says she is quite happy with her teaching and her organ. How did she get the situation? There would be a lively competition for the vacant place in a church like St. Gudule's."

"Your uncle has friends in the vestry, and exerted his influence. This Marie must not suspect. Much as she desired the place, she would throw it up to-morrow if she guessed to whom she owes it."

"How absurd, and how shamefully ungrateful! I must talk her out of that nonsense some day."

"Better leave the subject alone. The misguided child believes honestly that she does right to be angry with my brother. I imagine that one motive of her perseverance in trying to get the position of music teacher at Mrs. Marcy's and that of organist in St. Gudule's, was the desire to free herself from obligations to him."

"Which she can never do."

"She thinks that she can. We must leave her to nurse her fancied grievance until her eyes are opened by the logic of events, or until God touches her heart to gentler judgment of her best friends."

"Does she support herself entirely?"

"She has steadily refused to accept anything from me for a year. I have no idea what Mrs. Marcy pays her. Her salary at St. Gudule's is seven hundred dollars, but I should not have known that had not your uncle told me. She grows more reserved as time goes on."

The brother set his lower jaw sternly.

"Does she visit you often?"

"I contrive to see her at least once in ten days, but her duties prevent her from coming often to us. Of course she can no longer pass her Sundays at home. I am afraid," she went on reluctantly, "that she is inclined to be severe with herself in the matter of personal expense. Mrs. Marcy told me the last time I called there, while I was waiting for

Marie to finish a lesson, that 'Miss Paull had too little recreation. Except for the long walk which she takes every day unless in very stormy weather, she leaves the house but once during the week, and that is on Friday evening to attend choir-rehearsal. She declines all invitations to friends' houses, and to places of amusement such as most young people enjoy.' I mentioned this to Marie when she came in and Mrs. Marcy left us. She answered that she now belonged to the working classes, and had no time to squander upon pleasure-taking. She dresses very plainly, — almost shabbily. I do not think she has bought a new gown, or even hat, since she began to take care of her own finances."

"Marie miserly!" amused and incredulous. "She used to be an incorrigible spendthrift. Mother"— as if struck by a startling thought — "but no; that could hardly be!"

"That she is pinching herself in order to send money out of the country?" Mrs. Paull spoke out the suspicion he had repressed. "She would do it were there occasion, or if she imagined there were. I am sure that she has no foreign correspondent, or I should have discovered it during the two months she spent here this summer. She would hardly conceal the circumstance from me, I think, even had not the mail enlightened me. Indeed, had she opened communication with her father, I believe that her high sense of honor and of what loyalty to him demanded would have driven her to me with the intelligence. She is fearless in her very wilfulness. Poor child! she sees everything now through a distorted medium. Ah, well! In God's good time all will be right."

Another interval of silence followed. Such are unmistakable indices of perfect communion of spirit. Common friendship demands the reassurance, at decorous distances, of mutual regard and thoughtfulness.

Lanier leaned forward to pile more logs upon the sinking coals, putting them on one at a time, apparently interested in the consumption of each.

"Mother," without withdrawing his eyes from this operation, "may I ask you one question?"

"As many as you like, my son," steadily and cheerfully.

"You told me, a while ago, that, besides paying the interest to Uncle Roger, you had deposited in the savings bank, last year and this, six hundred dollars. At that rate you will have paid off the whole debt in eight years more. Should he who laid the debt upon you return to America then, — have you ever thought what would be your duty or your inclination?"

He could not see the sickly pallor the fire-glow did not veil, or the sharp quiver that shook the light from her eyes. He divined, through the nameless sympathy welding heart to heart, that a short, fierce battle against powerful odds kept her silent for the instant that elapsed before her hand rested upon his head.

"My darling, for months the thought never left me, sleeping or waking! When I began to learn how to take God at His word, and not to meddle with a future which is all His, and none of it mine, I asked Him — as I suppose Paul besought Him to take away the thorn in his flesh — to remove from me the dread and the doubt and the vain planning, to show me how to leave the wanderer and all pertaining to him in His safe, wise, loving hands. He answered my prayer, not as he answered Paul, — for Paul was stronger than I, and could bear more, — but by setting my thoughts free from that one torturing subject, that I might study and obey His will in and for me in the present. Should the hour ever come for decision and action, His grace will be sufficient for me, His wisdom will not be withheld. Until then, let the dead past bury its dead."

While mother and son talked together that stormy September night, the choir of St. Gudule's rehearsed the music selected for the approaching Sabbath. The new organist had been inducted into office but two months before. Her youth and sex had told against her in the judgment of musical critics in the congregation, and with at least two of the quartette choir. The correctness and brilliancy of her technique; the taste and spirit with which she interpreted the most difficult passage submitted to her, broke down the prejudice of the listeners below-stairs; the almost austere gravity of her demeanor, the respect with which she hearkened to suggestions, and her willingness to obey them, silenced her coadjutors. She was, apparently, bent upon, as the basso put it, "cold business," comprehending why she was there, and with no eye or ear for anything but duty.

She wore to-night a black merino gown, as simply fashioned as a nun's, and a close black felt hat, one blue velvet bow nestling in the puffs of golden hair the only touch of color in her costume. Her face, unsmiling and intent, as her eyes followed the score, might have belonged to a woman twice her years for any sign it gave of frivolity; there was not a tinge of coquetry in her reception of the greetings of her companions at her entrance, or of the encomiums passed upon her execution when the rehearsal was over.

"Thank you," to one, and "You are very kind," to another, were spoken without a rise of color, and with the least possible smile consistent with the fine breeding that marked every motion and syllable.

The tenor, who was, after the usual custom of tenors, young and thin, with fair hair and a sweeping mustache, did not venture upon an improvement of his very slight acquaintanceship with her, but got himself into his ulster and waited for the soprano to pull on her rubber sandals before offering to see her home. She was not very young, and not at all pretty; but she was accessible, and that went for much with a man who was bashful when not intrenched behind a sheet of music. The basso, being thicker-skinned, and a married man of forty, took courage to approach the organist, as she buttoned her gloves, preparatory to assuming waterproof and umbrella.

"I had nearly forgotten something which our excellent rector asked me to pass over to you this evening, Miss Paull," he said, in the rollicking way which men of his calibre confound with well-bred ease. "It frightens me to think what might have happened had I carried it home in my pocket. I dare say, now, you would never have spoken to me again, — maybe would have put me out in my best solo next Sunday."

Marie had listened politely up to this moment, her fair face composed and serious. The swift change that swept over it as she saw the superscription on the envelope extended by his pudgy hand, left him dumb and staring.

"It was more like a flash of lightning than anything else," he said to his wife when he got home. He did not even recollect whether or not she had thanked him by more than a bend of the head in passing him on her way to the gallery-stairs. "I shouldn't wonder if 'twas from her sweetheart abroad. The handwriting was a man's, and the postmark some outlandish place with a foreign stamp on it."

The rain was falling fast when Marie reached the street; the car which she hailed and boarded was full to both platforms. In obedience to the conductor's "Step forward there, please!" room was made for her just inside the rear door. She leaned, weak and sick, against the casing, the letter clutched tightly in her hand. It was addressed in her father's well-remembered handwriting, to "*Miss Marie Roché Paull. In care of Rev. Dr. Egbert Lee, Rector of St. Gudule's, New York City, N. Y., United States of America.*"

In the ten blocks that lay between the church and

Mrs. Marcy's door, she had time to review the futile attempts she had made to open communication with the exile since she had posted that first letter in Brooklyn to "Mr. Paul Morgan, Nice, France."

Carrie Storrs's device of setting the United States consul at Nice upon the track had elicited a civil reply from Mr. Oliver's secretary, to the effect that no American of the name she had given could be found in Nice. An Englishman calling himself "Ernest Morgan" had passed a winter there, then gone on to Monte Carlo. A guarded letter of inquiry to the far-famed gambling resort met with even less success, no reply being returned. Baffled and despairing, Marie desisted from other efforts until Carrie herself went abroad, a year ago, engaging not to abate her energetic attempts to find Mr. Paull until she could put his address in his daughter's hand. The rattle-brained, warm-hearted ally wrote regularly, and at surprising length for a traveller, to her whom she facetiously dubbed "Telemacha,"— always hopefully (it is so easy and pleasant to hope to all lengths when we have little at stake ourselves), always to no purpose, so far as the object of her search was concerned.

"If I had dared take papa into confidence, something might have been done through the police," she said to poor Marie upon her return. "But that would never have done, you know."

Marie did know, as well as if her only confidante had imparted the further information that once, when she "wondered," tentatively, to her father, "if they might not run over Mr. Paull in their travels," he retorted — tartly for a good-natured and well-trained American father — that "nothing was less likely, or, for that matter, less desirable."

It argued a depth of devotion which was pathetic, in view of the unworthiness of the object and the scant food that kept it alive, that the daughter's faith and love never wavered through all these eventless months. She had believed that her father still lived and loved her; affection and fancy hung fadeless wreaths above the visage enshrined in her heart of hearts, — idealized him into a stainless hero, an uncomplaining martyr. Her life had but one purpose, to make amends to him for all he had suffered, to repair with her young life the wreck his enemies had made of his. It was monomania, flourishing the more rankly, and striking its roots more deeply, for the shade in which she kept it.

Here was her reward! Clutching the letter still more tightly, she sprang from the car at Mrs. Marcy's corner, ran through the rain, without raising her umbrella, to the sidewalk, and up the steps, let herself in with her latch-key, and flew up two, three flights of stairs, to her room, to fall upon her knees and tear open the precious missive. She must read it thus — for God had sent it to her — at last! at last!

"My own sweet daughter —"

"I knew it! I knew it! oh, my darling, my noble suffering angel!" she cried aloud, kissing the words over and over. "O God! give me strength to read it all!"

It was long, — although, as he said, he was uncertain whether or not it would ever meet her eyes. He had seen in a New York paper a notice of the appointment of "Miss Marie Paull, daughter of the late Ernest Paull," to the position of organist in the church of St. Gudule's, Rev. Egbert Lee, D.D., rector. He had written to her before, and repeatedly, — letters which her silence proved to him had not reached her. This was one more crumb cast upon the waters. Perhaps the well-meant surveillance of her lawful guardians might extend even to communications sent under cover to a stranger. He prayed her, should she receive this, to tell him of herself, — his best beloved, — of her brothers and of Gladys (blessings on the baby, who must, by now, have forgotten her unhappy father), and of the mother, for whom he had not a word of censure.

"I, who know her Spartan integrity, her rigid sense of what she believes to be duty, her steadfast adherence to the road which she conceives is laid out by Right, expect nothing from her clemency. Believing, as she does, in the clever fabrications of my persecutors, she cannot act differently. I name her daily in my prayers as one of the noblest of women. It is not her fault, but that of the adviser who has her ear, that we are parted by half the breadth of the globe. I hope that your brother, as her favorite child, is the comfort and help she used to prophesy he would prove. If so, she misses me no longer. I am persuaded other things of you, my precious child, the little Marie who promised to marry papa when she should grow up, — my household fairy.

"You might not care to renew that promise now, could you see how gray I am, and what lines care, toil, and longing have engraved in the face you once loved to kiss. I have worked hard and against odds in strange lands, and am poorer now than when I left my native shore. I should not like to have my bonny bird see where and how I live, and how shabby are my clothes. The hunger and the husks are mine, but not the riotous living. The vision of your innocent eyes, if nothing else, would prevent that. And there is no earthly home for the exile whom you, at least, will never believe to be a prodigal. The knowledge of this should make the thought of the rest that remaineth the sweeter. I shall see you there, if never again here."

CHAPTER XV.

Is that beast better that hath two or three mountains to graze upon, than a little bee that feeds on dew or manna, and lives upon what falls every morning from the storehouse of heaven, clouds, and Providence?

JEREMY TAYLOR.

Drop thy still dews of quietness,
   Till all our strivings cease;
Take from our souls the strain and stress,
And let our ordered lives confess
   The beauty of Thy peace.

JOHN GREENLEAF WHITTIER.

CHAPTER XV.

"WAKE up, boys! and see what a white Christmas we have!" called Mrs. Paull from the foot of the stairs.

She was answered by the rush windowward of four naked feet upon the floor overhead, and shrill, joyous outcries from two pairs of healthy lungs. She opened the front door and stepped out upon the porch, where Lanier's shovel and Elspeth's broom were at work. It had snowed, not fast, but perseveringly, for fourteen hours. At three o'clock on Christmas morning the cold became too intense for any further downfall. The wind did not rise with the sun, — nor did the thermometer.

Mrs. Paull looked out upon a smooth expanse of what might have been down from a curlew's breast, soft, light, and delicately dyed into the purest shade of pink. The ice-chained lake was a spotless plain into which the lawn sloped by imperceptible degrees; the naked branches of the deciduous trees were outlined to the tiniest tip with the feathery fall; the pines bowed in dumb majesty beneath the weight of royal ermine. The still, keen air was a luxury to the respiratory organs, and stung faces and fingers with the prick of electric needles. Every mountain was a Mont Blanc against the fleckless azure of the vast hollowed firmament; from the laden roofs of a dozen farmhouses arose steady columns of smoke that caught the flush of the eastern horizon in clearing the shadow of the hills.

"Such a white Christmas!" repeated Mrs. Paull, in an ecstasy of enjoyment. "And such a gloriously beautiful happy world!"

Lanier tossed his last shovelful of snow upon the mastiff, — whom ozone, or some instinctive sense of unusual hilarity in the moral atmosphere, moved to extraordinary yelps and bounds, — and joined his mother in her rapid promenade of the paved floor.

"A pink Christmas, I should call it. Your glorious world is one huge, full-blown maiden-blush rose."

"Just now, — yes! In ten minutes the blush will be gone. It is fading now. Why should I be reminded of what the royalist said of the winter funeral of Charles I. ? ' And so went our white king to his burial.'"

"A grewsome association for Christmas-day!"

"Hardly that, when one recalls what he escaped. But we will have nothing but Christmas-day talk to-day. Breakfast will be ready at eight, did you say, Elspeth? Mr. Lanier is ravenous already. We will have luncheon, my son, at half-past twelve, that you may meet Marie at the two o'clock train. Do you know" — linking her hands upon his arm as they walked — "I accept her consent to keep Christmas with us as an augury of better things? She has looked happier, and spoken more gently when I have seen her lately. She sent no gifts for the tree except a book for each of the boys, and a doll for Gladys; but you and I prize more than expensive presents the signs that we are gaining back the dear, affectionate, winsome Marie of long ago. In His own good time all that is wrong comes right.

> "'For right is right since God is God,
> And right the day must win ;
> To doubt would be disloyalty,
> To falter would be sin.'

"And there is no place in God's world on this white Christmas-day — see, it is all pure white now — for faltering or for disloyalty."

Her eyes sparkled; her face was aglow with the dry, sweet coldness of the air; her step was as light and swift as her son's.

He stooped to kiss her, and meeting her arch glance, caught her around the waist, and waltzed with her to the other end of the piazza. The mastiff leaped and barked, Elspeth leaned on her broom to chuckle, and Gladys, appearing in the door, screamed with glee, and clapped her hands.

"Mamma is dancing! Come, Nursey, and look at her!"

"Was there ever another such boy!" ejaculated Mrs. Paull, freeing herself at length, and putting her hand to her head, breathless with mirth and exercise. "I am not quite sure that my hair is on my head, and my head upon my shoulders."

"There ain't many such, and more's the pity!" said Nurse Williams, from the doorway. "And such mothers are even scarcer, Mr. Lanier. You are real smart to make the most of yours. You can't make too much."

She had been a guest at Pinehurst for a fortnight.

"The first out-and-out holiday I've had in ten years," she told Lanier the night before, while he and she were trimming the Christmas-tree. "And it has built me right over again. I've had a right tough pull of it since last August. First off, two typhoids in New York, — in Mr. Stevens's parish. When you've said that you may be sure they had swallowed enough sewer-gas and stale vegetables — not to speak of decayed fruit bought cheap Saturday night, on account o' not keeping over Sunday — to give them typhoid as was typhoid. The two were in the one house. Mr. Stevens he come over for me on his own two feet. He couldn't trust the telegraph, he said. He waited until I could rush some things into my bag, and took me back with him. When he's on what he calls ' the King's business,' he has no manner of patience with ' fuss and frills.' That's the name he gives to pretences of all sorts, whether it's pretending to be too busy, or not well enough, or not competent to roll up your sleeves, as it might be, and go to work. I've heard it said that he has lettered on the inside of his watch: ' The night cometh!'"

"He borrowed that idea from Dr. Johnson, Nurse," said Lanier, banteringly. "He had the motto engraved in Greek upon his watch-case. But go on!"

He was never better amused than when he got the good soul mounted, and in full canter, upon one of her hobbies. He said she took such comfort in all sides of her life that it refreshed him to listen and to look. They were prime friends.

"Was he a medical or a minister doctor?"

"Neither; a doctor of philosophy and letters, and a dictionary-maker."

"Oh!" placidly concerned. "Then I suppose he *had* to talk Greek, poor gentleman! That 'Tales from Shakespeare' is for Master Edwin's branch, I think; 'Historic Boys' is for Master Tom. Their sister sent them, — and handsome books they are. Very improving, too, I guess.

"So, after the typhoids were up and 'round, — and they accounted for six solid weeks, — measles set in in our church. I had five children in one family, — one of 'em complicated with mumps, and the other with rheumatism for quite a spell. You would n't believe how often one disease lies in wait for another. There's nothing in natur', I verily believe and attest, more trying to patients and doctors than complications. It's like getting out of the woods to find yourself up to the waist in a ma'sh. And then there was that poor young married lady that had her skirts set afire with the stump of her husband's cigar he had thrown down on the hearth, thinking it was out, and he a-reading aloud from the newspaper to her, and she braiding a smoking-jacket for him, and neither of them mistrusting a thing amiss until she was in a blaze. She will be lame for life, but she did n't die, and he promised her never to touch another cigar. He said he'd had a 'sickener that would last him for a hundred years.' By the time she was able to walk about her room, I broke down clean for the first time since I put out my sign that I'd 'nurse, etc.' Mrs. Barnes she made me laugh when she come to see me on my back with a different sort of ache in every bone in my body, by saying that the 'and-so-forth had been too much for me at last.' Such a flow of spirits as that blessed woman has! Between ourselves and the post, Mr. Lanier (though what the post has to do with two people and a secret, I could never make out), her it was that put your mother up to dropping in upon me on the tenth of December, and nothing would serve her but I must bundle right up, without any more words, and come up here with her.

"She made me laugh, too, and cry together.

"'It's the King's business I'm on, Mrs. Williams,' says she, funny, and yet solemn. 'Pinehurst is the cup of cold water I'm sent here to offer you, my fellow disciple.'

"It's a drink that has put new life into me. Ah, Mr. Lanier, don't you fall into the way so many people have — 'specially young people who have n't the sign of a scar of trouble upon the skin of their hearts — of talking of this world as a sink of sin, and of their fellow-beings as worm-eaten by selfishness, from A to Amperzand. There's loads of specked fruit lying on the grass in the Lord's orchard, but it's oftentimes the sweetest that's knurly, or rotten on one side. I think the time will come when the Master, walking in the garden in the cool of the day, will cut off for His own use the good part, and throw the bad away.

"As for your mother, she's sound and ripe and fine-flavored, through and through. It's an education in grace and faith just to be with her from day to day."

The speaker was a goodly sight in herself on this holiday, than which no whiter had stood in her calendar for many a long year. The wholesome fare, bracing air, and cordial cheer of Pinehurst had, as she said, restored her to her normal self. Her cheeks had the bloom of a Spitzenberg apple; her laugh was the merry gurgle her patients found irresistibly contagious; her comfortable visage was an illuminated demonstration of "peace on earth, good-will to men." Over her gray gown was tied what was surely the smoothest apron in all the world where white muslin aprons are the badge of notable housewifery. She had been downstairs for over an hour, dusting the parlor, dressing the breakfast table with ground-pine and bitter-sweet berries, and in the kitchen contriving to help, without hindering, Elspeth, — not always an easy undertaking in another woman's kitchen.

When, at half-past seven, the household assembled in the parlor for prayers, she supplied a harmonious contralto to the soprano in which Mrs. Paull led the quaint old hymn that peals and echoes on one morning of the year around the globe: —

"While shepherds watched their flocks by night,
All seated on the ground,
The angel of the Lord came down
And glory shone around."

What a Christmas-keeping that was! From the pink rising of the sun to the crimson going down of the same, there was not one false note in the guileless mirth of childhood, not a sharp tone in the voices of their elders. Nothing went wrong. At breakfast the generous rivalry of Elspeth's spongy muffins and Mrs. Williams's smothered chicken added zest to the discussion of both; the clear black coffee in the cups of the grown people was mantled by whipped cream of like quality with that which slid slowly down inside of the glasses from which the children drank their milk.

Before anybody dreamed that the forenoon was half gone, the luncheon was served, — a luncheon which the children averred was quite as much fun as the Big Patch picnic: toasted bannocks and yellow buttermilk and home-made cream cheese, as smooth as butter, and far better than so-called Neufchatel, and hot corn-bread, and wafery slices of coralline ham, and doughnuts, — an early meal, that Lanier might set out betimes for Peddlington, which Marie would reach by the one o'clock train from New York. She could not get away earlier on account of the morning service at St. Gudule's. It was in voluntary compliment to her that her little brothers, and even Gladys, begged not to have the large parlor where the tree stood, opened until the afternoon. They had hung up their stockings overnight, and enjoyed overhauling the fruit, bonbons, and other trifles with which they were distended by morning. The Tree — the anniversary's Crown and Event — should not be touched, or so much as looked upon, before "Sister's" arrival.

Everything went upon velvet that day. The sleek roadster attached to the trim cutter, which was Uncle Roger's Christmas present to his sister, actually arched his neck, curvetted, and "stepped out" with an air a thoroughbred might have emulated, when Lanier got in and took up the reins. Not a capful of wind had dislodged the trim coping of snow from the top of the stone walls. The steady, still cold had held on, although the sun shone brightly. The four-inch-thick covering of the earth had not melted, but settled into compactness, making the sleighing excellent, without need of cutting roads in any direction. As the cutter spun out of the gate, — "spun" was not too strong a word in the boys' opinion, for the gallant way in which bay Prince carried off the new equipage, — the dry snow spurned by his hoofs hung in the air like silver dust.

"I wonder if it's too dry to make a snow-man with?" speculated Mrs. Williams, squeezing a handful in her strong fingers.

That was the inception of the famous statue of Santa Claus, which was erected at the right side of the piazza-step under the shelter of the porch, "ready to shake hands with anybody who called," said Gladys.

He was almost built when Mr. Morse drove around the corner of the house, the jingle of his sleigh-bells unheard in the clamor of talk and laughter, until he was abreast of the busy group. Wrapped up to their eyes, with just room between the folds of their comforters for the escape of clouds of eager breath, with thick gloves protecting hands that would else have been frosted, the boys brought and emptied upon the floor basketfuls of snow. Mrs. Paull and Mrs. Williams, also muffled beyond recognition but for eyes and voices, acted as sculptors-in-chief. Mr. Morse's companion was his Philadelphia brother-in-law, Dr. Lyell, a frequent and favored visitor at Pinehurst.

"Don't stop! Let us take a hand!" called the pastor, gayly, as the sleigh dashed on to the stable for shelter for the horse.

They were back in three minutes, and took a hand with a will equal to that of the most zealous, and skill that threw the best efforts of their predecessors into the background.

"Mould and pose are really classic!" observed Mrs. Paull, withdrawing to a suitable distance for contemplation, while the boys swept up the snow scattered about the base of the statue. "The Knickerbocker saint is classic by now, is n't he?"

"I flatter myself that his cloak has a togaesque droop," said Dr. Lyell, his head on one side, his hand funnelled artistically. "But the beard — of which Mr. Morse was sole architect — is the masterpiece. I wish we could borrow him as a figure-head for the big sleigh to-night" — was the adroit introduction to a petition the two had come to prefer.

The parsonage was full of frolicsome young people from Philadelphia and New York, for whom the Morses had planned a moonlight sleigh-ride. Would

Mrs. Paull spare her son and daughter for a few hours? The party would call for them at half-past seven, and return them in safety before midnight. Mrs. Morse was to matronize the affair, and Mr. Morse would allow nobody but himself to act as charioteer. They were to take supper at a hotel ten miles away, situated in the very heart of the snow-girt mountains, and renowned for excellent fare. This was the programme unfolded by Mrs. Paull over the Christmas dinner, served at five o'clock that the children might have time to digest it before bedtime.

Marie sat at her mother's right hand, dressed, as was her custom, simply in black. No conventual costume could have hidden the fact of her beauty to-day. Her nectarine bloom, the golden sheen of her luxuriant hair, the eyes, violet-blue in color, and eloquent in the expression of every fluctuation of emotion, would have made a pretty, even a brilliant-looking woman of her, had her features been less regular. In the holiday mood in which she indulged herself, she was bewitching in the sight of others as well as her mother, whose prideful love as she looked and listened to her wayward daughter gave watchful Mrs. Williams a heartache.

"She's taken lots of stock in that girl, in spite of all that's passed," she meditated. "Up to date, it is n't paying stock either; but, there! the love a mother puts into her children is most generally to be considered in the light of a permanent investment. There's no calculating what the dividends will be of shares that are below par sometimes six days in a week, and that a smile or a kind word can send up on the seventh day to thribble what they're worth."

Marie's eyes danced for one unguarded moment, and her color was heightened at hearing of the prospective frolic, but her reply was demure.

"I should like to go if Lanier is to be one of the party. Perhaps, however, mother would rather have us stay at home this evening?"

It was spoken carelessly, but the starved heart of the parent responded to the slight indication of regard for her wishes.

"By no means, love," she hastened to reply. "I shall have you with me all day to-morrow. If I were ten years younger, and had not played the sculptor so hard this afternoon, I should ask for a seat in the sleigh. The idea is simply enchanting."

"You would be the handsomest woman there, if you went!" said loyal Tom.

"That's so!" Edwin backed up his senior.

"And the youngest!" put in Mrs. Williams.

"And the most fascinating!"— this from Lanier.

"And the best and sweetest!" Gladys carried on the eulogy, reaching over from her chair at her mother's left hand to clasp her arms behind her neck.

"Certainly the richest!" responded Mrs. Paull, trying to laugh, while her eyes swam in a happy dew. "When I have all my children about me, I can say with all my heart that I do not envy the Baroness Burdett-Coutts, or Queen Crœsus, — if there was such a personage."

She said the same in substance again, as, having seen the big sleigh, heaped with furs and happiness, drive from the door, and listened until the last tinkle of the bells lost itself among the hills, she heaved a satisfied sigh in returning to the fireside with Mrs. Williams.

"My cup is very full to-night. The paths I have not known have brought me out into a wealthy place. These anniversaries are hill-tops where it is lawful to rest awhile and look back over the road we have travelled. How lovely Marie has been to-day! Don't you think so?"

"We are not the only people of that opinion. Unless I am mistaken, there's a young man of that party who could give us a point or two upon the subject."

Mrs. Paull had taken up a stick of wood to lay on the fire. The sentence arrested her. Still holding it, she looked around quickly:

"Do you mean Dr. Lyell?"

"Just that!"

The hostess adjusted the stick carefully in its place, brushed up the hearth, and pulled forward two chairs, one for her companion, one for herself.

"I have never thought of such a possibility," she said slowly. "She seems such a child to me."

"In her twentieth year, is n't she?"

"She was nineteen in October. Quite too young to be married."

"She looks and acts and feels like a woman of twenty-five. You won't take it amiss if I say what come into my head, seeing them two together? — before that, in fact, for the notion popped into my brain this afternoon while he was helping and talking to you over the snow-man. I think when he was holding snow in his hand to soften it enough to make a nose, and you begged him not to do it. 'I'd rather Santa Claus should have a snub nose than that you should freeze your fingers,' says you, in your nice, motherly way. And he flashed his eyes up at you so quick and grateful and affectionate-like, — just the look I've noticed in other young men in talking to women they wish were their mothers-in-law. That set me on to watch him with Miss Marie. He looked too happy to see her, and she made too much of an effort to behave to him exactly as she did to Mr. Morse, not to mean something out of the common. Mr. Morse, he may not have understood it. Ministers are the salt of the earth, as we all know, that is, the right sort are. (Salt that's lost its savor ain't to be compared in trashiness with the wrong kind!) But I've noticed a many a time that most of them — even the saltiest, as you may say — have got so into the habit of being put first that they kinder squirm when they are put second. Maybe it's the praise and reverence of the women in the congregation that's responsible for it. Maybe, again, it's being stood up above the people so constant, in pulpits and upon platforms and things. Anyhow, it's more than likely Mr. Morse took it as quite natural that Miss Marie squeezed his hand in both of hers, and said, ' May n't I please sit up there by you ? ' quite as if she meant it. His wife had different eyes and her own notions, so she had a fat elderly man on the raised front seat, and snuggled Miss Marie in the one just behind, ' out of the wind,' she said, and between her and Dr. Lyell."

"Is that ' the notion ' you hoped I would not mind your telling?" asked Mrs. Paull, smiling.

She was versed in her old friend's manner of leading up to a delicate subject.

"Well, then, it isn't, though it has a good deal to do with it, when you come down to the truth. This was what I was thinking of: The best way to get one thing out of the mind is to fill it with another thing. Ever since I knew her, Miss Marie has had her head and heart taken up with one idea. If this nice young gentleman, who, from what I can judge, is what he ought to be, could work himself into her favor — why, it would be a safer and happier filling up of her heart and her life than the other. You'll forgive me if I've gone too far, Mrs. Paull? Nobody knows better than me, ma'am, that some wounds ought not be meddled with, even after they're healed over. No matter how light they are touched, they inflame, and like's not, break out again. I've carried such a tender spot about me for nine-and-twenty years."

"Forgive you, dear friend!" said Mrs. Paull's mildest tone. "After all you have done for me and mine, could I take exception to anything you might say, even if my judgment did not tell me you are in the right, as it does in this instance? I could ask no better earthly blessing for my deep-hearted girl than to see her the happy wife of an honorable man, — be it Richard Lyell or anybody else. Pure love of a worthy object is a sovereign cure for morbidness. Next to this, I place active industry for others' good, — something to do, and to be doing it."

"You are in the right there. But for my work, — my profession, as some call it (I don't, but we mean the same thing), — work that's laid right down before me, and me to ask no questions, and to slight nothing, — day's work, cut and carved and measured out, same as the tale of bricks was to the Isr'elites, but by another sort of overseer, — I'd 'a' been in my grave or in the lunatic asylum ages ago. And since I've known and walked in the Royal Road, the yoke has been easy and the burden light. It's like day unto day uttering speech, a-whispering one to the other of the following of goodness and mercy, and angels coming to minister unto me in my darkest night.

> 'The sweet surrounding
> Of Thine angels' banding wings.'

Yes, I can truly say that the songs I have had in the house of my pilgrimage since I was let to understand what pilgrimage is, — and the house but a 'moving tent pitched each night nearer home,' — are more and joyfuller than in the days when, as one might say, my corn and my wine were increased."

"And you, too, have had a great sorrow?"

The question was scarcely above a whisper.

"Such a sorrow as has made every other seem light to me. Hark! they can't be back already?"

The clash and chime of sleigh-bells were loud and close at hand. With the instant apprehension that some accident had befallen the revellers, both women hastened to the outer door.

A livery-stable sleigh and a pair of horses were there; a tall man threw back the robes and alighted, as the lamp-rays from the hall streamed out upon the welcoming figure of Santa Claus.

CHAPTER XVI.

The Everlasting Arms! I think of that whenever rest is sweet. How the whole earth and the strength of it, that is almightiness, is beneath every tired creature to give it rest, holding us always! No thought of God is closer than that. — ADELINE D. T. WHITNEY.

In God's world for those who are in earnest there is no failure. — F. W. ROBERTSON.

> For him the silver ladder shall be set;
> His Saviour shall receive his latest breath;
> He walketh to a fadeless coronet
> Up through the gate of death.
>
> ANONYMOUS.

CHAPTER XVI.

"DON'T be frightened, Alice!" said the unexpected visitor. "I am only a Christmas trick."

"Roger! my blessed brother!" was the glad outcry with which the sister sprang to his arms. "This is a joyful surprise! I only needed it to make our white Christmas ' round and perfect as a star.' "

Voice and limbs tremulous with excitement, she stood in the embrace of his left arm, while he gave orders to the driver to put up at the village hotel and come for him at nine o'clock next morning. His sister interrupted him:

"So soon, brother? It has been so long since you were here!"

"I must be off in the ten o'clock train, my dear girl. As it is, I shall find a pile of work that has rolled up like a snow-ball during my twenty-four hours' vacation. Halloo!" — halting to survey the majestic snow effigy towering higher than his head. "You have a Pequod Michael Angelo, then?"

While she explained, Mrs. Williams slipped unobserved into the house. By the time he was relieved of his overcoat and muffler, and installed in an easy-chair before the roaring fire of hickory-logs, a tap at the door heralded Elspeth and the supper-tray, Mrs. Williams following with the coffee-pot.

In defiance of his remonstrances, the three waited upon him as they might upon a materialized spirit of Christmas. He began by protesting that he had no appetite, having eaten his holiday dinner in the bosom of his family at half-past five o'clock, and it was not yet nine, and had the reward of submission to his sister's solicitations in the discovery that the sharp air of the hills had enkindled and renewed genuine hunger.

"Now, I shall not dare seek my pillow until midnight!" he feigned to bemoan himself, when the remnants of the feast were cleared away, and Mrs. Williams and Elspeth had withdrawn. "I might have known that Elspeth's cookery would tempt me beyond my powers of resistance. I can hardly believe myself really here in body; the 'lark' has been such a veritable impromptu. I was sipping my after-dinner coffee in the library when Virginia regretted to me that she had promised to take the children to a Christmas frolic at her sister's, and my spirit moved suddenly and mightily within me toward *my* sister. 'My dear,' I said, to the best and most reasonable of wives, 'I am strongly tempted to make a rush in another direction, — to escape to the mountains, in fact. I have not seen Alice in a month, or the children in three months.' Her countenance cleared up on the instant, and I saw that she had been afraid that I would be bored at her sister's party. Genevieve is a fine woman, but she is not Virginia, and I had a hankering on Christmas night for my own kin and kind. So, here I am."

He looked happy and comfortable in the home he had made luxurious for the sister he loved. The chair in which he leaned back had been his father's; the cushioned stool on which his feet rested had been worked by his mother, — and he was a man upon whom the claims of early association were strong. Amid the toils and temptations of such an existence as a successful business career in America entails upon him who pursues it, he had kept a clean heart and pure hands, but the ceaseless grind of the mill had told upon his nervous forces. His handsome features were thinned into ethereal refinement; his dark eyes were quick and searching; the masses of brown hair pushed back from his broad forehead showed a white lining at the temples. Still his was a goodly and a stately presence, — noble beyond comparison in the sight of her whose earthly savior he had proved himself in her extremest need. Her eyes lingered fondly upon him; while they talked her hand wandered often to his knee or arm; once he turned to press his lips to it as it rested upon his shoulder. To the world, he was quiet, reserved, and self-contained; his wife and children and the sister he ranked second only to his Virginia as the embodiment of perfect womanhood, knew the passionate depths of the hidden heart.

She could not weary of telling him what full and exquisite delight the unlooked-for visit had brought to her, — "the beautiful outgoing of a perfect day," she called it. He would have all the particulars of the home-festival, an expression of profound gratification stealing over his face as she spoke of Marie's altered demeanor.

"To be frank with you," he owned, "had I supposed that her engagements would permit her to be with you to-day, I should have hesitated before obeying the spirit-impulse I told you of. The sight of me can hardly be agreeable to her, poor child!"

Without thinking why they did it, they all called the proud, self-reliant girl that when she was not present to be irked by their pity.

"I have heard no better news in a month of Sundays than that she is coming to herself. It is not a matter of moment that she should do my motives justice; it is a great satisfaction to look forward to the time when she shall know you, her mother, as you are, and appreciate at its true value the tender forbearance displayed toward her by you when you were yourself so sadly in need of all the love and sympathy your children could give you. I used to think, Alice, that the workman in the stony field of the world must wait until nightfall before receiving his recompense. At fifty, I am beginning to learn that if he be observant, he gets many an earnest, as he goes along, of what the final reward will be. I wish I had been on the look-out earlier. I have missed tokens which I ought to have picked up of the 'largesse' flung to his subjects by the King in passing."

"Good old Dr. George Junkin said to me once," replied his sister, "that one key to the enigma of the Father's apparently severe dealings with His children is that sin, by its very nature, must entail suffering upon the transgressor; and since there are no punitive fires in the world to come for His beloved, the chastening requisite for purification and healthful spiritual growth must be borne here. I believe firmly that we too frequently miss the benefit we might gain from what you speak of as an earnest of the 'reserved' treasure at which Saint Peter hints. We make too little of every-day joys, of daily deliverance, of sparkles of happiness, and glimpses of beauty granted to us, — not by accident, but as really 'sent' to us as the fall of manna was sent to the Israelites. What wealth of spiritual instruction there is in that story of the manna! 'He that had gathered much had nothing over, and he that had gathered little had no lack,' provided the gathering was according to the word of the Lord. It was only the hoard secreted for the morrow that spoiled into offensiveness."

Roger patted her shoulder, the corners of his mustache twitching roguishly: —

"I catch the hoof-beats of your hobby, my dear! Don't rein him in on my account. I may have laughed at him and at you, in a half-hearted way, sometimes, but often and often, when I have lain awake into the small hours, revolving this scheme of adding to my store, or anticipating the dreadful details of threatening losses to me, and to others who trusted in my sagacity, I have bethought myself of your Royal Road, and acknowledged that its ways are the ways of pleasantness, and all its paths are peace. If I had my life to live over again, I would curb imagination, and deny myself some of the pleasures of anticipation for the sake of knowing that peace. I would try to take God at His word, and cast at least a few tons of this load of daily care upon Him who careth for me. Even for me!" he added dreamily, with bowed head. "Even for me!"

He passed his hand over his eyes, and roused to a livelier tone.

"I do not know twelve lines of poetry in all, but two of the dozen sang and hummed themselves in my ears to a sleigh-bell accompaniment all the way from Peddlington. They are part of an old song our father liked to hear you sing: —

> 'I know Thou wilt not slight my call,
> For Thou dost mark the sparrow's fall.'

Would it awaken the children if you were to run it over for me now?"

Her answer was to arise and go to the piano Marie had left open. Elspeth, hobnobbing over the kitchen fire with Mrs. Williams, set the dining-room door ajar that they might hear more distinctly the rich vibrant notes that swelled and soared through the silent chambers and empty halls: —

> " Rocked in the cradle of the deep,
> I lay me down in peace to sleep;
> Secure I rest upon the wave,
> For Thou, O Lord! hast power to save.
> I know Thou wilt not slight my call,
> For Thou dost mark the sparrow's fall;
> So calm I lay me down to sleep,
> Rocked in the cradle of the deep.

> " And such the trust that still were mine,
> Though blasting winds swept o'er the brine,
> And though the tempest's fiery breath
> Wake me from sleep to pain and death, —
> Secure in ocean's cave with thee,
> The germ of immortality,
> Peaceful I'd lay me down to sleep
> Rocked in the cradle of the deep."

When the singer resumed her seat, Mr. Lanier laid his hand upon hers.

"Thank you!" he said. "When we join the everlasting song, I shall lower my voice to listen for yours. I think I should recognize it in the Hallelujah Chorus itself.

> ' We've lived and loved together,
> Through many changing years,' —

sweet sister! (There go two more of my dozen!) In all those years, and through all the changes they have wrought, have we ever exchanged a sharp word, or had a hard thought of one another?"

"Never!" she said earnestly.

"That is pleasant to think of while we are alive upon the earth. It will be a consolation to the one left behind when the other is yet more alive in the house where changes never come. While I am in the confessional" — with a little laugh —"I may as well admit that I should have been a healthier Christian had I taken and enjoyed the snatches of rest thrown into my way on the journey up-hill, instead of eating and sleeping in harness, and giving up an hour or so of Sunday, and more than an hour or so of the time that should have been spent every night in folding the hands together in slumber, — in longing for eternal rest. One verse I do know by heart. I should be hopelessly stupid if I did not, having repeated it some hundreds of times, in the heat of the day's battle, and in the night when sleep forsook my eyelids:—

> 'Oh, Land of Rest, for thee I sigh!
> When will the moment come,
> When I shall lay my armor by,
> And be in thee at home?'

A man gets so tired! so tired!"

"Every buckle and strap of that same armor ought to be let out," Mrs. Paull said decidedly. "Dear Roger! is such incessant toil imperative at your age, and in your circumstances? Surely you have accumulated enough to warrant this?"

"That is not the question. Riches are a responsibility, no less than a care, — a responsibility one cannot delegate to another. For money — for the money's worth — I would not give that," snapping his fingers. "As a means of doing good, of conferring happiness, of insuring the comfort of those I love; of enhancing the prosperity of the community in which I have made my fortune, — its value cannot be overstated.

"I did not come here to talk of money and money-making, but before quitting the subject, — there will be a desk in my office for Lanier when he is ready to take it. My elder boys being girls, it will be fifteen years before Roger, Jr., will be eligible for such a position. Shall we — you and I — live to read the style of the firm, — 'Lanier & Son,' — do you think?"

"It is altogether probable. Our father lived to be seventy-three."

"It is a long time to look ahead!" with a weary intonation.

"Happily there is no need to do it," said the sister. "The 'hoof-beats' again! The present is so affluent of mercies that I have no temptation to forecast the future, further than to thank you for your generous designs toward my boy. I can promise that he will serve you faithfully, to the best of his ability. He cannot serve you too well. He knows and feels this."

At eleven o'clock, hearing Elspeth moving about, shutting up the house, her mistress called her and Mrs. Williams into the sitting-room. Mr. Lanier sat at the table with the Family Bible open before him, — reverent and dignified as befitted the patriarchal office.

"*The steps of a good man are ordered by the Lord,*" he read: "*and he delighteth in His way.*

"*Though he fall, he shall not be utterly cast down: for the Lord upholdeth him with His hand.*

"*I have been young, and now am old; yet have I not seen the righteous forsaken, nor his seed begging bread.*"

He did not finish the Psalm, closing the book upon the thirty-seventh verse: —

"*Mark the perfect man, and behold the upright; for the end of that man is peace.*"

Perhaps he did not care, on Christmas night, to

direct his thoughts and those of his auditors to the antithetical doom of transgressors. His face was all peace as the four arose from their knees after the brief prayer, direct and devout, that committed the household and all dear to it to the Father's loving care.

"Your visit is the postscript to a love-letter for us all, from Him who was born in Bethlehem," said Mrs. Williams, in shaking hands with him for the night. "He sent you — straight!"

"I hope so!" reverently. "But the benefit is chiefly mine. I am younger by ten years than when I left New York. Mrs. Paull has a private cellar at Pinehurst where she keeps the Elixir of Life 'on tap.' You have been treated to it, I see, Mrs. Williams. I am glad to see you looking so well. Good-night! Christmas dreams to you, Elspeth!"

When his sister came back to the sitting-room after a conference in the hall with Elspeth, he was standing by the hearth, examining a photograph of Marie taken from the mantel.

"There is capital stuff in that girl," he said kindly. "You will get a world of comfort out of her yet. Wrap yourself up warmly, and take a turn on the piazza before going to bed, if you are not too weary. I shall sleep the better for an ozone nightcap."

The weather had moderated sensibly since the sun went down. Plumes of pale vapor were streaming up slowly from behind the hills; about the moon, round as a shield, and riding high in the zenith, was flung a vast halo, glittering with faintly prismatic crystals of snow,

"'A far-off halo, a near-hand storm!'" quoted Roger, drawing his sister's hand within his arm. "I hope it will be snow, and not rain, as my sleigh has no top. Yet a heavy snow-fall upon that which is already on the ground would be no joke to a man who must be in New York at eleven o'clock to-morrow morning. And there is no telegraph-station nearer than Peddlington!"

He looked so perturbed that Mrs. Paull tendered a morsel of comfort.

"Should you be snow-bound, — and I don't believe you will be, — a day of country-rest, winter-rest, would do you a world of good. I am not sure that there could be a better prescription for you, and other jaded men of affairs, than to be weather-locked for a solid week in a country-house. It would loosen the nerve-tension efficaciously."

"And loosen the credit-tension yet more effectually! No, my dear, I must stand in my office at eleven-thirty to-morrow, weather or no weather. Some exigencies are inexorable, and the law calling a business man to his post out-Dracos Draco.

"Borrowing trouble again, you will say! I will take the present pleasure without courting to-morrow's shadow. I am conscious at this precise instant of nothing but that I was a wonderfully clever fellow to plan this frolic, and that I am more than satisfied with the result of it.

"What a benignant air your snow sentinel wears in the moonlight! He really startled me, as we drove up to the porch; his attitude was so life-like and imposing. Do you recollect Hawthorne's charming story of 'The Snow Image,' and the scolding we got from our nurse one stormy afternoon for stealing out into the back-yard to build a little girl like that which the mother saw running about in the garden with her daughters? How we believed in things, then! There is no fiction in Child-World. There is a large hospitality in the outstretch of your Santa Claus' massive arm, and his beard is a stroke of genius. It would not surprise me out of my wits if our venerable friend were to break loose from his moorings, and fall into step with us."

Chatting, now jestingly, now seriously, they paced up and down for a good half-hour, watching the rising mists gather form and opaqueness, as they invaded the clear ether of the upper heavens. The horizon lines were blurred, and in the extreme distance blotted out; the moon grew wan and watery; there was a nearing change in the Christmas weather. Boding murmurs ran from bough to bough of the ermined pines; occasionally a deep, irregular growl, like subterranean thunder, shuddered to them from the ice-bound lake, — the struggle for freedom of imprisoned winds entrapped through some "breathing-hole" far up the gorge, and aroused to rebellion by the indications of approaching warfare in the free air above the dungeon.

The visitor expressed no further solicitude as to the chances of detention in his homeward journey. The clear shining of his holiday mood continued throughout the walk and talk.

Mrs. Paull paused for a last look at the outer scene before entering the house.

"Our white Christmas is over!" she said regretfully. "There goes the stroke of twelve! Ah, well! we have enjoyed every blessed minute of it. 'From early morn to dewy eve,' it has been without spot or wrinkle or any such thing. We give it back to God as pure as when we received it from His hand.

"'And so went our white king to his burial!'"

Her brother looked at her in surprised inquiry.

"You spoke of a ringing in your ears or brain of a certain snatch of a song. That sentence has haunted me all day. I read it in an account of the execution of Charles I., written, as you may know, by a devoted royalist. The snow fell upon his bier as they carried it to the vault; when it got there, the black velvet was as white as wool. 'And so went our white king to his burial,' are the concluding words of the narrative. That they should pursue me to-day is an absurd and, so far as I can judge, a causeless haunting, although I do not deny that I am a Stuart-lover. Now your lines are beautiful, comforting, and always apt."

Her brother hummed them in putting together the brands on the hearth, and piling on stout logs that would be ablaze by the time Lanier and Marie returned: —

"I know Thou wilt not slight my call,
For Thou dost mark the sparrow's fall."

"I don't know that I care to get away from my 'haunting.' I could lay nothing pleasanter to heart. And the inevitable association of '*Ye are of more value than many sparrows*' is a soft pillow for temples a-throb with the cares of this world and the deceitfulness of riches.

"Good-night, my Evangel! God bless and keep you, and give you many, many more white days!"

Mrs. Paull caught up his haunting rhyme, going over words and tune musingly, a smile upon her lip, as she laid off her dress, put on a wrapper, and went back to the parlor-fire. She stirred the bed of scarlet coals, lay back in her father's chair, her feet upon the embroidered stool, and thought her own happy thoughts until the merry-makers found her there, fully awake to the interest of the story of their drive and entertainment.

Marie kissed her of her own accord outside of her mother's chamber-door.

"You are too good to me, mamma! I wish I were a better child to you!"

"All dear and lovely things have come to me this Christmas-tide!" murmured the mother, as she laid her head on the pillow, and heard the toll of one from the hall-clock.

She was falling asleep when the hymning of a distant choir seemed to bring to her the fragment of the "old song our father loved to hear you sing." She could have fancied that she heard her brother's voice in the celestial music: —

> "I know Thou wilt not slight my call,
> For Thou dost mark the sparrow's fall."

She sat up, startled and but partially awake; then smiled and sank back among the pillows.

"Dear, dear old Roger! No wonder that I dream of him!"

The stillness of night and slumber enwrapped dreaming household and landscape. Except that the mourning pines responded fitfully to the captive winds under the ice, and that long brooding breathings stirred the unclothed limbs of oaks and hickories, nothing moved in the solemn amphitheatre within the rampart of the hills, until, at four o'clock, the snow began to fall.

Great flakes drifted straight earthward, and caught upon and clung to the trees, floating down and down, slow and large, until the nearest hills were invisible behind the wavering white veil. The trees ceased their sighing under the increasing weight of damp snow; the mysterious groans beneath the ice were muffled out of hearing; the earth, that had slept while the moon shone, lay dead in her misty shroud.

Over her, morning broke dimly and reluctantly. Everything in the landscape had suffered a snow-change; fences were buried out of sight, and all traces of highways were obliterated; the lake was no more level than the meadow beyond it; one half of the benignant snow-image presented to view a misshapen obelisk, majestic still in disfigurement. On the northward and lakeward sides of the dwelling there were embankments of snow against the foundation, darkening the cellar, and upon the roof pediments and turrets never built there by mortal architecture, and white "pointings" of bricks and stones that were not there yesterday. On one end and the front, the gray dawn could not penetrate the snow-incrusted windows, and the red shine of the newly-kindled fires showed murky from without, even after the inmates were up and stirring to make all ready for Uncle Roger's early breakfast.

The panes of the south-chamber casements were clear. Facing that which looked toward the east, — as one who watched to see the day break and the shadows flee away, with a smile that was not expectation, but fulness of satisfaction upon his lips, — lay a pale sleeper who would not arise with the rest at the call of the new day.

"And so went our white king to his burial!"

CHAPTER XVII.

Like a blind spinner in the sun
> I tread my days;
I know that all the threads will run
> Appointed ways.
I know each day will bring its task,
And — being blind — no more I ask.

I do not know the use or name
> Of that I spin;
I only know that some one came
> And laid within
My hand the thread, and said, "Since you
Are blind, but one thing you can do."

H. H.

CHAPTER XVII.

ROGER LANIER'S loving thoughtfulness for the sister thrown so sadly upon his generosity and protection, and whom he had cherished fondly to the end, was further exemplified in his will.

The property bequeathed to her by their father, and judiciously invested by the son, was committed to the care of his fellow and surviving trustee, who was also his business partner. For himself, he devised to Alice Paull, and her children after her, Pinehurst, with garden, orchard, and woodlands adjacent; in all, thirty acres; ten thousand dollars for her own use in fee simple, and two thousand to each of her five children, — Lanier's and Marie's legacies to be paid to them at once, those of the younger children to accumulate under their mother's management, until each should reach his or her majority. There was a long list of minor bequests, including one hundred dollars apiece to Mary Williams and Elspeth Boyd.

He had forgotten nobody whom want or worth had brought to his notice. From the grave in which they laid, that white Christmas week, all of him that could die, he continued to exert the beneficent influence that had been an essential part of his nature. Being dead, he yet spoke of the divine lavishness learned at the feet of Him who gave His all for an unloving world.

Above that grave there arose in due time a stately obelisk, bearing upon one side of the base the last text upon which his living eyes had rested, and which his reverent tongue had uttered: —

> "Mark the perfect man, and behold the upright,
> For the end of that man is peace."

Upon the obelisk, and beneath the brief record of his name and age, were the lines: —

> "I know Thou wilt not slight my call,
> For Thou dost mark the sparrow's fall."

"He has fallen as he would have wished, — with his full armor on," — wife and sister said to one another. "For him the exchange is all gain. For us — "

Words failed them there. Apart, and in her own home, each gathered her children under her wings, and, looking upon their helplessness, braced body and spirit to do a woman's part in her shattered life.

Upon the peaceful household of Pinehurst, the bereavement had fallen with terrible suddenness and weight. Mrs. Paull had herself gone to knock at her brother's door in season to awaken him for his breakfast and journey, and receiving no reply, entered, supposing that he had arisen and gone downstairs to make observations as to the depth of the snow-fall, and calculate the chances of reaching the city in time to keep his engagement.

When the numbness of the first shock passed before returning and poignant sentiency, nurse, son, and servant were alarmed for her health and reason. The exquisitely tender and vivid memories of Roger's latest words and looks, of the graceful play of fun and fancy that had enlivened the sweet counsel they had held together on that never-to-be-forgotten night; the full and affectionate confidence he had poured out upon her, — his "Evangel," — added keenest regret to natural grief at the loss of the strong staff of her worse-than-widowhood.

For ten hours after she had found her brother asleep, with the frozen sweetness of the smile that visits mortal lineaments but once, upon the finely moulded face, not a single tear softened eyes that were perilously bright; the flush of cheek and lips reminded Elspeth and Mrs. Williams of the earlier stage of the illness that had once nearly wrecked life and mind. Relief came strangely and unexpectedly.

Owing to the heavy fall of snow, not only the highway to Peddlington was blocked up, but the railway from that town to New York was not cleared for passenger-trains before the afternoon, and Mrs. Lanier did not reach Pinchurst until after dark. As the distant sound of sleigh-bells warned Mrs. Paull of her approach, she came out upon the piazza to receive her sister-in-law, and espied the fallen bulk of the snow image, hurriedly toppled over by the shovels that had removed the drifts, and now prone and unconsidered among the heaps thrown up in cutting a path to the carriage-drive. The arm, outstretched in welcome or benediction, was gone, and the lower limbs were confused with the surrounding masses; but trunk and head were distinguishable in the moonlight, and the indefinable expression of majestic calm the effigy had worn while upright.

"It would not surprise me out of my wits if our venerable friend there were to break loose from his moorings, and fall into step with us."

The gay laugh that went with the pleasantry rang anew in her ear, and the manly tones that were henceforth to be but an echo for all time.

"It is nothing but snow, and it has outlasted *him!*" she cried out, and lapsed into wild weeping in her son's arms.

"Thank God!" said Dr. Lyell, aside to his brother-in-law. "The worst is over!"

The two men, with Mrs. Morse, had been at the house, or attending to business connected with the sad event all day. They accompanied the remains to the city, and were present at the funeral and burial, — quiet, unobtrusive, and efficient, such friends and neighbors as prosperity seldom develops. The day of the interment was one of fierce tempest, — an ice-storm long remembered by those who were exposed to it. By request of the widow and sister of the deceased, Mr. Morse offered the prayer of committal at the grave, standing bare-headed during the brief service, and driving back to town in his wet clothes.

The next afflictive news brought to the mourners in the lakeside homestead was of his severe, and soon, his dangerous illness. Four weeks' suspension between his bed and the tomb left him the spectre of his hale and comely self. As soon as he could travel, his brother-in-law asked leave of absence for him of the church, which was instantly granted, and early in February he sailed under Dr. Lyell's care for the south of France.

All had come to pass with terrifying swiftness, when one recalls the jocund spirits of the parsonage and Pinehurst households on the Christmas afternoon, removed into the far past in the imaginations of the participants in the innocent revelry. It required no common exercise of will to readjust domestic machinery, and to lay again a firm hand upon the guiding lever.

As Mrs. Morse drove through the wood separating the Pinehurst house from the highway, one bleak March afternoon, she awoke abruptly to the conviction that, into the intercourse of the past few weeks which had ripened warm friendliness into intimacy, she had received rather than imparted hopeful courage. She had fallen into the habit of repairing to Mrs. Paull when she was lonely or despondent because of her husband's absence and ill-health; when an expected letter did not arrive; when a parishioner was captious, or over-sensitive, or there was sickness in her nursery, — and she never went away unsatisfied. She was ingenuous with herself as well as impulsive with her friends, and, her eyes once opened, she did not spare self-rebuke.

"One might suppose that I was deserted and bereaved, and not she!" jerking the reins upon the unoffending horse. "I have taken everything, and given nothing. I have talked of myself and my concerns like a selfish baby, and she has listened like a sympathizing angel. Just let me get a chance to turn the tables once, and won't I try to stand better in my own opinion?"

Not a human creature was in sight when she drew up at the lakeward front, and although the blinds were open, the dwelling had to her fancy a lonely aspect, enhanced by the trim order of grounds and out-houses which generally relieved the isolation of the location. She was about to tie her horse to the hitching-post at the right of the house, when a door opened in the barn, and a red-haired Scotchman, who had been employed upon the place for a year or more, issued from it.

"Is Mrs. Paull at home, Robert?"

"Na; and she's not, ma'am. I'm just back from driving her to Peddlington, — her and the wee missie."

"Then —" began the visitor, disappointed.

"Wull ye be sae gude as to walk in, ma'am?" said Elspeth, from behind her. "Robert! ye'll look after the beast. My mistress left a word for ye, if ye suld call, as she thocht like ye might. Wull ye step into the parlor, if ye please, ma'am?"

"Let me come right into the kitchen where you were sitting, Elspeth," — suiting movement to word. "I am always delighted to get a peep at it. Nobody's else kitchen is so neat and cheerful, — and indeed so pretty, now that your geraniums are in bloom. How do you coax them to blossom all the time? This is more like a greenhouse than a kitchen. And, I declare, your roses are in bud!"

An odd agitation in the woman's demeanor prompted her to talk on, to give Elspeth a chance to resume her usual manner.

"Robert says that Mrs. Paull has gone to Peddlington and taken Gladys with her. Will she come home on the stage, or stay all night in New York?"

Elspeth tossed her apron over her head and sobbed chokingly, still standing bolt upright in the middle of the floor.

"What has happened? Is there any bad news? Tell me, quick!" demanded Mrs. Morse, her heart sinking desperately low. "Oh, do try to speak!"

"Bad news, ma'am! There could hardly be waur for us a'! It's nane that wull mak' ye more than middlin' sorry!" faltered the handmaiden, between the gulps that essayed to swallow her emotion. "She bade me not to keep back the truth frae ye, who aye lo'ed the misguided lassie weel, and hae proven yersel' the true friend to us in a' our adversity."

Mrs. Morse whitened under an awful foreboding.

"You cannot be talking about Marie. She is not *dead?*"

"Mayhap it wad be better for us and for hersel' an' she war!" hopelessly Gaelic in the sloughs of her distress. "She's gane, Mrs! Morse! gane awa' to join hersel' to him! God forgie me! but I could wish he had sunken to the bottom o' th' seas when he crossed them himsel', before, like the eerie de'il he is, he temptit me bairnie wha I nursed i' these arms when she waur but ane hour auld — to follow him!"

Mrs. Morse felt the cold sweat ooze out upon lips and forehead.

"Elspeth, what are you saying? I cannot — I will not believe that Marie has eloped! she would not run away from home and friends to join any man alive. There is some frightful mistake in all this."

"It's heaven's ain truth, ma'am!" said Elspeth. "If the mistress had na' carried awa' wi' her to show to Mrs. Lanier, the bit letter that cam' by the day's mail frae th' puir childie hersel', I could read it oot to ye unner her ain hand and seal. Sae shakey and scratchet-like, Mrs. Morse, I could guess she war greeting sair the while she wrote it. I had it in me hand, whilst I could read it twice over, and I mind weel how it ran. That wha' sinks far in the heart by way o' th' een, aye lingers there lang.

"It war maistly like this she wrote: 'DEAR MITHER, — My feyther is ill in Paw' (did e'er a Christian hear o' sic an ill-begotten name for a toun?). 'Verra ill, and mayhap like to dee. I hae been in correspondence wi' him sin' last September. He is puir and an invaleed, wi' naebody to care for, or be wi', him. In his last letter just received — the whilk I eenclose — ye wull see that he hae little or nae hope o' getting weel. I hae plenty o' money to tak' care o' him while he is alive, wha' wi' my Uncle Roger's legacy and the bit I hae contrivit to save thae two years.'

"Did ye ever hear the like o' that, Mrs. Morse? She will hae fair starrved hersel' to put by siller for that — *de'il!*" sputtering with the vain effort to think up another and as forcible, if less hackneyed, epithet.

"Poor dear child! Go on! what else did she say?"

"That she had kenned a' th' while that he wad need her; that he had na askit her to come to him; that he war in nae cemmedceate danger, and that the medical man thought if he could get to Algeria, he might e'en recover. She kenned better than that, she said. Her feyther was trying to deceive her to keep her mind easy.

"At the last she set down this postscript: 'Mother, ye 'll forgie me when ye recklect how ye ance lo'ed him yersel'. I hae lo'ed him allers, — me dear, noble feyther! sae noble and sae unhappy! Ane day ye wull be conveenced of his cennocence, and wull bless me because I did no leave him to dee alane amang strangers. Kees the children for me, and beg Lanier not to be fashed wi' me.' And at the verra fut o' th' page, 'Love to Elspeth. She maunna' scold me.'"

Her voice went to pieces again in the surf of her sobs.

Mrs. Morse sat miserable and helpless for a minute, then a ray darted upon her mind.

"Was the name of the place where Mr. Paull is, Pau?" she asked eagerly. "Why, my husband and brother are going there — so a letter from Mr. Morse, received to-day, tells me. They will look him up."

The fire in Elspeth's eyes dried the tears.

"'Deed, ma'am, I've me doobts if he's ever been there, or ill at all. I've kenned him twenty year an' mair, an' the times he tellt th' truth war mair seldom than th' times he leed, an' kenned he war leeing. All he wants is to get mair siller frae the innocent baby. In the smooth, fause letter frae him slippet into hers, he speaks of money she's sent him, and that it saved him frae starving, and gat him meedical attendance, an' that the sight o' it aye gared him greet — ah! ma'am, is it ony wonder I lose me wuts an' me bonnie Engleesh in thinkin' o' my sweet, headstrong bairnie in the hands o' thot mon, and his maister, the de'il, only kens in what manner o' company beside?"

"It is all very sad — very terrible!" assented the listener, forced to collect her senses by the frenzied state of the whilom phlegmatic Scotchwoman. "But Mrs. Paull may get to New York in time to stop her. When was she to sail?"

"Yesterday. Mrs. Paull will gae straight to her sister-in-law, and the two will try to find by what steamer she's gane. They can do naught ilse. I'll carry the mither's face wi' me down to me grave. 'T was like one wha' had gat her death-call. An' never a bitter word or look! Only, 'Elspeth, ye 'll not tell the boys what's gane wrang? I'll leave them at hame. I maun tak' the dochter he's left to me with me to her aunt's. God will strengthen me for this day, also.' There maun be summat far agley in the warld, Mrs. Morse, when sic a mon can mar the life o' sic a woman."

"I cannot but hope that Mr. Morse can be of some service to her, and to our poor little Marie," said the pastor's wife, consolingly. "I will write to him to-night, and the letter will go out by Saturday's steamer. Whether her father is at Pau or not (the word was spelled P-a-u, was n't it?), Marie will go straight there, expecting to find him. What a wild, imprudent idea it was, — flying off to the ends of the earth alone! A young, pretty girl, who has never been a hundred miles from home!"

"She was aye as brave as brawss,— her mither's ain bairn for speerit, — and wha wad gae through fire an' water for love's sake. Ance he gets hold o' her, he'll ne'er let her gang till every bit and bittock o' her hard-got siller is in his pouch. God forgie me, a sinner, Mrs. Morse! but when I think o' it, I could stop his fausse breath wi' me twa auld hands, if he stood here before me!"

Mrs. Morse was a peaceable Christian woman, yet she did not look horrified at the bloodthirsty outburst. She asked quietly,—

"Where are Tom and Edwin?"

"In their play-shop in th' attic, happy as kings, wi' never a thocht o' what's come to their sister, an' th' mither's heart-break."

"Let me take them home with me for the night — until their mother comes back. My boys will be overjoyed to have them, and you will be more comfortable to have them away while you are so unhappy."

She bore the two lads off with her, delighted on their parts with the prospect of the visit, leaving Elspeth to nurse her grief and wrath, or to reason and pray herself into a gentler mood. There was literally nothing for her hands to do until it should be time to set about getting supper for Robert and herself. It was but four o'clock when Mrs. Morse departed; the house was in perfect order; the kitchen, her especial domain, was speckless and shining from the polished floor to the copper boiler to the left of the range, and the row of tins gracing the shelf above the dresser. Moreover, for perhaps the first time since she was a woman grown, she had no heart to work. All the inherited savagery of her Gaelic blood was in a ferment. The stern integrity and uncompromising judgment of her Covenant forbears were arrayed with her love for her stolen nursling and fealty to her beloved mistress against the author of this latest and foulest wrong to an unoffending household. She had never really believed in Ernest Paull, even when he won the unquestioning devotion of Alice Lanier's heart, yet in all her years of service in his family, she had held her peace as to this, her private opinion. Now she felt as if her soul were swollen blackly with the accumulated distrust and dislike of twenty-five years. He was the impersonation of all the sorrow that had followed her mistress, until, but for divine grace and the gallant championship of him who was now no more, she must have been hounded into her grave. At the thought of Roger Lanier, an odd constriction closed upon the faithful heart; two tears forced themselves from her hot eyes.

"If he war here, this wad na 'a come aboot!" she muttered. "It mak's me fair mad to think his money, that he meant suld be a peace-offering to the blind, doited bairn, suld fa' into sic dirty hands!"

A loud ring at the door-bell aroused her. She was sitting in the chimney-corner facing the windows that opened upon the piazza. When Mrs. Morse went away, the cautious care-taker had locked the main entrance door, leading into the hall, and the two parlors upon the left and right of this. Never a tramp had been seen about the place, but the canny Scot always made provision for the unexpected. Glancing from the window nearest her, and seeing no vehicle in the carriage-drive, she decided to answer the appellant by way of the kitchen door.

Opening it, and stepping beyond the threshold to get a better view of the visitor, she saw a well-dressed man standing with his back to the door at which he had rung. He faced the lake, and looked about him with apparent interest in the landscape or premises; his profile was turned to Elspeth; one hand, cast carelessly behind him, was gloved; the other held a cane, and was bare.

Elspeth believed, when she came to look back upon the scene and interview, that she recognized this ungloved hand and the easy grace of his attitude before she knew the face to be Ernest Paull's.

He had not heard her open the kitchen door. The March wind was blustering, and the pines made loud moan in his ears. When, drawn perhaps by the steady glare of her angry eyes, he looked toward her, she had shut herself out with him, and, her heels upon the sill of the stout door, had the mien of one defending a fortress.

He walked quickly down the piazza, his feet ringing upon the brick pavement. She recollected his gait so well! the slight roll that never degenerated into a swagger, and a springy rise upon the toes,— the carriage of a man who thought well of himself, and was used to being thought well of by the world.

In nearing her, he changed the cane into his left hand, and held out the bare right.

"Ah, Elspeth! how do you do?"

She folded her arms so tightly that nothing but her own will or a crowbar could have undone them; her stare was stony, yet lurid, like the "slag" of a smelting-pot; her mouth was a grim, straight line that gave her the physiognomy of a North American Indian. She neither budged nor spoke.

"Why, Elspeth! my good woman!" with a laugh of friendly patronage, "am I so changed that you do not know me?"

"I ken ye weel, — mair's the peety."

Her voice rasped like the sharpening of a saw.

He laughed again, less good-humoredly, and with a scornful cadence, and spoke like one who had no disposition to dally with whims.

"Where is your mistress?"

"She's awa' frae her hame. Where is me misthress's dochter?"

"See here, Elspeth! You cannot impose upon me with any of your high-tragedy airs. We know one another of old, and I am less inclined to submit to impertinence now than then. I asked civilly — more civilly than you deserve to be treated — where Mrs. Paull is."

"And I asked for Miss Marie, that ye 've tolled frae hame and freends and nateeve land to follow ye to th' eends of th' airth, and ye here in free and eenlichtend America, while she's gane to speir after ye in a place where ye 've niver set a fute, for a' I ken."

His change of color was perceptible through the bronze of a recent sea-voyage.

"What under heaven are you talking about?" he interrogated harshly.

"Just wha I hae tellt to ye! that my mistress, wha used to be yer wife before yer prefairred Jeczebeel to Esther,"—stingingly acrimonious,—"hae gane to th' ceety for tidings o' her child, wha sailit yestreen to tend ye on yer seeck-bed and mayhap to receive yer last breath (Heaven save and keep us frae sic awfu' prevairication and lees!),—ye having fuled the puir blind lassie's haid wi' sic stuff o' yer pooverty and seeckness as micht turn the stummick o' a cast-iron pot!"

"Do you really mean"—coming a step nearer, and speaking hurriedly—"that the silly child sailed yesterday for France, hoping to see me there? Why did her mother allow it? Was there no one to stop her? This is abominable!"

"Ye have used the reet word for ance! If me releegion allowed me to put in a harder, I wad fleen it at ye. And the abomination is at yer door, the sin upon yer heid, where th' puneeshment will be too in the Day when He maketh eenqueeseetion for the blood o' hearts and o' souls."

"Hold your tongue, woman! You say that Mrs. Paull is in town? Where?"

Elspeth was mute.

"Can't you understand English? Speak!"

No response.

"I'll make you answer!" Beside himself with anxiety and suspense, he put out his hand as if to take her by the shoulder.

Without shrinking so much as a hair's breadth away from him, she drew herself up to her full height, until she towered above him; her eyes glowed dangerously.

"Lay th' weight o' yer cowardly finger upo' me, and I'll stretch ye at me feet, ye fausse carle! Ye bade me 'haud me tongue!' and I hae haud it. I'll rend it oot by th' root before I'll tell ye where me mistress is. What are ye to her? What is she to ye, wha desairted her and deesgraced the bairns she had borne to ye, and wad hae let them starve had it na been for him wha made ye afraid to veesit America unteel his body war unner th' sod, and his speerit in heaven, where the likes o' ye wull be lang in meeting him, while there's a God o' justeece to rule th' airth and th' heavens! If ye hae ane grain o' good in ye, gae ye back to the far countree where ye hae been spending that poor lassie's substance in reeotous leeving, and send her hame again!"

"When will Mrs. Paull be at home?" as if he had not heard a word of denunciation or counsel.

"I dinna ken. If I did, ye wad be nane the wiser."

"Where are the children?"

"They're nane o' them within."

"Did they go with their mother?"

Obstinate silence again.

"Elspeth!" persuasively.

Not a syllable.

He walked up the piazza, close to the wall of the house, eying the closed shutters sharply in passing, his hands behind his back, turned at the far end, and came directly up to her, with the mien of a man willing to reason, yet resolved to end a debate by stringent action.

"You must comprehend, Elspeth, being an unusually sensible woman, that you cannot keep up this sort of thing with me. The children are mine, and I can get out a writ that will give them to me. If you go too far, I will do it. No power on earth can hinder me. It is as well that your mistress should know this. If she is in New York, I advise you to communicate with her at once and inform her as to my intentions. If, as I more than suspect, she is in this house," — stepping back to survey the upper windows, and raising his voice, — "you may tell her that I will call again in a week for her answer."

Misled by Elspeth's immobility and down-dropt eyes, he went on more threateningly, —

"In point of fact, I have the right, legal and moral, to search the premises for myself. You certainly have not the right to prevent me."

"I'll tak' it, then! Ye'll enter this door over my deid body. And suld ye try it, a skreel from me wad fetch a lang-legged laddie from yon barn, wha'd think na mair o' tossing ye, neck and crop, oot into the loch over there, than if ye were a mad dog. I may not ken muckle o' th' la', but I ken wha hae the stranger body o' twa men, an' ye are nae Goliath o' Garth!"

"You run a great risk," returned Mr. Paull, with affected coolness. "I have warned you. Upon your head be the consequences. I have crossed the ocean to see my wife and to claim my children — and I shall do both. You may deliver my message to Mrs. Paull, or not, as you like. It makes no difference to me."

He sauntered deliberately off the porch and along the drive to the road leading to the highway, striking at stones and fallen leaves with his cane, in an idle, lounging fashion. Between tree-trunks and naked branches Elspeth saw him get into a buggy in which sat another man, and the two drove away together.

She was left in victorious possession of the field.

For how long?

CHAPTER XVIII.

Be not deceived; God is not mocked; whatsoever a man soweth that shall he also reap. — SAINT PAUL.

>A pitiful thing the gift to-day
>   That is dross, and nothing worth.
>Though if it had come but yesterday,
>   It had brimmed with sweet the earth.
>   M. E. SANGSTER.

CHAPTER XVIII.

IN one particular, at least, Elspeth's skepticism with regard to the statements made by her former master was, in a measure, unjust.

The man who strode moodily through the Pinchurst Woods on that blustering March afternoon was not in robust health. Had her excitement suffered her to use her eyes as faithfully as was her custom, she must have observed that he was thinner than when she saw him last, and that a peculiar hollowing of the chest caused him to stoop slightly in walking. He breathed fast, and not regularly, after swinging himself up into the hired carriage awaiting him; leaned back, slouched his hat over his brows, and remained silent until he alighted at the railway station at Peddlington.

He was bitterly chagrined at the result of his expedition. Just two weeks before, he had picked up a copy of a New York paper two months old, in a barber's shop in Monte Carlo. The paper contained what purported to be an abstract of the will of the late Roger Lanier, wherein his estate was estimated at over two million dollars. In the list of legacies was one of thirty thousand dollars and a handsome country-seat in New Jersey to his sister, Mrs. Paull, and two thousand dollars to each of her five children.

Marie had written briefly in her weekly letter, of her uncle's death, — brevity her father was incapable of attributing to her remorseful disinclination to dwell upon the event. She had not alluded to the will at all, and the news was momentous to the exile. The tidings of Roger Lanier's decease could not be otherwise than welcome. So far as Ernest Paull had ascertained, his brother-in-law was the only person, except, perhaps, his former employer, who was acquainted with all the particulars of his dishonorable flight from America. A better man than he to whom it was addressed, would have found it difficult to forgive the letter that followed him to Nice. The writer had wasted no words in giving the refugee to understand that his expatriation was perpetual.

"I have refunded the stolen money," he wrote tersely. "I did this to save my sister's name from open disgrace. Should you attempt to return to this country, or in any manner annoy her or her children, you will be given up to justice. The sum you stole was put into the hands of your late employers with this distinct understanding. They will prosecute you without mercy. Your crime is not condoned by their acceptance of what they consider, in such an event, 'hush-money,' to be returned to me. If, as I have reason to believe, you added forgery to theft, the prosecution would be a yet graver affair."

The gate of return to home, country, and a show of respectability was double-locked and barred. He had no resource but to live by his wits. When Mr. and Mrs. Paul Morgan became notorious as card-sharpers in one place, they removed to another, and assumed another *alias*, until his partner wearied of the precarious existence and of him, and left him to speculate alone. It would have been surprising in these circumstances had poor Marie's piteous epistles reached him. With all his keen watch of New York papers, he never saw one line relative to him or his family, until his eyes lighted upon the notice of his daughter's appointment as organist in St. Gudule's. His letter to her was a cast into the water that proved unexpectedly profitable. Her answer enclosed a bill of exchange for one hundred dollars, and she had sent him two hundred since without intimating that the amount represented self-denial on her part that was actual hardship. He had played unscrupulously upon her passionate attachment to the parent idealized by memory and imagination. The child evidently had resources and a fat private purse. To whom was her tribute due, if not to him?

The letter containing the grievous story of his invalidism, and the physician's recommendation of Algeria as the one hope of saving his life, was a mixed tissue of truth and deceit. He was feebly convalescent from a seizure of what the English doctor, summoned hastily to the gambling hell in which he fell ill, pronounced a menace of "angina pectoris."

"You have been living at the pace that kills, my friend," he warned the patient. "Pull up, or you will make short work of the rest of the way."

Without the remotest intention of tempting his young daughter to come to him, he had written in his best style that he had been nigh unto the gates of death, and could not obey the doctor's advice for want of means. He calculated upon the receipt of another and a larger check than the previous remittances, and was counting the days before it could reach him, when the paragraph in the old journal gave a new phase to life and expectation.

That his enemy was dead had meant something in the line of fortunate possibilities for him. He had little fear of prosecution or disgraceful publicity from the men he had robbed, now that their inflexible prompter was out of the way, yet he felt but a slight drawing homeward. Marie's money would go farther on this side of the ocean. In New York he must work, or feign to work for a living, and he loved foreign Bohemianism better than domestic respectability.

Thirty thousand dollars, added to the sum settled upon Alice by her father, would bring a tolerable income, even in America, when one had a roof over her head. He would go home and get his share of the goods provided. He was positive, with his knowledge of his wife's character, that she would not turn him from her door. If he had sinned against her, he had expiated his transgression by living from hand to mouth, and by enforced separation from his children. His eyes watered at the latter thought. His was an affectionate, shallow nature, and such make a specious show to the world and to themselves. In the light of his interesting discovery, his love for the darlings of his fireside approximated heart-hunger. He convinced himself that impatience to clasp them once more to his bosom impelled him to risk his fate upon one audacious venture. With the superstition common to weak natures, he resolved to hazard the remnant of Marie's last remittance at rouge-et-noir that night. If he won, he would on the morrow buy a ticket to New York. If he lost, he could not go, — therefore, Destiny had decreed a different lot for him. He won four times the sum he laid upon the table.

His first call, after landing in New York, was at Mrs. Marcy's fashionable Boarding and Day School for Young Ladies. His inquiry for Miss Paull was answered by the information that she was not in, and that the footman could not say when she would be. She had been called out of town by the illness of a friend. He "believed it was her mother."

"Can I see Mrs. Marcy?" asked the stranger.

"Mrs. Marcy is not at home."

"One of the teachers, then. I must know where to find Miss Paull."

With dexterity acquired by foreign practice, he slipped a dollar into the man's hand, and was forthwith ushered into a reception room. To him presently descended an under-teacher, hurried and fagged, who knew nothing beyond what Mrs. Marcy had dropped incidentally in her hearing; namely, that a substitute must be found for Miss Paull, who had been summoned to the sick-bed of a relative.

"I asked no questions," added the drudge, who looked too tired to be inquisitive. "But, knowing that Miss Paull's family reside in New Jersey, I took it for granted that she had gone there."

She was not especially interested in her fellow-teacher, or chronic fatigue made her unobservant, else she might have noted the striking resemblance between the inquirer and the absent girl. The footman had made better use of his opportunities, for, at luncheon, he reported in the kitchen his impression that the disappointed visitor was Miss Paull's uncle from abroad, who had probably come to America to give her a fortune. "He was a genuine swell and a perfect gentleman, and enough like Miss Marie to be her father forty times over."

With the dazed sensation of a dreamer, who must awake presently and find himself at home in bed, Ernest Paull trod the once-familiar streets without seeing a friend he knew, or being recognized by any one. He had landed early in the morning, and had time to dine at his hotel before taking an afternoon train to Pequod.

The aspect of Pinchurst pleased him more than he had expected. It was a cosey corner in which to recover strength, and to be rehabilitated by degrees from the effect of circumstances. During the drive from Peddlington he had speculated as to the possible seriousness of his wife's illness, if she were the ailing relative. A sensation-lover inborn, he arranged a tableau of reconciliation in the sick-chamber — perhaps, even, at the death-bed — of an otherwise exemplary woman, who had lent too ready an ear to the worldly maxims of a designing brother. Should Alice die, would it be found that her brother's bequest was hers in fee-simple? or would it be ungenerously lodged with trustees, or entailed upon the heirs of her body? In any event, he could depend upon his sweet Marie's disposition toward him. It might perhaps be as well — in the mind of Providence — if the noble girl were to become the head of the household. He could be very comfortable in the country until next winter, with little Marie to cater for and nurse him.

This conclusion was prominent in his thoughts, as, turning to contemplate the wing of the picturesque colonial homestead, he met Elspeth's blazing eye.

The dialogue with her was the kick of the dreamer to the basket of Alnaschar. Even while he vapored to her of his rights and his determination to maintain them, he was aware that she must discover, ere long, the absurdity of his position. Roger Lanier was dead; but his wife, a woman of much force of character, was fondly attached to her sister-in-law, and rather than allow her to be imposed upon by the returned husband, was quite capable of enforcing his warning to the banished man. His only hope lay in her unwillingness to make public a page of family history that might wound her pride. He wished, when it was too late, that he had forced an entrance into the house which was morally his own. If Alice were really there and ill, Marie's place was at her bedside.

Unless — and subsequent reflection made him more and more fearful of this — the story of her departure for France were true, and not a fabrication of the Scotch virago. He had never known Elspeth to tell a lie; he had known her to be truthful to her own disadvantage. Her excitement was unfeigned, and what would arise from the loss of one of the children she had brought up.

His heart stood still in the horror of the admitted probability. Next to himself, he cared more for his eldest daughter than for any other living thing. He comprehended far better than untravelled Elspeth could divine, what must be the position of a beautiful young girl, alone and unsophisticated, who should set on foot in Pau, unaided and bewildered, inquiries concerning "Mr. James Ellis," the name he had worn there for a few months, and to which Marie had addressed several letters, one of which contained a bill of exchange. He was not utterly depraved. Few men are. Bohemianized to the core though he was, callous in sensibilities and conscience as only such a career as his had been abroad can make a human creature who once yielded outward obedience to moral principles, — he would rather have resigned the hope of future pecuniary aid from his daughter than introduce her into the scenes that had known him most intimately of late. He had not scrupled to rob his child; he would not demoralize her even in thought. America and the parental roof were the places for girls.

The more he thought of the awful possibilities contingent upon what he stigmatized as "a mad, romantic escapade," the more the horror grew. He drank heavily as bedtime drew near, to court sleep and respite from the visions multiplying and looming before his imagination. At midnight he arose from an uneasy pillow to dose himself with an opiate prescribed by the English physician. He had hardly lain down before terrible pain seized him with tiger-like fierceness. He knew the teeth and grip of his enemy. It was part of the price that he paid for "the pace that kills." After repeated attempts to rise, the dread of dying in agony alone nerved him to a mighty effort. He rolled from the bed, and, by partly dragging, partly rolling himself across the room, reached the bell, pulled himself up to it, rang and rang, then fell upon the floor.

Three days of unspeakable suffering had elapsed when he left his chamber, haggard and feeble, as from as many weeks of illness. When pain and alternating stupor let him think during this confinement, his mind ran with feverish persistence upon one topic.

Marie, on the sea, — a friendless wanderer, landing at a foreign port with no one to welcome or care for her, distraught and terrified amid the pushing, curious crowds of the popular resort where she had hoped to find him. Always she was a sacrifice to filial devotion. Sometimes he was angry at the unworldly recklessness with which she had thrown up her position in the school and probably in the church, to fly to him. Oftener he could have dashed his head against the wall in mad regret for his overstrained appeal to her love and compassion that had resulted so calamitously.

Calamitously to him, — alone, suffering, and nearly penniless in a city where his nearest of blood would repudiate, or, at best, merely tolerate him! He had blundered atrociously in letting temper get the better of discretion when provoked by Elspeth's insolence. Whatever relentings might, under favorable circumstances, have visited his wife's heart, he had antagonized her by threatening to deprive her of her children. Empty as she might know the menace to be after his wilful desertion of his family and two years of silence, she would accept the gasconade as a token that he was prepared for war rather than for peace. He had put her on her guard and presumably on her mettle, and he knew the quality of the Lanier spirit. Twice he wrote to her; once in the doughty strain of an injured man, demanding an interview and opportunity for explanation. The letter lay on his table all night, was re-read in the morning, and burned. It offended his taste, and was undiplomatic. The second was studiously incoherent, and sincere only so far as he represented himself as distracted at the rash step taken by their daughter. His florid appeals to the love his wife had once professed for him, his protestations of remorseful tenderness and entreaties to be received back into some measure of regard as the lover of her youth and father of her children, — were so strained and artificial as to disgust himself before the message was completed.

He could imagine how Alice would look while reading it. She was a true Lanier in her lofty disdain of sham sentiment. He had never been afraid of her in the old times. He quailed at the idea of meeting her clear, honest eyes now that she knew him for what he was, — forger, thief, liar, and bigamist. Roger Lanier had frankly applied all of these titles to him in the scathing letter addressed to "Mr. Paul Morgan, Nice, France." Marie had written respectfully of her mother, but with no affectation of concealment of her uncle's influence over his sister. "Uncle Roger has settled mother and the children in one of his country-houses, which he has spared no money or pains in making comfortable, and is advisor-general in everything that concerns the household." "He and I are distantly polite to each other," said another letter. " While he is your enemy, he can never be my friend, and this he has been made to understand more than once. All the same, I cannot question his attachment to mother and to Lanier."

On the sixth day after the attack that had stolen so much of his strength and energy, Ernest Paull paid his week's board, and had exactly one dollar and thirty cents left in the world. The doctor's fees had been unexpectedly large, and illness in a city hotel is a costly indulgence. Under the spur of the discovery, he made up his mind abruptly to call upon Roger Lanier's widow.

Putting upon the errand the face which he imagined it would be dressed in by conscious innocence, he sent up a card upon which he had pencilled his real name.

Mrs. Lanier came down at once; a handsome woman, doubly dignified by widow's weeds; collected and serious in demeanor, and so utterly free from discomposure of any kind that he was instantly aware of her knowledge of what Elspeth could tell.

Her next action, after acknowledging his respectful salutation by a silent bend of the head, defined their relative position. She remained standing in an easy, expectant attitude by a table near the front windows of the drawing-room, thus compelling him to remain upon his feet. He had retained his hat, and not removed his overcoat, and felt awkwardly isolated in the exact middle of the apartment. A tax-gatherer or a plumber would have had more gracious audience. Supersensitive to trifles, he appreciated her advantage and his loss at the outset.

His manner, under the trying circumstances, was self-respectful and deferential, without a symptom of embarrassment.

"I have called, Mrs. Lanier, upon confidential and personal, that is, family, affairs. Can we talk in some less public place?"

"It is my wish to hear what you have to say here, Mr. Paull. Our interview will be, of necessity, short."

Polished ice would have been as fur compared with her accents; her eyes were steady.

He had known this woman from her childhood and his; as his sister-in-law, he had jested familiarly with her, had been wont to kiss her at meeting and at parting. His head whirled, and a pang shot from the left to the right lung like a fiery needle. He must be master of himself,— at any rate, while here.

"I take your meaning, madam, and will be as brief as is compatible with the gravity of my communication. I have been extremely ill since my unfortunate visit to Pequod, or I should have seen you before. I learned then, to my astonishment and regret, that my daughter Marie had sailed for France to rejoin me,— an extraordinary step which I should have opposed strenuously had I anticipated it. It is my earnest desire to repair, as far as may be, the indirect injury I have done the poor child in writing somewhat freely of the precarious state of my health, thereby inducing her — most unintentionally, as I solemnly declare — to come to me. I wish to sail by to-morrow's steamer to Havre; proceed thence to Pau, and bring her back to her mother and her home. It is the least that I can do and — I am grieved to say — the utmost."

"It is unnecessary to put yourself to so much trouble, Mr. Paull. We have sent a cable despatch to friends on the other side to meet my niece upon her arrival at Havre and send her, under a suitable escort, back to New York. You may be quite easy with regard to her."

A movement, slight but expressive, intimated her impression that, his business having been despatched, he would take his leave. Words would not have been a more explicit dismissal. The blood rushed impetuously to his pale face; the tremor in his voice, if artistic, was genuine, albeit his ejaculation was more rhetorical than devout.

"Thank God! I have suffered untold agonies in reflecting upon the possible consequences of my child's rash generosity. You have taken an intolerable burden from my heart. I will detain you but a minute longer: Virginia! Mrs. Lanier! is there no mercy in the heart of a good woman for a penitent sinner?"

Another gesture, more decided and expressive than the former, arrested him on the word. The cold severity of her gaze did not change.

"I must decline to discuss abstract subjects with Mr. Paull," she said pointedly.

He raised his head haughtily.

"I might have known what measure of Christian charity I should meet with in this house. I was a fool to hope for anything else. I came here with a heart full of sorrowful and loving thoughts, — the broken and contrite spirit which pietists despise.

I am hungry for news of my wife and little ones; I am ruined in health and a beggar; and you, who could tell me all I long to know, — you, who profess to follow in the footsteps of Him who called sinners to repentance, — sneer at me in my extremity, trample me under your feet with cold cruelty that reminds me whose pupil you are. I should have known better than to expect one crumb from any table in Roger Lanier's house. He hated me while he lived. I might have comprehended that, as his wife and a Christian, you must meet confession and petition with holy insult."

Furious as he appeared, angry as he really was, he had put the harangue together cleverly until his mention of her husband's name. She lifted the hand that had rested lightly upon the table; chill civility was exchanged for severity as frigid.

"You have set your action in entering this house in the proper light by your last sentence. I have only, in closing this interview, to express my regret at having granted it."

She moved toward the bell.

"You need not summon your footman to put me into the street," he said with biting emphasis. "To be driven off the premises of the elect twice in one week should convert even such a reprobate as I. Whatever becomes of the ruin the Laniers have made of what was once a man, the Creator of us all — if you will admit that He had a hand in my make-up — knows where the responsibility will rest —"

The rapid patter of small feet sounded on the stairs; two little girls appeared in the arched doorway.

"Mamma!" twittered the taller of the two, "may Gladys and I — Oh! I beg pardon!" as she perceived that her mother was not alone.

Her black frock showed her to be a daughter of the house; the golden silk of her companion's curls, her limpid blue eyes and delicate features, were Marie's and her father's.

He took one eager step toward her. Mrs. Lanier interposed her stately figure, and spoke with mild decision: —

"Alice, dear, I am engaged, as you see. Take your cousin into the library, and shut the door when you go in. I will be there in a moment."

She was disappointed if she had anticipated a further scene. The wretched man walked directly to the front door, laid his hand on the lock, and glanced back.

"Is her mother here too?" he asked.

"She is not."

He stumbled on the stone steps, and caught at the railing to save himself. A man who was passing, after a quick glance at the handsome house he was leaving, and a keener at himself, stopped and came back.

"Excuse me, sir, but are you ill? Is there anything I can do for you?"

A hot oath flew from Paull's lips. "What business is that of yours? Do I look like a tramp?"

"Not a bit! not a bit!" rejoined the would-be helper, jocularly. "I beg your pardon! The man who needs me is my neighbor. If you don't — you're *not!* Good-afternoon."

It was afternoon by now. People who had homes, and liberty to return to them, clogged all the uptown avenues of travel; the sea-air bit at him at every cross-street, raw with salt, and numbing to flesh and bone. Down these shorter streets he had glimpses of the west, where the sun was going down and staining the river-fogs a dingy red. This would be one of the nights when it was wise to take the bridge-route to Brooklyn instead of the ferry.

The thought of Brooklyn strayed again into his mind, three hours later, as he emerged from a place he used to frequent when the exchequer was low. It was well down-town, and he had had a hot supper there for thirty-five cents, several drinks at the bar, and the chance to gamble with the remaining half-dollar. The man who won it, laughed brutally in handing back eight cents.

"Three for the bridge and five for the street-car!" He was drunker than Paull, and disposed to be liberal. "You belong over the river, don't you? I won't give the New York cops a chance to run you in."

Paull pocketed the coins, and passed into the street. The fog was foul in that quarter, leaving a taint of oily uncleanness upon the tongue. Brooklyn would be sweeter, — to breathe, — and was a cheaper place to live in. He would go over and "prospect" this very night. He must leave that first-class hotel. He would go back after he had secured lodgings over the river, and get his trunk. It was full of handsome clothing. A man in his profession could not afford to be shabby.

Apparent prosperity was a part of his capital. Still

he must look up a Brooklyn pawnbroker to-morrow, and "hock" a few things. He must have food and shelter until he could turn himself. He lived in Brooklyn once — or his family did. He would go to Brooklyn by all means. After all — might not Alice have kept her town-house? It was not likely that she lived all the year round in that beastly country hole. A cunning gleam lit his watery eyes. She was probably there now — in hiding. He laughed outright at the thought of how he would circumvent Virginia Lanier, — the cold-blooded snake!

His thoughts were getting hazy. American drinks were "heady."

He had walked very far, and was tired in legs and head. At 363 Mendebras Avenue they answered rudely his civil inquiries for Mrs. Paull.

"No such person had ever lived there so far as they knew."

He decided to walk back to New York; that is, if he could "run" the ferry. He had had a watch when he called at Mrs. Lanier's. He recollected looking at it in a saloon on the Brooklyn side of the bridge. A saloon with scarlet curtains at the windows, and frescos on the inner walls. A band was playing "Razzle Dazzle;" and girls with pointed bangs and red cheeks were waiting upon men who sat with their hats on, and drank beer and cocktails, and smoked strong cigars. He had his watch then, and no small change to pay for his drinks. He mentioned this to the bar-keeper, and promised to call in to-morrow, early, and settle. The bar-keeper — or somebody else — had said that was "all right." He had his watch in his hand then, and did not recollect putting it back into his pocket when he got into the street. He would call at that saloon the first thing in the morning, and see if he had left it on the counter.

This was a nasty night, and Brooklyn had the beastliest climate on the globe, — catarrhal, consumptive, neuralgic. That must be neuralgia that stabbed him to the heart every few minutes. The beefsteak he had for supper was as tough as sole-leather.

Ten knives instead of one were struck into his chest, and a red-hot iron band seemed to crush in his lungs. With a despairing groan, he sank down upon a door-step, tearing at his clothes to loosen the awful pressure.

CHAPTER XIX.

Definite work is not always that which is cut and squared for us, but that which comes as a claim upon the conscience, whether it is nursing in a hospital or hemming a handkerchief. — E. M. SEWALL.

> Christ in His heavenly garden walks all day,
> And calls to souls upon the world's highway,
> Wearied with trifles, maimed and sick with sin;
> Christ by the gate stands, and invites them in.
> F. T. PALGRAVE.

CHAPTER XIX.

"I AM sadly afraid that Marie has not been quite candid in this affair," said Mrs. Barnes, with a look of real concern. "I am very fond of that child, with all her faults. She has a heart as deep as a well, and generous impulses. The very devotion to her wretched father, which has warped one side of her nature, springs from a worthy root. But I cannot excuse her for telling her mother that she has been in correspondence with him since last September, and leaving her to infer that she had not written to or heard from him until then. Why, the first time I ever met her was in the post-office in Fulton Street, when she was asking for a stamp that would take a letter to Nice, in France. She stamped it as it lay on the counter; and in the casual way in which one sees such things, I observed that it was addressed to 'Mr. Paul Morgan.' That was one of his aliases, you know. I should never have thought of the incident again had not her voice sounded so like her mother's that I looked at her, and followed her out to ask if her name were Paull. When Mrs. Paull told me yesterday that her husband had been known abroad as 'Mr. Paul Morgan,' it all flashed upon me. Of course, I said nothing to her of the meeting and the letter.

She has sorrow enough without it. But I wish — I *wish* Marie had not said that!"

Mrs. Williams shook her head dolorously.

"I can't see through it — nor, for the matter of that, far into it. I'd have said, if asked, that while the child is headstrong and high-strung to that extent that when her blood is up, I've thought to myself that I'd as lief strike matches on a powder-keg all day as live in the house with her, there isn't an atom of deceit in her. She's too outspoken for her own comfort and that of other people. If she has circumvented the truth this time, it's the outcropping of the father's blood in her. Her teeth are set on edge, and sharpened to make mince-meat of facts, because such sour grapes have been 'the chief of his diet,' as Mother Goose says, for all these years."

"He has much to answer for, if only for the wrong done to this one child."

"You may say it. I declare for it, Mrs. Barnes, when I get to studying over what depends upon the way fathers and mothers behave and think and feel, I think that if I had children to raise, I'd begin to preach to them of their responsibility as parents by the time they could say, 'Now I lay me.'"

"One poor wife, who labored prayerfully to bring up her children in the right way, is reaping a woful harvest of her husband's sowing," returned Mrs. Barnes, sadly. "And here comes trouble upon trouble in his return to America. It was a bold thing to do, and yet, as it now appears, safe enough. Roger Lanier was the only man to be feared, and he knew it. But for her heroic faith, and her practice of trusting God, in deed as well as in theory, to care for the interests she commits to Him, she must have gone wild over Ernest Paull's cowardly threat to claim the custody of the children. Of course, as Dr. Barnes says, it was all talk, intended to frighten women and children, but it shows the temper and spirit of the man."

"Where are the poor babies now?"

"Mrs. Morse has the two boys still. She carried them off with her on a visit to her mother in Philadelphia the day after Mr. Paull was in Pequod. Elspeth went to the parsonage and told her all about it, then took the nine-o'clock train to New York, with a letter from Mrs. Morse to Mrs. Paull in her pocket, suggesting the very best thing to be done in the circumstances, — a cablegram to Mr. Morse. He answered Mrs. Paull within six hours after the despatch left New York: 'Will care for your bird.'"

"Isn't that like Mr. Morse? Who knows — don't laugh and tell me again that I have a keen nose for providence — but *wouldn't* it be a providence if this wild-goose chase of the dear child's should be the means of drawing her and Dr. Lyell nearer together? If ever a girl needed a steady, kind, right-minded husband, she does."

"I wish I could hope for such an ending to her mad folly. From what I have heard of Dr. Lyell, he considers the price of a discreet woman above rubies. Mrs. Lanier very considerately added to the despatch, 'Her father is here.' Otherwise, no entreaties or commands would have brought Marie home."

"Gladys is still with Mrs. Lanier, you say?"

"She is. The poor mother went back to Pinehurst alone three days ago. I spent yesterday and last night with her. She is brave and trustful, but worn to a mere shadow by these latest trials. It was bad enough to learn that her daughter had gone off alone to such a man as we know her father to be. It was worse, if possible, to think of her landing, unprotected and friendless, in a foreign country. But the hardest effort of faith is to believe that good can come of the appearance in the home given her by her brother (where she has toiled so nobly to defray her husband's debt to that brother), of this bad-tempered, vindictive, broken-down adventurer, whom she cannot present to her boys as their father. If he had returned penitent and decent, I believe — I am sure — that she would have received him. Her views of the might of the marriage-contract are exceedingly and righteously strict. As it is, so far as we can see, nothing but misery and disgrace can come of it. The Royal Road" — a smile breaking through the cloud — "is the only way that is not hedged up for my afflicted friend."

"That never is hedged up, His Holy Name be praised!" responded Mrs. Williams, devoutly. "It is the highway where the redeemed of the Lord can always walk. She finds the burden of this dark day as much as she can bear with all the help she can get."

"It is all she can carry. I told her so, and she answered, 'Unless the Father should see fit to add to it. Then He would have to increase the supply of daily grace. I am living up to my allowance.'

You can think how she would say it, and smile in saying it. As for me, I caught myself listening by day and by night for that man's step upon the porch. If a shadow passed the window where we were at work, I started with the fear that he might be there armed with a search-warrant, or a writ of *habeas corpus*, or determined to see and talk with her.

"As for our brave Elspeth," — Mrs. Barnes's love of fun getting the better of her sympathy in an actual laugh, — "she stalks about the place like a grenadier, eyes alert, and ears pricked up, and nostrils quivering, ready for battle. I have my suspicions that she feeds that big dog upon raw meat to make him savage. I know that she keeps him chained by the kitchen-door all day, and that he patrols the premises all night. I used to hear his heavy feet marching up and down the piazza, and once an hour making the rounds of the house. Even Robert had a watchful look I had not believed him capable of. Up to ten o'clock to-day, nothing more had been heard of Paull than if Elspeth had throttled him, and thrust him under the rotten ice which is beginning to float down the lake. My husband does not like the looks of this. He thinks that Paull is planning some ugly surprise that will annoy, if it does not terrify his wife, — such as spying out the children's hiding-places, and trying to seize them. *I* think that he is waiting to get legal advice, or, what is more likely, hoping to wear out Alice's spirit by a mysterious silence. There is nothing harder to bear than a vague dread. I believe him to be capable of anything," added the whole-souled little woman, who, like most warm lovers, was a good hater.

"If I had any opinion on the subject — which I don't presume to have," Nurse Williams announced, folding up her knitting, preparatory to going home, — "it would be that he has taken vessel and gone back where he came from, to see if he can get hold of his daughter. He's maybe uneasy about her, knowing the ways of foreign parts as he does, and that women can't go kiting round there alone — especially when they are young and pretty — as they can over here (and particularly, as I will and must always say, in Brooklyn!), and he must have some natural feeling for the poor child. Leastways he knows that she is the best card in his hand.

"Will you listen to me using gambling talk in my old age when I don't know queens from spades, nor hearts from jacks? It must be the talking and thinking so much about a man who's made his living that way. There's more things that's catching than measles and cholera. You'll let me know if you've any further news of them all? They are in my mind and prayers all the time I'm awake."

She had run in for an hour that evening expressly to inquire as to the case of her Pinehurst friends, and she carried them upon her great heart in her homeward walk. The weather was much colder than when she went into her pastor's house. The salt yellow fogs were rolling seaward before a brisk nor'wester; the stars blinked frostily overhead.

"March will die like a roaring lion!" soliloquized the good soul, "stepping out" at a rate of speed disporportioned to her years and weight. "His teeth are sharp too!"

The nor'wester was a young gale when she faced it, bullying all weaker things after the manner of March winds, capricious, and no respecter of persons. Substantial as was her build, she had to duck her head, and shoulder the blast sidelong in crossing the streets. Thus advancing, she brought herself into contact with a stout man at the junction of the Avenue with Post Street. Both staggered, and he seized her arm to save her from falling, with —

"I beg your pardon, madam!"

"If it ain't Mr. Stevens!" cried she, with what breath the gale and shock had spared to her.

The home missionary laughed, — a right round, jovial laugh that must have come all the way from his heels.

"This is one of the things people who know no better call ' wonderful ! ' " he said jollily. " Such things as are all the time happening to me — and to anybody who is on the lookout for them. I am on my way to your house. Just got off the car at the corner below."

"King's business?"

"That's as you look at it. Busy?"

"Just home from a bilious-remittent yesterday, and pretty well rested out last night. Why! what's this?"

Mr. Stevens said "Halloo!" and both halted at the bottom of the steps leading up to the sign of "Mary Williams, Nurse, &c." A man crouched there, doubled up until his forehead rested on his knees, not — as the practised eye of the two spectators at once discerned — in the limp attitude of the drunkard, but tense with physical anguish. Mr. Stevens took him gently by the shoulder. He moaned, and tried to raise himself. The light of the street-lamp showed a face like chalk, made keen and old by extremity of pain.

"Aha!" escaped the missionary.

He let go of the shoulder, and beckoned the nurse a few steps apart.

"I've seen this man before to-day. He swore at me then. That brings him fairly within the category of 'them that curse and despitefully use you.' So my duty is to bless him. Can you take him in for an hour or so? He has a convulsion of some sort, and ought to be attended to at once."

"I'll see if the men-folks downstairs are at home. They can help you up to my sitting-room with him," mounting the steps hastily.

The "men-folks," a father and grown son, willingly lent a hand in the charitable deed. Whatever Mrs. Williams ordained respecting sick people was law and gospel to them. The three men got the groaning and almost unconscious sufferer up to the second floor, and laid him upon the lounge under the illustrated poem, Mrs. Williams's pride. At her next behest the son ran off for Dr. Bacon.

"It's angina pectoris!" said Mr. Stevens, presently, watching the fierce spasms.

"We used to call it 'breast-pang,'" said the nurse, in the same guarded key. "There's few worse things that the human body can endure. He's been drinking hard too. Maybe to try to quiet the pain, poor fellow! I've known people to mistake it for cramp in the stomach in the first stages. He looks like a gentleman."

The missionary nodded, his grave, pitying regards upon the convulsed features. Used as he was to witnessing every form of suffering, he appreciated that this was an extraordinary case, and that the peril was imminent. Hot fomentations were applied to his chest, and hot water-bags to his feet, without mitigation of the symptoms. It was a tedious half-hour that rolled by before the bustle of the physician's arrival was heard upon the stairs. For the next hour little was said in the room besides the quick, authoritative directions of the chief in command, and the queries of the subordinates.

In that time medicines were brought in; a folding-bed was lowered and made up, the sufferer undressed and laid within it, apparently unconscious of everything except the intolerable torture of his mysterious malady. It was twelve o'clock when his groans ceased, and he lay in the stupor induced by anodynes and exhaustion.

Dr. Bacon picked up the coat he had taken off the better to handle the writhing man, and whistled.

"By Jap! that was a near thing. I thought he was off a dozen times. Who and what is he? and how came you two in charge of this private hospital?"

"He was taken upon my steps," said Mrs. Williams.

"And you took him in. You may be thankful if he does n't turn the tables. Such impulsive charity is pious, but poor policy, so far as the life that now is goes. What do you know of our patient, Mr. Stevens?"

"He is a traveller on the Jericho road, and my neighbor. The priest and the Levite had probably had their look and their say about him, but they were out of sight before we came up."

The doctor's eyes twinkled with merry malice.

"S-o-o! a pair of good Samaritans, eh? The sacred drama is likely to cost you more than a pocketful of tuppences, and more time than you calculated upon. He can't be moved to-night, or to-morrow, without endangering his life, — which is n't worth taking odds upon, in any event. You've got a white elephant on your hands, my good sister. My advice (unprofessional) is that you examine his clothing for some clew to his identity. If he has friends, they ought to be informed as to what has happened."

The search was futile. Not a letter, or so much as a handkerchief, was in the pockets, and none of the garments were marked.

The doctor whistled again.

"That saying about the Jericho road was n't amiss. Our *un*certain man has certainly fallen among thieves, and thieves without honor at that."

The smile he turned upon the hostess was a broad grin of mischievous satisfaction.

"Here's a station on the Royal Road for you! Not having taken a ticket on that line myself, I humbly propose that you bundle him out of this to the hospital the minute I can say with any degree of truthfulness that he is n't likely to die on the way. If he dies here, there will be a newspaper inquest, and there's no telling what amount of talk and fuss."

"That's for to-morrow to decide, — not you, nor

yet me," rejoined the nurse, composedly. " But this much I do say, — until it's safe to move him, here he stays! A human life is a human life, and I have n't lived to be fifty-seven years old to be scared by newspaper powder. They are mostly blank cartridges."

" Oh, I know you of old! No matter whom you are dealing with, you always write yourself down as ' No. 2.' See here, my friend, — for I am your friend, whether you are foolish or sensible, — this man is not one of your kind. There is n't a sign of the disciple about him. We doctors see enough of the side of life the knots are on, to make us keen in these matters. He's a genteel ' tough ' — that's what he is — and just off of a hard ' tear.' Don't set your heart upon nursing him into a sheep. He's an out-and-out goat. I don't say you're to put him into the street to-night, but I'll look in to-morrow with a hospital permit in my pocket, and an elastic conscience in my manly bosom.

" Did you ever behold a more obstinate countenance in your born days?" pointing to Mrs. Williams, who was quietly setting the disordered room into its accustomed condition. " She's a respectable woman, with a professional reputation to maintain, and it really won't do for her to be housing stragglers in this promiscuous manner. She ought, in the first place, to have sent off post-haste for an ambulance and shipped him to the hospital."

" Or station-house," put in Mr. Stevens, smiling quietly. " There were probably none on the turnpike to Jericho, or the priest and Levite would have thought of one. The Royal Road I heard you speak of just now is lined with Houses of Mercy and Ready Reliefs, and so on. That comes of living in the nineteenth century, I suppose."

The doctor was not disconcerted.

"As to charity, real charity, I believe in it as truly as any man. But these works of supererogation are outside of my province — and comprehension. I dare affirm — for I know you and respect your principles — that five out of every ten cases of so-called distress you relieve, prove, when you come to look into them, to have been frauds, or, at least, exaggerated for the purpose of working up your sympathies to the alms-point. There is a continual pull upon your nervous forces and purse-strings, and for what? To further pauperize paupers, to instruct designing scamps in hypocrisy and cunning, and deplete good men's pockets. Am I right?"

"Better that ninety-nine guilty men go free than that one innocent man should be punished," quoted Mr. Stevens. "My conscience is easier for not taking the chance against the innocent one. As to the unworthy whom I feed and clothe, believing that I am obeying the Master's precept to provide for the destitute, — what follows the action performed in this spirit is none of my business. It is done unto God, not unto man."

Dr. Bacon shrugged his shoulders and spread out his hands.

"And it is none of my business, you might say, to dictate to whom you are to give and when and how. Only, I beg you to believe that I am sincerely interested in our excellent Mrs. Williams, and I don't fancy the contract she has on her hands just now."

He moved toward the bed. The conversation had been held in the sub-tones trained nurses understand (or ought to understand) how to use, audible only to the interlocutor and free from the sibilations that arouse a sleeper more readily than a loud call.

The man lay like one dead, but for his low, labored respiration, — the ground swell after the storm. His face was livid, the cheeks had fallen in; his jaw hung loosely.

"Send for me should the pain return," said the doctor, in leaving his side. "Should you find him sinking, don't call me up. It would be over before I could get here. It is touch-and-go with him for the next few hours."

Mr. Stevens took his departure half an hour later. He had left a sick man in New York to whom he had meant to send Mrs. Williams. He must secure another nurse before he could go to his own home.

"I will look in upon you to-morrow forenoon," was his parting promise. "Keep up a brave heart, my sister — and may the Sleepless Eye watch with you!"

He had made his call, and Dr. Bacon his, before the patient gave any sign that he knew where he was — or indeed that he was at all. It was then the recurrence of the horrible grip upon his chest that aroused him from the protracted stupor. The paroxysm was slighter and briefer than the former, and when it was relieved, he moved and spoke with comparative ease. Another long night of lethargic slumber succeeded, and the Sabbath day dawned brightly.

"Treacherous, but delicious," Dr. Bacon pronounced the weather. "Nice, while it lasts, and profitable to the profession when it is over. I wish you could get a mouthful of the outer air before the storm it is breeding comes."

For answer, she looked at him across the stranger's pillow.

"Oh, I suppose so!" he retorted crossly. "I feel like shaking you, all the same!"

The patient seemed unobservant of the by-play, although he was rational and fully awake, replying coherently and in well-chosen terms to the physician's questions as to his physical condition. He suffered little actual pain, he said, but there were moments of distressing prostration when his heart stopped beating for a moment, and resumed action with difficulty. He supposed that, with returning strength, this sensation would pass away. He thanked the doctor for his kindly attentions, and complimented him, briefly but courteously, upon his skill.

"I was more dangerously ill from the same cause in February. I am not alarmed as to the final result."

After the doctor had gone, Mrs. Williams was slightly confused by the unexpected query: "Why did he want to shake you?"

"Pshaw! you mustn't mind Dr. Bacon's nonsense. He and I have worked together so many years that he says pretty much whatever comes into his head. Will you take your broth now?"

He complied, said "Thank you!" as she laid his head again on the pillow, and was so still she would have believed him drowsy, but for the wide gaze of the eyes straight forward into vacancy.

"You and Dr. Bacon consider me extremely ill, do you not?" he asked, at length, without apparent emotion. "You may be nearer right than I."

"Nobody can suffer as you do, without becoming seriously ill, sir. There's always more or less danger in such attacks. I am very thankful to see you so much easier."

"You do not say 'better,' I observe! Why are you taking care of me?"

"You fell ill at my door at ten o'clock at night. What could a Christian woman do but see that you did not die there? Then, too, I am a professional nurse, and there seemed to be a providence in it."

In the next interval of silence between them, the church-bell began to chime for the morning service; that of the Jeremy Taylor Memorial sonorous and clear, because close at hand. Mrs. Williams's head was reverently inclined as the final toll sounded the call to worship in the sanctuary of her love; believing herself unnoticed by her lodger, she folded her hands and joined in spirit in the invocation which she knew was said at that minute over the congregation bowed in prayer.

"It is Sunday, is it not?" came from her companion presently.

"Yes, and a beautiful Sabbath, sir. I'm always grateful for a lovely Lord's Day."

"You were praying just now. Did you pray for me?"

"Yes. I have been praying constantly for you all the morning — and yesterday — and night before."

"Thank you!"

The weak voice she could have fancied was weaker every time she listened to it, spoke again after a long pause.

"Are you not in the habit of reading your Bible on Sundays when you do not go to church?"

"Always." She arose with alacrity, and took the well-worn Book from its cushioned stand. "If you don't mind I should like to look over a Psalm, or a bit of the Gospels. They hearten a body up amazingly."

He waited until she settled her eye-glasses and opened her Bible.

"Would it weary you to read a few verses aloud?"

"Not at all." She would not display too much eagerness lest he should shrink back into the shell of polite reserve. "Have you any choice, sir?"

The answer was not prompt, and was enunciated lingeringly, indescribable pathos in the last inflections: —

"If you please — the story of the thief on the Cross!"

He lay perfectly still while the pleasant voice, solemn with the weight of pious awe, rendered the tale: —

"*And when they came unto the place which is called The skull, there they crucified Him, and the malefactors, one on the right hand and the other on the left.*

"*And Jesus said, 'Father, forgive them; for they know not what they do.' And parting His garments among them, they cast lots.*

"*And the people stood beholding. And the rulers also scoffed at Him, saying, 'He saved others; let*

Him save Himself, if this is the Christ of God, His chosen.'

"*And the soldiers also mocked Him, coming to Him, offering Him vinegar, and saying, 'If Thou art the King of the Jews, save Thyself!'*

"*And there was also a superscription over Him, 'This is the King of the Jews.'*

"*And one of the malefactors which were hanged railed on Him, saying, 'Art not Thou the Christ? save Thyself and us.'*

"*But the other answered, and rebuking him said, 'Dost thou not even fear God, seeing thou art in the same condemnation? And we indeed justly; for we receive the due reward of our deeds: but this man hath done nothing amiss.'*

"*And he said, 'Jesus! remember me when Thou comest into Thy kingdom.'*

"*And He said unto him, 'Verily I say unto thee, To-day shalt thou be with me in Paradise.'*"

The reverent accents ceased, and there was a stillness that might be felt. The sunken eyes appeared to gaze upon a pencil of sunshine slipping stealthily along the wall; the lips murmured no thanks; Mrs. Williams crossed the room with her soundless step to lay the Bible upon its pillow.

"I remember," she said softly, to herself as much as to the possible auditor, "hearing an old preacher say once that ' we had one such story given to us in God's Word, that none might despair, and only one, that none might presume.' You may have heard too, sir, of John Wesley's answer to the lady who told him that there was no hope of her salvation;

she felt herself to be a lost sinner. 'I am glad of that, madam,' says Mr. Wesley, 'very glad of it.' 'How can you say so?' says she, quite horrified. 'Because I read in my Bible that Christ came to seek and to save that which is lost.' That anecdote has been a comfort to many a poor soul, I don't doubt. It has helped me more than once, I know, when I got down in my mind."

He shifted his position to bring her within eye-range.

"Do you believe, then — Where did you get that picture?"

A fine cabinet photograph of Mrs. Paull stood upon a miniature easel on the low mantel-shelf, a second and broader sun-ray lying athwart it.

As the nurse afterward related the incident, a light as bright broke in upon her mind; her heart beat suffocatingly; odd zigzags of flame hindered her vision. Professional caution and tact did not fail her, however.

"There, now!" in her creamiest legato; "I don't wonder it catches your eye. That's a lovely lady I nursed through brain fever a little over two years ago. She's had lots of trouble and sorrow, — enough to kill most women, but she has been wonderfully supported through it all. I set a deal of store by her, and she knows that so well, she gave me her picture last Christmas. Maybe you'd like to look at it nearer, sir?"

He snatched rather than accepted it from her, grasped it with both shaking hands, his eyes kindling hungrily. Eyes and fingers seemed as if they would never let it go.

"Excuse me for a minute, please!" said Mrs. Williams, the "&c.," in entire command of speech and action. "I must see how that beef-tea is getting on in the kitchen."

When out of his sight she fell upon her knees: —

"Dear Lord! give me light enough for the next step! Thou, who canst save to the uttermost, have mercy upon this wandering soul!"

A strange, choking cry — a horrid rattling sound — made her fly into the outer room. Ernest Paull had raised himself upon his elbow; his right hand plucked convulsively at his breast; his eyes, wild and imploring, besought help which mortal skill could not render.

The struggle was fearfully brief. Even as she raised him in her arms that air might enter the closing lungs, his frame relaxed; with one last effort he lifted his wife's picture to his lips, and the life fluttered forth.

CHAPTER XX.

What could I do, O blessed Guide and Master,
        Other than this ?
Still to go on, as now, not slower, faster,
        Nor fear to miss
The road, although so very long it be,
        While led by Thee.
Step after step, feeling Thee close beside me,
        Although unseen;
Through thorns, through flowers, whether the tempest
        hide Thee,
        Or heavens serene, —
Assured Thy faithfulness cannot betray,
        Nor love decay.

                      SUSAN COOLIDGE.

CHAPTER XX.

EIGHTEEN months after Ernest Paull's death, his widow and eldest son drove one moonlight evening down to the village post-office for the late mail. There were two mails a day in Pequod now, and a railroad in building on the other side of the lake from Pinehurst. The old Dutch neighborhood was waking up to the appreciation of the consequence, real and prospective, of a mountain retreat within an hour by rail of the metropolis. "The store" had arisen a story in the world, and had a brand-new coat of paint that glistened under the full moon. There was a smarter look about the knot of village loafers gathered upon the porch and steps, some smoking, some whittling.

While Mrs. Paull waited in the buggy for her son's return from the interior of the building, she heard them talk of factory work, crops, and general rural news. They were neither worse nor better than the average of men and lads who frequent the country store; but, as the idle chit-chat went on, the lady was disagreeably impressed by the bovine drawl, the slovenly dialect, and low range of ideas of men who had passed their lives in a community where church-going was respectable, and schooling was, by law, obligatory. She had striven unostentatiously to do missionary work among these people, recognizing, at the outset, what many as earnest never perceive, and thereby fail in their ministry to those they would lift to higher levels; to wit, that the native-born American, no matter what his birth, station, or means, is never a peasant, and ignores resentfully the existence of such a class on this side of the Atlantic. She had discovered other things that pained and surprised her far more than the suspicious spirit of independence that, if rightly directed, leads to the right sort of self-respect. The tone of every-day morality among the "village people" was not a whit higher than in the slummiest quarters of the so-considered wicked city. The men and boys, with lamentably few exceptions, drank bad liquor, smoked and chewed vile tobacco, and that incessantly, gamed and swore freely. The women were coarse and bold in their demeanor, and notoriously lax in principle. It was not uncommon for girls of thirteen to marry boys but a few years older; wife-beating was a frequent occurrence, and a more common sight was husband and wife drinking together, while their children, ragged, barefoot, and dirty, learned profanity and vice in the public roads. There were three churches in sight of the "Crossroad store," and pastors and Sunday-school teachers who sought to draw in learners and co-workers. The common people stood aloof and on the defensive.

Aided by Marie and Mrs. Morse, Mrs. Paull had established a sewing and cooking class which met twice a week in a house in the village. Not a woman or girl would have walked the half-mile to

Pinehurst to be taught anything. The attitude — conscious and habitual — of the "native-born" ignoramus is patronage of those who would help him to rise. Women washed and scrubbed for their better-to-do neighbors with the air of conferring a favor, receiving payment for the same with supercilious toleration irresistibly funny to those who had too much sense to let it irritate them. If it pleased Mrs. Paull to teach the children to sew, and to give them the aprons and frocks they made; to invite the wives of the operatives to help her play cook two afternoons in the week, and to let them carry home the food they prepared, — they let her have her way, some good-humoredly, some contemptuously, none gratefully. The same state of feeling prevailed with respect to the Bible class held on Wednesday night in the new "hall" over the store. When they felt like it, they came; when they did not feel like it, they stayed away.

The field was not encouraging. She had confessed this to Lanier on the drive down: —

"I do not lose heart, simply because I know that I owe a duty to my neighbor, and that I am trying to fulfil it to the best of my light and knowledge. It is the 'duty that lies nearest my hand.' Hence it is God's will that I should do it. As Mr. Stevens says, what comes of it is none of my business. Each of us is a soldier in the ranks. When the Commander says, 'Come,' or 'Go,' 'Do this,' or 'Do that,' we have no choice but to obey. Human nature in Pequod is Water-Street human nature. The rural district is not Arcadia, but it is good for me to find here what Byron coveted when he began the study of German, — 'something craggy to break his mind upon.' I have learned long ago, that merely sentimental Christianity cannot labor effectively in a severely practical world, where dirt and poverty go hand-in-hand, and those who are in the direst need of moral and spiritual help are the most averse to receiving such help."

"A clear case of 'I will be drowned! Nobody shall help me'?"

"Exactly! Fortunately there is One who sees the end from the beginning, and appoints to each day its 'tender tasking.'"

She had bowed pleasantly to the group of loungers when the buggy drew up at the store, and Lanier had lifted his hat. The men nodded, not a hand moving to the brim of hat or cap. Then they had gone on talking, rather more loudly than before, to prove how uncowed they were by a refined presence.

Mrs. Paull comprehended the drift of all this by this time, and did not feel indignant or wounded by behavior that would have offended her sense of fitness had the boorishness manifested itself in men of a different stamp. She noted, instead, with silent gratification, that not an oath was uttered in her hearing, or an unclean word. The mind, free from carking preoccupation in the morrow, discerns and gets all the sweetness out of such grains of comfort.

The end of the upper story, inhabited by the storekeeper's family, was lighted, and a window was open in one room, the evening being bland. Presently somebody — the wife or daughter of the proprietor — began to play upon a melodeon.

She did not play even mechanically well, tripping once in a while over a key, and hurrying or retarding the time according to a system of her own; the instrument wheezed asthmatically when certain keys were pressed; and twice in one tune, which was unfamiliar to the performer, the wind gave out through her forgetfulness of the duty her foot owed to the pedal.

But when a woman's and a man's voice arose in a hymn-tune, the hum of talk upon the porch ceased. Not a man moved while the sacred song went on. It was taken, of course, from a Moody and Sankey collection. Nos. 1, 2, and 3 of "Gospel Hymns" are to be found in every farm or village house, as surely as churn and sewing-machine.

In the windless night they heard every word. The heart of one listener was a harp, with each chord tense and a-thrill in response to the remembered strain: —

> "I need Thee every hour,
> Most gracious Lord!
> No tender voice like Thine
> Can peace afford."

Several voices among the lower group joined in the refrain very softly, not to disturb the musicians above stairs: —

> "I need Thee, oh, I need Thee!
> Every hour I need Thee.
> Oh, bless me now, my Saviour!
> I come to Thee!"

It was the "cry of the human" of every degree.

Lanier was in his seat by his mother while the first verse was in singing. He did not touch the reins until the last repetition of the chorus died away, and neither of the two spoke before the top of the first hill was reached. The road skirted the edge of the lake, which was full from the autumnal rains. The head of water pouring over the dam raised a deep-toned shout, which was taken up by the listening hills. Clouds of spray were rising from the rocks, glittering like diamond-dust, and beading with pearls the outermost boughs of the hemlock wood on the other side of the rocky way. Just where the lake gathered itself into a smooth sheet for the plunge, a thicket of witch-hazel was studded with numberless blooms. The hills dreamed upon the horizon; the stars pale, but constant, held to their courses in the gray-blue canopy of a world at rest.

"It will be four years next month!" Mrs. Paull mused aloud. "That hymn brought it all back so vividly that for a moment I thought I could not bear it. I held still, and the pain passed, as all pains must pass by His grace.

"My boy! never distrust Him! Paul meant much when he told his neophytes that he 'would have them without carefulness.' It was the echo of the Master's will."

"I saw something to-day that made me wish that you were with me," answered Lanier. The accord between their spirits was perfected with the passing of years. "Close by the Peddlington station, right in the thick of wheels, horses, and people, within six feet of the rails where locomotives were drilling up and down, were two sparrows picking up scattered grain that had fallen from freight car or wagon. The chippiest, chirpiest pair of busybodies you can imagine, so happy over their ' find ' that they chattered as they ate. I stood still for fully five minutes to watch them. It was a sermon in song and feathers. The roar of traffic and the jargon of voices went for less than nothing to the wise midgets. God had put their dinner — such a big dinner! — just there, and they took it, asking no questions."

"The dear little types!" smiled the mother, tenderly. "I never see one without wishing he knew how honored he is, — far above the other birds of the air. How careless of me not to notice that you are cumbered with all these letters and papers, and have to hold the reins besides! We have a lordly mail! Let me take it!"

"The heaviest, and it goes without saying the most important, part is for Marie, including the usual corpulent envelope from Philadelphia. The postal service of Pequod will be lighter after November fifteenth. I am to be best man, she tells me. You must advise me what to get for a wedding-present. Lanier & Co. must have had the event in view when they raised my salary the first of the month. You will miss our bonnie girl."

"More than I could have believed possible two years ago. The shock that awaited her upon her return from what we all considered an ill-starred voyage, threw her back into her mother's arms, and

I have kept her there. Her friends are very good to her. Her Aunt Virginia has given her all her linen, and Mrs. Barnes is embroidering her initials upon each piece, ' stitching love into every letter,' as she says, in her graceful way. I shall not let Mrs. Williams leave us until after the wedding. I shall convince her that we cannot get ready for it without her help. That is true as far as it goes, but she ought to have the change and rest."

"Has she been ill? I was actually appalled at the alteration in her when I met her at the station this afternoon. She must have lost fifty pounds of flesh since I saw her in July. But for her voice and laugh I should hardly have known her. I asked her through what mill of self-sacrifice she had been putting herself lately."

Mrs. Paull uttered an exclamation of regret, then checking it midway, asked with interest, —

"What did she say?"

"That she was no fonder of peas in her shoes and hair-cloth shirts than other folks. For her part, she thought the most dangerous part of spiritual vanity was that people felt in making martyrs of themselves. 'It's a great honor to be a martyr when God calls you to the stake, or to the gallows,' she went on to improve the occasion by remarking; ' but a great piece of presumption when one grabs at the martyr's crown before it is offered to him. Even our Lord passed through the midst of them that wanted to throw Him off the hill on which Nazareth was built. The very city in which He was brought up, too!' What a Bible scholar she is!"

"What a noble, plucky Christian heroine she is!" said Mrs. Paull, much moved. "No martyr ever went to the torture more unflinchingly than she has walked the cruel stones of her appointed pathway of life.

"Drive slowly, dear! I must tell you a sad, true story before we reach home. You should hear it, that you may not wound our dear friend by thoughtless questions. She would never allow you to suspect it if she did, but she has borne so much that we must shield her in every possible way. Mrs. Barnes told me the sorrowful tale last week when she was here. She said that Mrs. Williams wished me to hear it, but could not trust herself as yet to talk of it.

"She was married at twenty to a smart young fellow, — a machinist by trade, and in a good business. Within six months she knew that he was a drunkard, — a confirmed sot. He had loved liquor ever since he was a boy, as his father had before him, so he told her. On her death-bed his mother had begged him to promise her that he would never touch another drop, and he had vowed upon her Bible that he would not. This was a year before his marriage, and before he met Mary Johnson, who became his wife. He was good-looking, Mrs. Barnes says, with a kind heart and sweet temper, one of the most lovable of men when sober, and industrious and ambitious. A few glasses of the accursed stuff converted him into a demon, quarrelsome, violent, and cruel. His wife kept the knowledge of his besetting sin to herself as long as she could, hoping with all the strength of her sanguine nature to bring about his reform. When one fall after another would have discouraged any other woman, she clung to the belief that the good in him would get the upper hand of the evil.

"'He never said a cross word to me when he was himself,' she told Mrs. Barnes; 'and when the crazy fit was over, he was fairly broken-hearted for what had happened. Many's the time I've known him spend half the night praying, with his Bible open before him, when he felt the terrible thirst coming on him. It was like a sly devil creeping up to him, and then, all at once, seizing him and carrying him off. I know now they say it is a disease, and to be treated like a disease, and not as a crime. Maybe so, but I call it being possessed by devils, — sometimes by one, sometimes by a whole legion of them, — as many as entered into the swine. It makes swine of some men; it made a wild beast of my husband. His eyes would get deeper set in his head, with red fire burning down in them, his forehead was lower and ridged down to his eyebrows, and you would n't have known the voice for his, that was almost like a woman's for gentleness when he was right.'

"Stop here, my son ! I never weary of that picture set in the opening between these trees."

They were upon the upper slope of the hill on which the homestead was built. The lights from the windows twinkled through the thinned foliage; below the house and lawn, the lake spread, an irregular sheet of silver-gray, shading into black where the banks were high. The blasted oak to which the mother had compared herself formed one side of the view; the shadow of the branchy crown projected upon the white road. The air was fragrant with the odor of fallen hickory leaves, and pulsated with distant music. Marie was at the piano, her glorious voice carrying far through the placid night.

"It is not the time or the place for a tragic story," resumed Mrs. Paull. "We will get it over quickly. They had been married several years, and had two children, — a boy and a girl. Times were hard with them, in consequence of the husband's habits, and Mary was obliged to go out sewing by the day to help support the family. When she did this, her sister, a girl of eighteen, used to stay with and take care of the children. Williams came home one noon, while his wife was absent, drunk and raving. It is supposed that his sister-in-law, who was spirited and fearless, reproached him with his condition; or she may have interfered to protect the little ones from their father's violence. The neighbors heard her scream, and ran to her help, — too late to save her. He had killed her and the children with an axe, and was raging about the room, cutting up the furniture with it.

"We read of similar deeds every week, but the revolting details and all the attendant horrors mean comparatively nothing to us, who hear of them afar off. Think of this happening to a woman like our dear Nurse Williams, — a clean-lived, God-fearing wife and mother!"

"Mother! are you quite sure it is true?"

"Dr. Barnes was her pastor then, as now. He was sent for to break the news to her. She fainted when the full force of the calamity fell upon her. Her first inquiry upon reviving was for her husband.

"'Drink murdered them, not he!' she said. 'When he comes to himself, he will not recollect anything he has done. He must be watched, or he will take his own life when he finds it out. He has the lovingest heart ever put into a man's bosom.'

"The thought that he would be tried for the triple murder seemed not to occur to her. She was in the court-room when he was sentenced to imprisonment for life. For thirty years she has visited him regularly, once a month, and written to him whenever she was allowed to send a letter. He died a fortnight ago. By the favor of the penitentiary officials, who were acquainted with his history, she was appointed his nurse in the prison hospital, and had been with him for a month when the end came.

"When Mrs. Barnes wrote to me how sadly shaken the noble woman was, I insisted that she should pay us a visit, writing directly to Mrs. Williams. Her presence ought to bring a blessing to any house. I covet the privilege of helping to mete out to her the measure she has given into other bosoms.

"Not a word of this to Marie, or to the children! I knew I could count upon your sympathy and cooperation."

They drove slowly and silently through the gate and wood and around to the front door. Marie had left the piano, and was watching for them — and the mail — upon the porch. A glance in at the kitchen window showed Tom and Edwin measuring the chestnuts gathered that day into a great basket, under Elspeth's approving inspection, and the mother passed through sitting-room and hall to her own chamber. The sound of voices met her on the threshold. The door was not fast and she pushed it aside noiselessly.

Mrs. Williams sat by the fire with Gladys — a slight weight for her years — in her arms. The child was wrapped in a dressing-gown; the golden head rested confidingly upon her friend's shoulder.

"There's one more verse," she pleaded. "I used to think it the nicest of all. Don't you remember, when I was a wee bit of a girl, I was never satisfied if you did not sing it clear through? You can't cheat me now, dear old nursie!"

With her cheek — less plump and rosy than in the times of which her favorite reminded her — nestled among the flossy curls, the shining of a great peace in her eyes, the nurse finished her song: —

> "It may be the sweet surrounding
>   Of Thine angels' banding wings
> May define fair meads, abounding
>   In the dew from Baca's springs.
> If, instead of beauty, burning
>   Be the measure of Thy will,
> May eyes, made by faith discerning,
>   See the shining ones there still."

FINIS.

WHOLESOME READING.

HOW THEY KEPT THE FAITH. A Tale of the Huguenots of Languedoc. By GRACE RAYMOND. 12mo, cloth. $1.50.

"We have rarely met with an attempt to reproduce a past epoch, so true to historical fact and firm in its grasp of the inner springs of action, as this tale as to how the Huguenots kept the faith in the time of Louis XIV. and the Dragonnades. The story is wrought out skilfully and naturally, the different characters stand out boldly on the canvas, the adherents of the Reformed faith, from principles of honor and heredity, are well contrasted with those whose attachment rested on conviction and conscience, and it is made plain that only a living faith in Christ, a power stronger than man's, could hold one steadfast under the stress of such tests as believers in those days had to endure.

"It must needs be that the story should abound in scenes which stir the blood with indignation and move the heart to pity, else it would not be true to history; but needlessly harrowing details are avoided, there are rifts of light in the clouds, and the end is one of chastened joy and peace. There is about the whole book an air of reality—of truth to life—which raises it much above the average novel or historical study, and bespeaks literary skill of a very high order. The novel ought to attain a wide popularity and increase the growing reputation of the gifted author."

LEAH OF JERUSALEM. A Story of the Time of Paul. By EDWARD PAYSON BERRY. 12mo, 388 pages. Cloth. $1.25.

A literary lady who read the manuscript says: "The style is strong; the story of intense interest; the atmosphere of the period well caught. I like the book better than any of the kind I have read except Ben-Hur."

"This is a very finely written story of the earliest days of Christianity, which is sure to give the reader a great deal of useful information concerning Jewish and Roman life and customs. It opens with the boyhood of St. Paul, which is described in a brief chapter. The second chapter introduces the heroine, Leah, at a date some twenty years later, who is cured of a fever by St. Stephen. The first martyrdom quickly follows, with Saul, now a young Jewish Rabbi, standing by. The life of the great Apostle is then mainly followed to its end in Rome, the sad experiences of Leah and her lover, who is St. Luke, being woven into the narrative. It is a sweet, pure, and strong story, which will do much in the way of quickening religious feeling in all who read it."
—*Providence Journal.*

AN OLD CHRONICLE OF LEIGHTON. By SARAH S. HAMER. 12mo, cloth, illustrated. $1.50.

"This is an interesting and well-written story of English life and character in the early part of the present century. The characters are well drawn and the incidents have about them all the flavor of the olden time. The writer has a pleasant, sprightly style which will at once win upon the reader, and there is not a dull page to be found between the covers of her book. We commend it to our readers as a book above the average."—*The Christian at Work.*

Published by **ANSON D. F. RANDOLPH & COMPANY** *(Incorporated),*
182 Fifth Avenue, New York.

⁎⁎⁎ Sent by mail, post-paid, on receipt of price.

THE CHILD OF THE PRECINCT. A Story by SARAH DOUDNEY. With four illustrations. 12mo, cloth. $1.50.

"Here is a beautiful English story, the scene laid partly in the city and partly in the country. This 'Child of the Precinct' is a sweet-faced orphan girl who, finding her way back, when days are dark, to her old friends and acquaintances is adopted into their circle and becomes a part of their life. How bright and winsome a part she plays is well told, and the sentiment that appears is of a pleasing and wholesome sort."—*The Standard.*

"The book is full of incident, is healthy and moral in tone, and depicts the trials of a young girl, first with an invalid mother, then an orphan. It shows her good judgment, and heroism, and womanly character. Altogether it is a very readable book, and one that will be an acceptable present."—*Journal and Messenger.*

GODIVA DURLEIGH. A Story by SARAH DOUDNEY. With four illustrations. 12mo, cloth. $1.50.

"A good, pure, bright, and well-written book by an English writer who is well known. Godiva Durleigh, the only daughter and sole companion of her father, a philanthropist of no little note, who spent his life and gave it for the rescue of several small children from their brutal father, and thereby he received his death-blow. Godiva, stunned by the loss of her father and companion, and alone in the world, save an uncle and three cousins, to whose care her father committed her. Sad and lonely were the days this lovely character spent in uncongenial surroundings, stung by the taunts of her jealous cousins; she was thrown upon her own resources, until an accident occurred to one of the cousins which nearly sapped her life; then it was that Godiva became all in all to every member of the family. For years her lover's life and her own drifted apart, but after many vicissitudes kind fate brought them together. But the book will have to be read to find out her end and that of many other characters in this book."—*Southern Churchman.*

THE ONLY WAY OUT. By LEANDER S. KEYSER. 16mo, cloth. $1.00.

The purpose of the author is to present a faithful portrait of the honest doubter; to describe his experiences, perplexities, and mental phases in general, and to point out the *only way* of escape from doubt. He believes that there are many earnest and intelligent young men and women in our colleges and elsewhere who honestly doubt the Divine authority of the Bible, and who would gladly welcome the truth if they were persuaded that it is to be found. Such persons will find many of their perplexities depicted in the story, while their objections are dealt with as fairly and thoroughly as possible. Other sceptics, not so sincere, may yet be benefited if the truth is presented to them in the proper manner. There is more fact than fiction in the spiritual experiences delineated; for the author has only described a land through which he himself has travelled, and is, therefore, familiar with the trials of the journey. The morally depleting influence of doubt, the inadequacy of modern materialism to satisfy the higher rational needs of the soul, and the gradual descent of the sceptic into pessimism and despair, are also described.

Published by ANSON D. F. RANDOLPH & COMPANY (Incorporated),
182 Fifth Avenue, New York.

⁎ *Sent by mail, post-paid, on receipt of price.*

STUBBLE OR WHEAT? A Story of more Lives than One. By S. Bayard Dod. 16mo, cloth, $1.00; paper, 25 cents.

A dramatic and original story, the purpose of which is to face the tide of pessimism that is sweeping through our literature, and ask men to listen to both sides of the question. It is a domestic story, showing the outcome of a life modelled on the pessimistic philosophy; and how, under ordinary circumstances, an earnest nature will be led who adopts this as the guiding influence of his life; the inevitable trend of its teachings. The principal character is a man who deliberately and carefully allows his better life to be destroyed by a corroding disbelief in all things good, true, and beautiful, and the story of whose career is carried on through school and college and after graduation. In contrast are other lives in the same circumstances grandly overcoming difficulties, and growing stronger and gladder. The characters are finely differentiated, and each one bears the stamp of a distinct personality. The exhibition of the pessimist's theory, contrasted with that of a sound Christian philosophy, suggests the answer to the question of the title: Which makes of life a field of barren stubble, and which a harvest of ripened grain?

STORIES BY SOPHY WINTHROP WEITZEL.

Faith and Patience; or, The Harrington Girls. 16mo, cloth. Illustrated. $1.00.

"The *petite*, graceful proportions, and fair, chaste apparel of this little book, will delight a critical eye. It appears outwardly to be designed especially to carry captive the hearts of juvenile readers; but inwardly it is adapted to please every cultivated mind. The story is not pretentious either in subject or dimensions, but it is very neatly told, and in both matter and manner will give abundant satisfaction."—*New York Tribune.*

Renee of France, Duchess of Ferrara. 12mo, cloth. $1.00.

"The terrible trials to which devout souls were subjected in attempting to escape from the toils of the mother-church in the first century of the Lutheran Reformation, and especially of one born in a royal family, as was the Princess Renée, the daughter of Louis XII., are vividly presented in this volume."—*Christian Weekly.*

"An appreciative woman's efforts to do justice to another woman, whose modest post in history has not attracted the attention her character merits."—*Troy Times.*

Sister and Saint. A Sketch of the Life of Jacqueline Pascal. 12mo, cloth. $1.00.

"There is an indescribable charm in each of the several characters here pictured, and the story as a whole will come like a refreshing influence into the hot and hurried life of this nineteenth century. It opens up a field new to most readers, and everybody will find it pleasant."—*Churchman.*

"The book, besides being a charming story, is a valuable review of the religious life of the period."—*Christian Union.*

Published by **ANSON D. F. RANDOLPH & COMPANY** *(Incorporated),*
182 Fifth Avenue, New York.

*** *Sent by mail, post-paid, on receipt of price.*

STORIES BY MARGARET M. ROBERTSON.

By a Way She Knew Not. The Story of Allison Bain. 12mo, cloth. $1.50.

A pleasing story of Scotch life among humble people, somewhat unusual in outline, and containing strongly drawn representations of character. The descriptions of the simple, honest life in the little town of Nethermuir make *genre* pictures of uncommon merit, and one is not likely to straightway forget the household at the manse, or the school-mistress and her pupils. A religious tone which pervades the book adds dignity to the story, while it in no way weakens the perfect art of the whole.

Eunice. A domestic Story of New England Life. With 12 illustrations. 12mo. $1.50.

A domestic story of New England persons and life, which sets forth vividly some of the trials which, although they occur to people everywhere, yet will be recognized by all New-Englanders as in a real sense characteristic of New England. The problems to be faced are outlined strongly, the religious spirit of the book is good, and is united with a story of real power.

Janet's Love and Service. 12mo, cloth. $1.50.

"It is rarely that we read a story which gives us so much satisfaction and so little cause of complaint. It is the story of just such a life as has occurred again and again in the past, and will occur again and again in the future. In form and style and method of treatment the volume is as simple as it is select. . . . . It is rather genial than witty or humorous, and it will be a satisfaction to know that there is a public who prefer this romance of real life to that of the cheap fire and sheet-iron thunder to be found in many modern novels."—*Harper's Magazine.*

THE STARLING. A Scotch Story. By NORMAN MACLEOD. Paper, 30 cents.

"A Scottish tale rich in humor, of absorbing interest, sufficiently instructive, and altogether edifying. Dr. Macleod is more apt in delineation of Scottish character than George MacDonald, and he never proses; there is nothing the reader wants to skip."—*The Occident.*

THE OLD LIEUTENANT AND HIS SON. By NORMAN MACLEOD. Paper, 30 cents.

"A charming story, told in the author's most winning way. Dr. Macleod needs no introduction to the reader."

Published by **ANSON D. F. RANDOLPH & COMPANY** *(Incorporated),*
182 Fifth Avenue, New York.

⁂ Sent by mail, post-paid, on receipt of price.

Stories by Elizabeth Prentiss.

Stepping Heavenward. Printed from new Stereotype Plates in 1880, and enhanced by a brief sketch of the author. Cloth, 12mo, 430 pages, $1.00; paper, 25 cents.

It is the story of the Life of Faith, with the charm of naturalness and human sympathy. This makes it acceptable as well as pure, strong, and helpful. — *New York Observer.*

Pemaquid. A story of Old Times in New England. Cloth. 12mo. 370 pages. $1.00.

We regard it as one of her best books. — *The Evangelist.*

The Home at Greylock. 12mo. Cloth. 338 pages. $1.00.

As wholesome as it is entertaining, and conveys many instructive lessons in its graceful and flowing narrative. — *Christian Intelligencer.*

Urbane and His Friends. Cloth. 12mo. 287 pages. Enlarged edition. $1.00.

Full of kindly and genial counsel, marked by great tenderness and simplicity of spirit, and very earnest and helpful. — *Boston Journal.*

Aunt Jane's Hero. Cloth. 12mo. 300 pages. $1.00.

"Aunt Jane's Hero" is so like people we meet, that we are anxious to have them read the book, in order to profit by its teachings. We like it and believe others will. — *The Advance.*

The Flower of the Family. A Book for Girls. Cloth. 16mo. 400 pages. $1.00.

"It aims to exact trivial home duty, by showing how such duty, performed in the fear of God and the love of Christ, may lead upward and onward through present self-denial to the highest usefulness, peace, and joy."

New York: ANSON D. F. RANDOLPH CO. (Incorporated),
182 FIFTH AVENUE.

A GIRL'S WINTER IN INDIA.

By MARY THORNE CARPENTER.

12 Full-page illustrations. 12mo, ornamental cloth. $1.50.

A GRAPHIC book by an American girl who spent last winter in India and Ceylon, and had the *entrée* to the Viceroy's entertainments and the Indian Zenanas. Her descriptions of the country and objects of unusual interest, as well as of life and character, cover a rather unusual range of observation, preceded by a record of a three weeks' voyage on a P. and O. steamer, with a donkey ride at Port Said, and an exceptional experience on the camels at Aden.

Three weeks were spent on the Island of Ceylon, and included a trip to the Kandian Mountains, the pleasure retreat of the English officials. Thence to Bombay, and on to Allahabad, with an Indian servant, whose original qualities were alike striking and ingenious. There is a vivid description of the Hindu Melah festivals on the banks of the Junna River, and of hundreds of holy Fakirs gathered there, with an account of the medical missions and the Christian schools. At Calcutta she saw the intense Oriental atmosphere heightened by the visit of the Russian Czarovitch, and at the grand ball, the high water-mark of Eastern magnificence, when the Rajahs and Indian princes appeared in the native costumes, bedecked with brilliant jewels.

In the descriptive bits of real life at Delhi, there is a characterization of mercantile life, and the peculiar methods of the native trading with foreigners. The wonderful ruins, the matchless Jumna Musjid, the imperial palaces, carved lace-work screens, the marble mosques, etc., all are portrayed in graphic terms. From Delhi, an excursion was made to the Kootub,—a unique monument of fluted sandstone of Arabic design.

Jeypore was a marked contrast to all previous sights. Here is a pink and white city. Elephants, caparisoned as in the Arabian Nights, tread softly in the streets; there are peculiar street scenes and customs, and the atmosphere is that of an intensified East. The traveller took an elephant ride to Amber and the deserted palace of the Rajputs. The mountain roadways were lined with white mosques, and shrines overgrown with dense creepers, through which darted wild peacocks and chattering monkeys.

New York: ANSON D. F. RANDOLPH & CO. (Incorporated),
182 FIFTH AVENUE.

Sent post-paid on receipt of price.

www.ingramcontent.com/pod-product-compliance
Lightning Source LLC
Chambersburg PA
CBHW030359230426
43664CB00007BB/657